Modern Critical Views

Chinua Achebe
Henry Adams
Aeschylus
S. Y. Agnon
Edward Albee
Raphael Alberti
Louisa May Alcott
A. R. Ammons
Sherwood Anderson
Aristophanes
Matthew Arnold
Antonin Artaud
John Ashbery
Margaret Atwood
W. H. Auden
Jane Austen
Isaac Babel
Sir Francis Bacon
James Baldwin
Honoré de Balzac
John Barth
Donald Barthelme
Charles Baudelaire
Simone de Beauvoir
Samuel Beckett
Saul Bellow
Thomas Berger
John Berryman
The Bible
Elizabeth Bishop
William Blake
Giovanni Boccaccio
Heinrich Böll
Jorge Luis Borges
Elizabeth Bowen
Bertolt Brecht
The Brontës
Charles Brockden Brown
Sterling Brown
Robert Browning
Martin Buber
John Bunyan
Anthony Burgess
Kenneth Burke
Robert Burns
William Burroughs
George Gordon, Lord
  Byron
Pedro Calderón de la Barca
Italo Calvino
Albert Camus
Canadian Poetry: Modern
  and Contemporary
Canadian Poetry through
  E. J. Pratt
Thomas Carlyle
Alejo Carpentier
Lewis Carroll
Willa Cather
Louis-Ferdinand Céline
Miguel de Cervantes

Geoffrey Chaucer
John Cheever
Anton Chekhov
Kate Chopin
Chrétien de Troyes
Agatha Christie
Samuel Taylor Coleridge
Colette
William Congreve & the
  Restoration Dramatists
Joseph Conrad
Contemporary Poets
James Fenimore Cooper
Pierre Corneille
Julio Cortázar
Hart Crane
Stephen Crane
e. e. cummings
Dante
Robertson Davies
Daniel Defoe
Philip K. Dick
Charles Dickens
James Dickey
Emily Dickinson
Denis Diderot
Isak Dinesen
E. L. Doctorow
John Donne & the
  Seventeenth-Century
  Metaphysical Poets
John Dos Passos
Fyodor Dostoevsky
Frederick Douglass
Theodore Dreiser
John Dryden
W. E. B. Du Bois
Lawrence Durrell
George Eliot
T. S. Eliot
Elizabethan Dramatists
Ralph Ellison
Ralph Waldo Emerson
Euripides
William Faulkner
Henry Fielding
F. Scott Fitzgerald
Gustave Flaubert
E. M. Forster
John Fowles
Sigmund Freud
Robert Frost
Northrop Frye
Carlos Fuentes
William Gaddis
André Gide
W. S. Gilbert
Allen Ginsberg
J. W. von Goethe
Nikolai Gogol
William Golding

Oliver Goldsmith
Mary Gordon
Günther Grass
Robert Graves
Graham Greene
Thomas Hardy
Nathaniel Hawthorne
William Hazlitt
H. D.
Seamus Heaney
Lillian Hellman
Ernest Hemingway
Hermann Hesse
Geoffrey Hill
Friedrich Hölderlin
Homer
A. D. Hope
Gerard Manley Hopkins
Horace
A. E. Housman
William Dean Howells
Langston Hughes
Ted Hughes
Victor Hugo
Zora Neale Hurston
Aldous Huxley
Henrik Ibsen
Eugene Ionesco
Washington Irving
Henry James
Dr. Samuel Johnson and
  James Boswell
Ben Jonson
James Joyce
Carl Gustav Jung
Franz Kafka
Yasonari Kawabata
John Keats
Søren Kierkegaard
Rudyard Kipling
Melanie Klein
Heinrich von Kleist
Philip Larkin
D. H. Lawrence
John le Carré
Ursula K. Le Guin
Giacomo Leopardi
Doris Lessing
Sinclair Lewis
Jack London
Frederico García Lorca
Robert Lowell
Malcolm Lowry
Norman Mailer
Bernard Malamud
Stéphane Mallarmé
Thomas Malory
André Malraux
Thomas Mann
Katherine Mansfield
Christopher Marlowe

Modern Critical Views

Gabriel García Márquez
Andrew Marvell
Carson McCullers
Herman Melville
George Meredith
James Merrill
John Stuart Mill
Arthur Miller
Henry Miller
John Milton
Yukio Mishima
Molière
Michel de Montaigne
Eugenio Montale
Marianne Moore
Alberto Moravia
Toni Morrison
Alice Munro
Iris Murdoch
Robert Musil
Vladimir Nabokov
V. S. Naipaul
R. K. Narayan
Pablo Neruda
John Henry, Cardinal
  Newman
Friedrich Nietzsche
Frank Norris
Joyce Carol Oates
Sean O'Casey
Flannery O'Connor
Christopher Okigbo
Charles Olson
Eugene O'Neill
José Ortega y Gasset
Joe Orton
George Orwell
Ovid
Wilfred Owen
Amos Oz
Cynthia Ozick
Grace Paley
Blaise Pascal
Walter Pater
Octavio Paz
Walker Percy
Petrarch
Pindar
Harold Pinter
Luigi Pirandello
Sylvia Plath
Plato

Plautus
Edgar Allan Poe
Poets of Sensibility & the
  Sublime
Poets of the Nineties
Alexander Pope
Katherine Anne Porter
Ezra Pound
Anthony Powell
Pre-Raphaelite Poets
Marcel Proust
Manuel Puig
Alexander Pushkin
Thomas Pynchon
Francisco de Quevedo
François Rabelais
Jean Racine
Ishmael Reed
Adrienne Rich
Samuel Richardson
Mordecai Richler
Rainer Maria Rilke
Arthur Rimbaud
Edwin Arlington Robinson
Theodore Roethke
Philip Roth
Jean-Jacques Rousseau
John Ruskin
J. D. Salinger
Jean-Paul Sartre
Gershom Scholem
Sir Walter Scott
William Shakespeare
  (3 vols.)
  Histories & Poems
  Comedies & Romances
  Tragedies
George Bernard Shaw
Mary Wollstonecraft
  Shelley
Percy Bysshe Shelley
Sam Shepard
Richard Brinsley Sheridan
Sir Philip Sidney
Isaac Bashevis Singer
Tobias Smollett
Alexander Solzhenitsyn
Sophocles
Wole Soyinka
Edmund Spenser
Gertrude Stein
John Steinbeck

Stendhal
Laurence Sterne
Wallace Stevens
Robert Louis Stevenson
Tom Stoppard
August Strindberg
Jonathan Swift
John Millington Synge
Alfred, Lord Tennyson
William Makepeace
  Thackeray
Dylan Thomas
Henry David Thoreau
James Thurber and S. J.
  Perelman
J. R. R. Tolkien
Leo Tolstoy
Jean Toomer
Lionel Trilling
Anthony Trollope
Ivan Turgenev
Mark Twain
Miguel de Unamuno
John Updike
Paul Valéry
Cesar Vallejo
Lope de Vega
Gore Vidal
Virgil
Voltaire
Kurt Vonnegut
Derek Walcott
Alice Walker
Robert Penn Warren
Evelyn Waugh
H. G. Wells
Eudora Welty
Nathanael West
Edith Wharton
Patrick White
Walt Whitman
Oscar Wilde
Tennessee Williams
William Carlos Williams
Thomas Wolfe
Virginia Woolf
William Wordsworth
Jay Wright
Richard Wright
William Butler Yeats
A. B. Yehoshua
Emile Zola

Modern Critical Views

PAUL VALÉRY

Edited and with an introduction by
Harold Bloom
Sterling Professor of the Humanities
Yale University

CHELSEA HOUSE PUBLISHERS
New York ◊ Philadelphia

© 1989 by Chelsea House Publishers, a division
of Main Line Book Company

Introduction © 1988 by Harold Bloom

Printed and bound in the United States of America

10   9   8   7   6   5   4   3   2   1

∞ The paper used in this publication meets the minimum
requirements of the American National Standard for Permanence
of Paper for Printed Library Materials, Z39.48–1984.

Library of Congress Cataloging-in-Publication Data
Paul Valéry / edited and with an introduction by
Harold Bloom.
    p.   cm.—(Modern critical views)
    Bibliography: p.
    Includes index.
    ISBN 1–55546–315–0 (alk. paper)
    1. Valéry, Paul, 1871–1945—Criticism and interpretation.
I. Bloom, Harold.   II. Series.
PQ2643.A26Z7259   1987   87–18363
841'.912—dc19   CIP

Contents

Editor's Note   vii

Introduction   1
     Harold Bloom

"La Dormeuse"   7
     Geoffrey H. Hartman

Two Prefaces   31
     Wallace Stevens

Introduction to *Poems in the Rough*   47
     Octave Nadal

Modulation and Movement in Valéry's Verse   61
     Lloyd James Austin

La Promenade avec Monsieur Teste   75
     W. N. Ince

La Jeune Parque   89
     Charles G. Whiting

Valéry and the Poetics of Language   103
     Gérard Genette

Paul Valéry's Poetic Theory   117
     René Wellek

Craniometry and Criticism:
Notes on a Valéryan Criss-Cross   131
     Jeffrey Mehlman

"An Ever Future Hollow in the Soul"   151
    James R. Lawler

Poetic Construction and Hermeneutic Tradition
in "Le Cimetière marin"   161
    Anselm Haverkamp

Chronology   181

Contributors   185

Bibliography   187

Acknowledgments   191

Index   193

Editor's Note

This book brings together a representative selection of the best criticism of the writings of Paul Valéry available in English. The critical essays are reprinted here in the chronological order of their original publication. I am grateful to Rhonda Garelick for her assistance in editing this volume.

My introduction centers upon Valéry's own criticism, with a particular emphasis upon the link between poetic self-awareness and poetic originality. Geoffrey Hartman begins the chronological sequence with his youthfully exuberant reading of Valéry's sonnet "La Dormeuse," which is viewed by Hartman as an unmediated vision, or pure act of knowledge.

Our strongest modern American poet, Wallace Stevens, pays tribute to Valéry in two appreciative prefaces to the dialogues *Dance and the Soul* and *Eupalinos*. Valéry's poems in prose are then introduced by Octave Nadal.

The subtle euphonies of Valéry's verse are investigated by Lloyd James Austin, after which W. N. Ince analyzes Valéry's peculiar but crucial personage, Monsieur Teste. *La Jeune Parque,* at once a masterwork and Valéry's crisis-poem, receives an exegesis from Charles G. Whiting, while the noted rhetorician Gérard Genette achieves an overview of Valéry's poetics.

René Wellek's survey of Valéry's position in critical history is followed by Jeffrey Mehlman's deconstruction of Valéry's critical stance. James R. Lawler, confronting Valéry's self-awareness, sees it in relation to Mallarmé. In this volume's final essay, Anselm Haverkamp gives a very full reading of Valéry's strongest single poem, the justly renowned "Le Cimetière marin."

Introduction

In the preface to his *Leonardo Poe Mallarmé*, Valéry calls these precursors "three masters of the art of abstraction." "Man fabricates by abstraction" is a famous Valéryan formula, reminding us that this sense of abstraction is Latin: "withdrawn, taken out from, removed." *It Must Be Abstract*, the first part of Stevens's *Notes toward a Supreme Fiction*, moves in the atmosphere of an American version of Valéry's insight, but the American is Walt Whitman and not Edgar Poe:

> The weather and the giant of the weather,
> Say the weather, the mere weather, the mere air:
> An abstraction blooded, as a man by thought.

Valéry fabricates by withdrawing from a stale reality, which he refuses to associate with the imaginings of his masters. These "enchanted, dominated me, and—as was only fitting—tormented me as well; the beautiful is that which fills us with despair." Had Valéry spoken of pain, rather than despair, he would have been more Nietzschean. The genealogy of imagination is not truly Valéry's subject. Despair is not a staleness in reality, or an absence of it; it is the overwhelming presence of reality, of the reality-principle, or the necessity of death-in-life, or simply of dying. Valéry's beautiful "Palme" concludes with a metaphor that seems central to all of his poetry:

> Pareille à celui qui pense
> Et dont l'âme se dépense
> A s'accroître de ses dons!

The palm is the image of a mind so rich in thinking that the gifts of its own soul augment it constantly. That may be one of the origins of Stevens's death-poem, "Of Mere Being," but Valéry's palm is less pure and less flickering than Stevens's final emblem. The two poets and poetic thinkers do not much resemble one another, despite Stevens's yearning regard for Valéry.

1

Perhaps the largest difference is in the attitudes towards precursors. Valéry is lucid and candid, and he confronts Mallarmé. Stevens insists that he does not read Whitman, condemns Whitman for his tramp *persona,* and yet he cannot cease revising Whitman's poems in his own poems. But then that is how Whitman came to discuss his relation to Ralph Waldo Emerson—clearly they order these matters differently in America.

In a meditation of 1919 on "The Intellectual Crisis," Valéry memorably depicted the European Hamlet staring at millions of ghosts:

> But he is an intellectual Hamlet. He meditates on the life and death of truths. For phantoms he has all the subjects of our controversies; for regrets he has all our titles to glory; he bows under the weight of discoveries and learning, unable to renounce and unable to resume this limitless activity. He reflects on the boredom of recommencing the past, on the folly of always striving to be original. He wavers between one abyss and the other, for two dangers still threaten the world: order and disorder.

This retains its force nearly seventy years later, just as it would baffle us if its subject were the American Hamlet. Valéry's fear was that Europe might "become *what she is in reality:* that is, a little cape of the Asiatic continent." The fear was prophetic, though the prophecy fortunately is not yet wholly fulfilled. When Valéry writes in this mode, he is principally of interest to editorial writers and newspaper columnists of the weightier variety. Yet his concern for European culture, perhaps a touch too custodial, is a crucial element in all his prose writing. Meditating upon Descartes, the archetypal French intellect, Valéry states the law of his own nature: "Descartes is above all, a man of intentional action." Consciousness was for Valéry an intentional adventure, and this sense of deliberate quest in the cultivation of consciousness is partly what makes Valéry a central figure of the Western literary intellect.

Valéry deprecated originality, but his critical insights are among the most original of our century. His *Analects* are crowded with the darker truths concerning literary originality:

> The value of men's works is not in the works themselves but in their later development by others, in other circumstances.

> Nothing is more "original," nothing more "oneself " than to feed on others. But one has to digest them. A lion is made of assimilated sheep.

> The hallmark of the greatest art is that imitations of it are legit-

imate, worthwhile, tolerable; that it is not demolished or devoured by them, or they by it.

Any production of the mind is important when its existence resolves, summons up, or cancels other works, whether previous to it or not.

An artist wants to inspire jealousy till the end of time.

Valéry's central text on originality is his "Letter about Mallarmé" of 1927 where his relation to his authentic precursor inspired dialectical ironies of great beauty;

> We say that an author is *original* when we cannot trace the hidden transformations that others underwent in his mind; we mean to say that the dependence of *what he does* on *what others have done* is excessively complex and irregular. There are works in the likeness of others, and works that are the reverse of others, but there are also works of which the relation with earlier productions is so intricate that we become confused and attribute them to the direct intervention of the gods.
>
> (To go deeper into the subject, we should also have to discuss the influence of a mind on itself and of a work on its author. But this is not the place.)

Everywhere else in Valéry, in prose and verse, is the place, because that was Valéry's true topos, the influence of Paul Valéry's mind upon itself. Is that not the true subject of Descartes and of Montaigne, and of all French men and women of sensibility and intellect? What never ceases to engage Valéry is the effect of his thought and writings upon himself. Creative misunderstandings induced in others were not without interest, but Valéry's creative misunderstandings of Valéry ravished his heart away. Texts of this ravishment abound, but I choose one of the subtlest and most evasive, the dialogue *Dance and the Soul*. Socrates is made by Valéry to speak of "that poison of poisons, that venom which is opposed to all nature," the reduction of life to things as they are that Stevens called the First Idea:

PHAEDRUS

What venom?

SOCRATES

Which is called: the tedium of living? I mean, understand me, not the passing ennui, the tedium that comes of fatigue, or the tedium of which we can see the germ or of which we know the limits; but that perfect tedium, that pure tedium that is not caused by misfortune or infirmity, that is compatible with apparently the happiest of all conditions—that tedium, in short, the stuff of which is nothing else than life itself, and which has no other second cause than the clear-sightedness of the living man. This absolute tedium is essentially nothing but life in its nakedness when it sees itself with unclouded eyes.

ERYXIMACHUS

It is very true that if our soul purges itself of all falseness, strips itself of every fraudulent addition to *what is,* our existence is endangered on the spot by the cold, exact, reasonable and moderate view of human life *as it is.*

PHAEDRUS

Life blackens at the contact of truth, as a suspicious mushroom blackens, when it is crushed, at the contact of the air.

SOCRATES

Eryximachus, I asked you if there were any cure?

ERYXIMACHUS

Why cure so reasonable a complaint? There is nothing, no doubt, nothing more essentially morbid, nothing more inimical to nature than to *see things as they are.* A cold and perfect light is a poison it is impossible to combat. Reality, unadulterated, instantly puts a stop to the heart. One drop of that icy lymph suffices to slacken all the springs of the soul, all the throbbing of desire, to exterminate all hopes and bring to ruin all the gods that inhabited our blood. The Virtues and the noblest colors are turned pale by it in a gradual and devouring consumption. The past is reduced to a handful of ashes, the future to a tiny icicle. The soul appears to itself as an empty and measurable form. Here then are things as they are—a rigorous and deadly chain, where each link joins and limits the next. . . . O Socrates, the universe cannot endure for a single instant to be only what it is. It is strange to think that that which is the Whole cannot suffice itself! . . . Its terror of being what it is has induced it to create and paint for itself thousands of masks; there is no other reason for the existence of mortals. What are mortals for?—Their business is *to know*. Know? And what is *to know*?—*It is assuredly not to be what one is.*—So here are human beings raving and thinking, introducing into nature the principle of unlimited errors and all these myriads of marvels!

The mistakes, the appearances, the play of the mind's dioptric give depth and animation to the world's miserable mass. The idea introduces into what is, the leaven of what is not. . . . But truth sometimes shows itself, and sounds a discord in the harmonious system of phantasmagorias and errors. . . . Everything straightway is threatened with perdition, and Socrates in person comes to beg of me a cure for this desperate case of clear-sightedness and ennui! . . .

We are close again to Stevens's appropriations from Valéry in *Notes toward a Supreme Fiction*. The "clear-sightedness of the living man" does not belong to Stevens or to us; it is the particular gift of the reductively lucid Valéry, who is capable of seeing "life in its nakedness." If Socrates here is Valéry the writer, then Eryximachus is Valéry the reader of—Valéry! "A cold and perfect light" is what Valéry has taught himself to see—in Valéry. Reality here is not so much the reality principle of Freud, as it is the next step after the nothingness of the abyss or final void in French Poe and in Mallarmé. A pragmatic Gnosticism, implicit in Poe and developed by Mallarmé, triumphs in Valéry's ironic sermon about "what is *to know*." The universe's terror of its own nothingness causes it to proliferate mortals, as if each one of us were only another desperate figuration. Our errors, our marvels, introduce "into what is, the leaven of what is not."

We encounter here again the vision of "Palme," since we hear the influence upon Valéry himself of:

> Parfois si l'on désespère,
> Si l'adorable rigueur
> Malgré tes larmes n'opère
> Que sous ombre de langueur.

"There is a strict law in literature that we must never go to the bottom of anything." Valéry almost did not take his own counsel in his endless quest to explain the preternatural prevalence of his intentional self-awareness. He seems now the last person-of-letters in the French tradition to have been capable of reconciling acute consciousness of one's own consciousness with the grand fabrications made possible only by abstraction, by a withdrawal from heightened rhetoricity. Compared to him, Sartre and Blanchot, let alone Derrida, come to creation only in the accents of a severe belatedness.

GEOFFREY H. HARTMAN

"La Dormeuse"

La Dormeuse

Quels secrets dans son coeur brûle ma jeune amie,
Ame par le doux masque aspirant une fleur?
De quels vains aliments sa naïve chaleur
Fait ce rayonnement d'une femme endormie?

Souffle, songes, silence, invincible accalmie,
Tu triomphes, ô paix plus puissante qu'un pleur,
Quand de ce plein sommeil l'onde grave et l'ampleur
Conspirent sur le sein d'une telle ennemie.

Dormeuse, amas doré d'ombres et d'abandons,
Ton repos redoutable est chargé de tels dons,
O biche avec langueur longue auprès d'une grappe,

Que malgré l'âme absente, occupée aux enfers,
Ta forme au ventre pur qu'un bras fluide drape,
Veille; ta forme veille, et mes yeux sont ouverts.

The Sleeper

To what secrets in her heart does my young friend set fire,
Soul breathing in through the sweet mask a flower?
From what vain nourishments may her indwelling warmth
Draw this radiance of a woman fallen asleep?

From *The Unmediated Vision: An Interpretation of Wordsworth, Hopkins, Rilke and Valéry.* © 1954 by Yale University Press, © 1966 by Geoffrey H. Hartman. Harcourt, Brace & World, 1966.

> Breath, dreams, stillness, O invincible calm,
> Peace of more power than a tear, yours is the triumph
> When the slow wave and ampleness of sleep
> Conspire on the breast of such an enemy.
>
> Sleeper, gold mass of shadows and yieldings,
> Your redoubtable rest is weighted with such gifts,
> O hind with languor long beside a grape cluster,
>
> That, though the soul is absent, busy in the depths,
> Your form's pure belly draped by the fluid arm
> Is awake; your form is awake, and my eyes are open.
>
> (*Charmes*)

The poet meditates on a sleeping woman. He wonders at the cause and effect of her repose, one so powerful that, though the soul is hidden, her "form" is awake and perceptible to his open eyes.

The poem has a fine but precarious stability. Each stanza, each verse, each word almost, seems to take a new beginning and exist for its own sake. The straight line of sense is continually suspended by precariousness or beauty of phrase. Most readers will be surprised at the opening verse which, with a rhythm reminiscent of Racine, stops short on *brûle,* suddenly perceived as the verb belonging to *ma jeune amie.* This inversion is the first of many to compel a withholding of the conventional sense of the words. Nothing betrays the meaning of a verse which seems to have emerged from a natural yet nonverbal movement of consciousness. Each line seems to carry the emphasis of the voice as voice, before it has become speech, words, differentiated feeling. We are led to reflect how the single verse with its character of independent, inner equilibrium is joined to the next.

In the first quatrain the soldering is achieved by apposition; also by the assonance of, for example, *amie* and *âme.* But there is also an inner parallelism. The second line of the quatrain is characterized like the first by an inversion ("par le doux masque"), and by a slight continuing of the alexandrine accent from the sixth syllable (*masque*) to the seventh (*aspirant*), a weak syllable, strengthened to this emphasis by its assonance with *masque* and *âme.* Thus, in both lines the predominant accent is found not on the sixth syllable but on both the sixth and seventh; this and inversion give the lines their quality of equilibrium at every point. If we go on to verses three and four we find in addition to assonance of the sixth syllable (*aliments, rayonnement*) that their linking is effected through the verb, suspended at the beginning of verse four, but absolutely without climactic result, for the line is almost at once pulled to the center by the long *rayonnement,* and made finally stable by the double, rising anapest of *d'une femme endormie.* And the first stanza as a whole is of course strongly joined by rhyme and by the parallelism of the two questions.

Apposition, inversion, suspension, assonance, to which in isolation no significance may be attached, are the more evident means ensuring the cohesion not only of the first, but of every stanza. Their mutual effect is to remove the poem as far as possible from the pathos of natural speech, preferring a spontaneity more stable and strange. This may be the spontaneity of a mind in resourceful play with the probabilities of rhythm and word.

For each stanza, like the first, develops out of a sudden verbal gesture or apostrophe promising climactic development ("Quels secrets . . . Souffles, songes, silences . . . Dormeuse"), a gesture that each line shares to a lesser degree; but the promise is deceptive, for equilibrium is at once reestablished by the retarding influences of inversion, apposition, and assonance. In the second stanza the tendency toward a free rhythm is so strong that we have one of the rare lines of French poetry composed of three nouns with asyndeton, and in its second part an adjective-noun combination (*invincible accalmie*) with an elision rarely used by Valéry. But the movement is not freed: it subsides as soon as we recognize that all these nouns which seemed independent are mere appositions to "ô paix plus puissante qu'un pleur"; while the stanza concludes with another retarding inversion ("Quand de ce plein sommeil").

Valéry is most sensitive to what he once called the parthenogenesis of the mind. These retardations aim first to render the spontaneous yet equilibrist motion of consciousness, its fundamental yet precarious continuity, then to cause in the reader a withholding of the commonplace sense of the words. Valéry, like Mallarmé, has broken with the French tradition of expository clarity, though he is clear enough in his own way. An initial obscurity is essential to "La Dormeuse." The poet uses every means to retard in us that faculty of the intellect often named induction, by which we are enabled to make a quick or conventional guess at the referent of a phrase.

Fullness of sound that seems to cause a perception of rhythm without a simultaneous perception of the literal sense is additional evidence that we are faced with an amiable conspiracy to retard induction. The suspension of sense by sound seems to increase in each stanza until we reach the climax of the third: "Dormeuse, amas doré d'ombres et d'abandons." There is such vocal joy in this verse that no one would be surprised to find "do-re-mi."

Yet to say of this line "here sense is suspended by sound" is only approximate. If its sense were merely "do-re-mi" we would not bother about it. The meaning, though retarded, is finally reinforced by what at first seems an entirely *arbitrary* effect of sound. These words are given a surprising resonance as if we heard them echoing not through the ordinary air, but through an unusual medium, such as water, though far more mysterious. The idea therefore arises, stimulated by Valéry himself, that poetry is, by essence, incantation; for, if the value of poetry lies in the indissolubility of sound and sense, and if this sound is largely arbitrary to the sense, then the significance of sound must be of an order other than intellectual—one that could be called magical. We would recall the fact that "La Dormeuse" is taken from a collection whose title is *Charmes*.

But with a deal of patience, as indispensable to comprehension as to analysis, we may render this charm fully accessible to the understanding. The line beginning "Dormeuse" is characterized by an unusual collocation of metaphor which destroys an immediate grasp of the literal sense. In what way is the sleeper a "mass," that is, a lifeless group of elements? Is it not the height of coldness to call this woman, full of dreams and quiet breathing, a "gold mass of shadows and yieldings"? This question is, of course, to a certain extent rhetorical, for the beauty of the sound protects the line, and *amas* still retains a note of seventeenth-century préciosité. But the yoking together of visual and spiritual qualities is strange; the woman is seen almost with a painter's eye as a combination of line and light intimating a purely decorative effect.

Indeed, the mixture is so subtle and the appeal of sound so evident that it may prompt the reader to reverse the usual order of cognition and instead of seeking the sense first in the general meaning of the words to search for it in the sound. This sound is more than a fine variation of similar elements forming the basis of all aesthetic charm.

French poetry since the appearance of romance intonation has had to both fight against and capitalize on the excessive lilt of its language. The classical alexandrine which Valéry modifies brings one solution, for in it, as opposed to that alexandrine which Ronsard found prosy, spineless, and without nerve, the upward movement is severely curtailed by a caesura, and by placing the main accents on the sixth and twelfth syllables, so that while the line wishes to fly away with the natural impulse of French speech, it gains order and intensity by the knowledge of a new commencement at the point of highest pitch. But when we read, "Dormeuse, amas doré d'ombres et d'abandons," a further development is felt. This line has, like most of Valéry's verse, a marvelous stability making it difficult to pick out the main accents of intensity. Every word seems so charged that the line affects us like a pattern of musical syllables, purified of the arbitrary emphases of speech, but not deprived of its own general and intense accent. In this line, and in the poem as a whole, there is an attempt at what may be called continuity by syllabic sound.

Valéry, in other words, evolves a poetic line truly both "poetic" and "line," that is to say, one whose rhythm, sound, and accent are continuous and stable, with the same continuity and the same stability as the melodic line of Gluck, where in spite of passion the only sign of it is in the sustained beauty of the voice's course, and the only sign of discontinuity is in the poignant vibrato of the voice that sings. But how can it occur in language that a syllable (i.e., a fragment of sound without sense except in a word) and a succession of syllables free themselves from that unit of sense we call a word and proceed to carry and perhaps determine meaning? Here, however, we arrive at a most general problem of verse, for Valéry has only made extreme use of poetry's general tendency to endow the sound of a word with a meaning independent of that word's ordinary signification.

The apparently arbitrary relation between the sound of a word and its sense intrigued Valéry. He reflected on it continuously, and this concern parallels his wish to retard the mind's conventional responses to language. Not by caprice, dandyism, or philosophical prejudice does he inveigh against the commonplace, but because he feels to an extreme degree the arbitrary nature of all conventional signs. He therefore insists on drawing attention to the fortuitous and indefinite character of signs in which we often see inherent significance or which we take on trust; and the highest praise he knows is to say of someone (as he did of Mallarmé) that this poet used language as if he had invented it. Can the connection between the sound of words and their sense, between conventional signs and their referents, be shown as more than arbitrary, since it is, no doubt, a more than arbitrary process that brought it, and still brings it, into being?

"La Dormeuse" gives an example of how an arbitrary yet necessary and perhaps even at base natural relation is constructed between sound and sense. One is impressed on reading the poem by the importance of the vowel *a* and its combinations. To list those more evident: *amie,* followed by *âme* and *aspirant; naïve chaleur; grave et l'ampleur; amas; âme, absente.* It is also difficult to distinguish between a shorter and a longer *a,* their length being equal because of the equilibrium and inner tension of the line. One may therefore find that the poem causes a fusion in the mind between the *am* of *âme* and the *am* of *amas,* probably aided by the association of the vowel *a* with the idea of *aspirant,* and of the consonant *m* with the idea of repose as in *femme endormie, sommeil,* and *ampleur,* so that on reaching the *amas* of stanza three the reader feels the tranquil breath of the sleeper. But though such single vowel or consonant effects are found always anywhere in poetry and are too delicate to isolate, the decontexualization of *am* as a sound unit is made possible by the verses' prompting of what has been called syllabic continuity. And coming to *amas,* we find that *âme* is present, simply through a sound syllable *am* that has, so to say, migrated.

But supposing this to be correct, that contained in *amas* is the meaning of *âme,* then we have found, by attention to sound, the persistent theme of the poem which at first resists logical analysis. For the indeterminate sense of *amas* leads us to the poem's fundamental theme: that the beauty of things is independent of our sense for what is human, the sleeper affecting not by her soul (*âme*), here hidden by sleep, and perhaps if genuine, always hidden, but by her quality to sheer sight, the word *amas* then denoting the indifference of the eyes to the human appeal of the subject.

Just as the poet withdraws words from common currency, and charms us into a retarding of their conventional sense, so the soul itself is withdrawn, and we are shown its secret influence not as a simple, commonplace, and sentimental object (as in Mme de Staël's "chantez votre âme"), but as something most beautiful when almost inhuman, affecting most powerfully when most unconscious or deprived of its displayed human sense, the object not of the mediate and sentimental, but of the immediate and aesthetic vision. In the impressionist and abstract painters the rendering of a human figure as human is no longer a pictorial value. In Valéry the rendering of a human figure as human is no longer a poetic value. Despite *âme,* the sleeping woman affects as *amas,* and it is this dehumanization as a result of which a thing or a person is seen only in terms of light, line, or visual quality, that gives the beauty of such lines as "Dormeuse, amas doré d'ombres et d'abandons" and "O biche avec langueur longue auprès d'une grappe."

Though we have approached this meaning by an analysis of rhythm and sound, it is there also and very strictly in the logical development. The unity of theme and style rests on a withholding from view of all human, that is to say, of all immediately moral, emotional, or sensual, attributes, and it is precisely this kind of retardation which is often termed aesthetic. The "burning" of the first quatrain, for example, does not produce heat but light (*rayonnement*); in "l'onde grave" a moral attribute is employed in its formalistic sense, and in "biche avec langueur longue" a sensuous quality delimited by a formal adjective.

Indeed, everything tends to this quality named in the last line "form." This is the thing that endures and remains awake in the sleeping woman, even though the soul is hidden and busied with a strange alchemy. What is "form"? It is evidently that which suspends hasty rationality or commonplace recognition, and which grants what may be called pure visibility. There is no doubt that the poem deals with a concrete and very sensuous experience, but the senses are touched as if they all had the objective and luminous vision of the eyes: "ta forme veille et mes yeux sont ouverts." The poem is concerned with the nature of contemplation, and probably aesthetic contemplation; the girl is revealed in the form of her body—"ta forme au ventre pur qu'un bras fluide drape"—yet this form does not express the organic reason of the body, but one touching the mind with the directness, luminosity, and coolness of a sight touching the eyes. The result is repose: neither sexual nor mental avidity but an indefinite suspension of the act of knowledge in favor of sheer visibility.

II

There is in Valéry's work an exceptional permanence of theme to which "La Dormeuse" gives only a single, if perfect, expression. We may choose works from any period of the poet's life—of the earliest poems such as "Eté" (*Album de vers anciens*), or later ones like *La Jeune Parque* (1917), "Le Cimetière marin" (*Charmes* 1922), the *Cantate de Narcisse* (1938), or the fragments of crude poetry (*poésie brute*) stemming from various dates and found in *Mélange*—the result is the same: every major poem presents the same experience, namely of a type of contemplation in which all knowledge about things is suspended, only their "form" remaining as the object of knowledge. We shall now define the nature of this contemplation, and of "form," its sole immediate object.

Each poem represents a conflict between the appeal of sensuous beauty as an image of fertility and its appeal as an image of self-sufficient purity. Let us take first the poem "Eté," then "Le Cimetière marin," and finally *La Jeune Parque*. In "Eté" the perfume of summertime is said to be as heavy as rock yet as pure as a rock of air, while the drowsy rumor of the sea is likened to that of a hive of busy bees. These comparisons, and the rest of the poem, both in sound and image, show the poet regarding summer as indistinguishably a figure for fertility and a figure for a luminous, self-sufficient beauty:

> Eté, roche d'air pur, et toi, ardente ruche,
> O mer! Eparpillée en mille mouches sur
> Les touffes d'une chair fraîche comme une cruche,
> Et jusque dans la bouche où bourdonne l'azur.

(Summer, rock of pure air, and you, ardent hive, o sea! scattered
like a thousand flies upon the tufts of a flesh cool as a pitcher,
and even into the mouth where hums the azure.)

In the "Graveyard by the Sea" the image of fertility which haunted
Valéry in his youth is now generalized as the image of an experience that
the mind cannot satisfy by contemplation, the *emprakton* of Pindar. There
is a restatement of the conflict between the active and the contemplative life.
The sea—that changer, bitch, resounding whore!—suggests by its perpetual
motion both the renewal at the source of perception which is the mark of
the active life, and the repetitive sameness which is the fate of the thinker
who would forestall experience by systematic thought. "La mer, la mer,
toujours recommencée (The sea, the sea, always restarting)."

As for *La Jeune Parque,* this poem has for its subject a mysterious person
of almost indifferent gender (we shall simply call her JP) who reflects on the
conflicting purposes of her body, a figure for love, fertility, and experience
as well as a figure for contemplation, self-sufficient purity, and narcissism.
The opening verses

Qui pleure là, sinon le vent simple, à cette heure
Seule avec diamants extrêmes? . . . Mais qui pleure,
Si proche de moi-même au moment de pleurer?

(Who weeps there, if not the simple wind, at this hour alone with
extreme diamonds? . . . But who weeps so close to myself at the
moment of weeping?)

already contain in full the theme and magic of the entire poem. JP wakes to
hear a cry and to perceive light in that twilight moment of the birth of
consciousness which Valéry delights to picture. It is actually JP who has just
cried beneath the bite of the serpent, but her body with its breath and tears
is felt as a strange body: perhaps it was the wind that cried, and perhaps
her tears, the "extreme diamonds," are really stars, "extreme" because set
far away in the sky, or shining at the extreme surface of her body, in her
eyes. Here again is that distancing effect also found in "La Dormeuse," the
dehumanization of the body by means of a purely visual perspective that will
not recognize the evident organic structure of movement and life. So the
poem as a whole may be considered the Odyssey of Consciousness in search
of its true body.

JP is met on her way by many temptations that would persuade her to
consider her own body as she considers the body of others, i.e., as a sensual
and practical thing with no other purpose than life or fertility. These temp-

tations are the bite of the snake, betokening sensual self-knowledge; memories of childhood and spring; the flesh itself and its lassitude; and finally, the sea's sharp call for rebirth. But consciousness, in love with the impersonal beauty of a body moving in space, overcomes every temptation until the very end of the poem, where there is an ambiguous and forced gesture toward an experience of things beyond contemplation and outside of the original body, an "il faut tenter de vivre."

Thus the body perceived under the sign of contemplation is contrasted to the body under the sign of experience or fertility. And there is always one quality through which physical beauty is enabled to become the object of a purely visual contemplation, and which Valéry describes as *clair* or *lumineux*. That phenomenon which Descartes made a quality of adequate ideas is made by Valéry into the quality of fully perceptible bodies. His entire output of verse gives the effect of being a continual meditation on the nature of space and the distribution of light. Everything appears to have *éclat de matière,* "brightness of matter." Even the air, space, *Cher Espace,* is felt as incandescent. We see midday as alchemist in "Le Cimetière marin," and one of its stanzas uses the term "immaterial fire" in description of the graveyard: "Fermé, sacré, plein d'un feu sans matière / Fragment terrestre offert à la lumière" (stanza 10). Now the sleeping woman's body was also termed luminous, and form represented as the result of a special burning. It is described as *rayonnement* and seems to affect the eyes alone, insofar as these are the luminous sense. Indeed, form as the immediate object of Valéry's special contemplation is not distinguishable from the sensation of radiance. The phenomenon of radiance as a constant of perception has only recently become a subject for empirical study by the eidetic school; but Valéry practised the phenomenological method as a matter of course, and is unafraid to base his poetry on simple psycho-physical observations. So the radiance in question is at origin a physical light, not Milton's "before the Sun / Before the Heavens thou wert." It results from this physical law, that we perceive the outgoing light of another body, but not of our own. Yet our own eyes surely have the outgoing light, even if we cannot perceive it. Valéry knew of this intuitively. The constituent character of that special contemplation the experience of which he seeks to express is that it causes the eyes and the intense mind to become aware of their emergent light, to desire its pure reflection by the thing about to be perceived. So Valéry goes in search of that material thing which might in fact show the desired quality of pure reflection; and almost finds it in the burning gulf of the cemetery, reflecting the zenith light of a southern noon:

> L'âme exposée aux torches du solstice,
> Je te soutiens, admirable justice
> De la lumière aux armes sans pitié!
> Je te rends pure à ta place première:
> Regarde toi!

(My soul exposed to the torches of the solstice, I bear up under you, admirable justice of a light whose arms are merciless! I give you back, pure, to your original place. Look at yourself!)

Is not Valéry in search of a body having the quality of pure or total reflection? For the image that he pursues is not for him a Platonic abstraction but a perfectly perceptible, and therefore intuitable, body, not an *eidos* simply, but also an *eidolon*. The poet of "Le Cimetière marin" stands in the same relation to the light as the sleeper's radiant body in "La Dormeuse" stood to his eyes. The torches of the solstice seek a being that would return their light as purely and strongly as it came; the poet sought a body that would answer entirely to the notion of his eyes. Valéry's reaction to the light is "Je te rends pure à ta place première: Regarde toi," and the form of the sleeping woman seems also to suggest "Regarde-toi," for he tells us not that he has understood the function of her beauty, but merely, "Your form is luminous, awake; my eyes are open." Just as the poet ideally returns the light to its source, and the sleeper the light to his eyes, so form is that which by some quality of pure reflection returns to Valéry the image of his mind.

The poet of course never finds the magical body of his quest. But he is always on the point of finding it: "ta forme fraîche, et cette claire écorce ... Oh! te saisir enfin ... Plus pur que d'une femme et non formé de fruits. (Your cool form and this light-colored bark ... Oh! if at last I could seize you! ... Purer than a woman's and not formed of fruits.)" The form sought by Valéry in the special contemplation is always almost visible, and "visible" must be understood in an absolute sense; it is the very same thing that Narcissus looks for, the always potential embodiment of the mind. Just as this contemplation, which perceives a radiance that cannot be perceived except in an almost unlighted mirror, which suspends every suggestion of the fertility or use of an object, is only virtual, never actual, so its object also is only virtual and never more than possible. Sight is experienced by Valéry as an unfulfilled condition, as *visibility,* and the object of sight as an unfulfilled existent, as *possibility.* And in order to convey the virtual quality of consciousness Valéry uses a specific method of style.

Few writers neglect so systematically the commonplace and sentimental quality of words, and combine such incongruous images as Valéry in his mixtures of metaphor. The technique which generally leaves in the mind a sensation of brilliance may be named the *metamorphosis* of metaphor: Valéry refuses to take any one image or metaphor seriously: the shimmering waves suggest mysterious sheep, a white flock of tranquil tombs, a swarm of doves, inquisitive angels. Such metamorphosis is also found on the level of sound; here it could be called modulation. But since we have to do with poetry and not music, we should find a term adequate to the fact that poetic sound never attains the freedom of the note, being limited by signs having direct referents in experience. The metamorphosis of metaphor, on the level of sound, is syllabic continuity.

An important example of syllabic continuity was suggested in our analysis in "La Dormeuse" of *âme* and *amas*. Now the syllables which in Valéry construct meaning through sound are not unlimited; there is in fact only one principal series, and this series may be considered as modulated from the root sound of *am*.

A first variation of *am* is that of *aime, même, extrême*. The couplet *même: extrême*, in particular, parallels the meaning of *âme: amas*. But the major variation of *am*, the fundamental, the most persistent, is that of *amer, mer, air, or*, etc. It could also simply be looked at as a modulation of a vowel-plus-*r*.

We remember the beginning of "Eté": "Eté, roche d'air pur, et toi, ardente ruche / O mer. . . ." One can make an impressive list of all the words ending in a vowel-plus-*r* that are found in this poem. *Air, pur, mer, sur, chair, azur, cher, perd, mer, odeur, purs, matière, lumière, hennir, pleurs, perd, amour, purs, l'or, éphémère, chair, splendeur amère, miroir, préfère, amour, l'heure, futur, sacrificateur, jour, azur, dur, autour, obscur, mer, jour, dore, air.*

The length even of this list makes it improbable that the variation is merely part of the aesthetic charm to be found in any poem. Our ear is haunted by syllables in vowel-plus-*r* until we tend to neglect continuity by word and sense for continuity by syllable and sound. Is there here a construction of meaning through sound similar to that found in "La Dormeuse"? We may safely say that a subtle identity is gradually induced between the concepts corresponding to the sound of *air, mer,* and that corresponding to the sound of *or*.

Thematic evidence may be added. A wave spilling onto sand is described as "a power, losing as tears all its diamonds." We are reminded of the "peace more powerful than a tear" invoked in "La Dormeuse." *La Jeune Parque* commences with "Qui pleure là" and includes the beautiful canticle of the tear. *Pleur* is one of the vowels-plus-*r* that echo through many of Valéry's poems. Nor is the poet's admiration for the tear an eccentric interest; it has a long literary tradition going back to the blazon of the Renaissance. Why is Valéry so concerned with weeping?

He is concerned because a tear is grief or passion made visible and therefore powerful, for nothing, according to Valéry, has power unless it also has visibility. But though the tear is compared to a diamond, it is less powerful than the simple imminence of grief, for its appearance already signifies a passing into act of what was in the highest degree virtual. That is also why the repose emanating from the sleeping woman is described as more powerful than a tear, because it is more virtual. In all things Valéry seeks this quality of the virtual, one recalling the emergent yet unrealizable character of consciousness, a state where intense expectation is not as yet betrayed by event.

The tear, then, has power insofar as it has visibility, but its very appearance already suggests the passing of this power. By emerging from the depth of invisible feeling or the depth of the unlit sea, tear and wave become visible and brilliant like a diamond. This act of gradual emergence parallels the gliding of vowel and concept between *mer* and *or:* gold, or rather, gold purified, gilt, representing what is most precious to sight. And the last line of the poem hints at the transmutation of even *air* into *or*—"Toute la peau dore les treilles d'air."

Thus gilt is taken as the property of everything that has become—like wave, tear, air and skin—visible, significant to sight. Numerous examples could be adduced to show this Midas touch of the eye, its gold-radiation:

> Je me voyais me voir, sinueuse, et dorais
> De regards en regards, mes profondes forêts.

(Sinuous, I saw myself seeing myself, and gilded with glance after glance my deep woods.)

Indeed, in one stanza of "Le Cimetière marin" this gold-glance of the eye is the actual subject, and its magnificent last line expresses the paradox of the instantaneous look understanding discontinuously and ever anew the moving sea—an analogue of the moving and ever-changing world as well as of the perceiving eye:

> Stable trésor, temple simple à Minerve,
> Masse de calme, et visible réserve,
> Eau sourcilleuse, Œil qui gardes en toi
> Tant de sommeil sous un voile de flamme,

O mon silence! . . . Edifice dans l'âme
Mais comble d'or aux mille tuiles, Toit!

(Stable treasure, simple temple to Minerva, mass of calm, and
reticence that can be seen; lidded water, Eye that keeps hidden
under its veil of flame so much sleep—O my silence! . . . Mansion
in the soul yet Roof with a thousand-tiled climax of gold!)

The exclamation "O mon silence!" informs us how intimately this
stanza bears on Valéry's experience as poet. Its every image is a bead on the
same string. The sea appears as a visible reserve or reservoir of visibility, as
an eye sheathed in light yet dark and inexhaustible within, as the invisible
and indivisible edifice of the soul revealed as a resplendent but splintered
surface. All these metamorphosed metaphors are but analogues to the poet's
famed silence, and this silence itself is but a synonym for Valéry's primary
experience, of *possibility as such:* of the mind insofar as it forms only imminent desires, of the body insofar as its power seems greatest when still
potential, of both mind and body insofar as visibility is their ideal fulfillment
and certain betrayal.

But another analogue to this silence striving for expression, this power
of sight unrealized under its veil of light, this gold-spotted sea calm and
inexhaustible in the depths, is the sleeping woman's invincible and radiant
calm:

Dormeuse, amas doré d'ombres et d'abandons!

At the heart of "La Dormeuse" is the fusion of *dor*mir and *dor*er. For
Valéry's desire is to have this repose, common to body and mind at the
height of power before the act, made visible, and gilt is the poet's major
image of transformation causing visibility without loss of purity—"It is, in
fact, the most abstract agent that exists, after thought: while thought may
metamorphose and envelop only images, gold has the power to excite and
favor the transmutation of all real things, changing one into the other; and
yet it remains incorruptible and, passing through all hands, pure."

Valéry shares in the general crisis of the aesthetic consciousness which
would suspend all relational knowledge of things in order to know the indefinite moment between possibility and act, but knows only the dispos-
session of a mind for which no visible form is visible enough.

III

O moment, diamant du Temps.... Contemplation in which time flashes like the diamond sea (and revery is indistinguishable from knowledge) is a rare experience, or else is swiftly lost among utilitarian thoughts. Valéry's special contemplation is all the more strange for having not God as its transcendent object, but any phenomenon of consciousness as such. What is found in consciousness cannot therefore be referred to anything but consciousness or itself. Valéry encounters the same problem as Rilke concerning the possibility of symbols. For the objects of perception cannot be represented in terms other than those directly given in perception. The body speaks its own language. Do "La Dormeuse" and the other poems of Valéry give evidence of a reflection on the possibility of symbols?

Two types of disproportionate movement are often represented by Valéry: that of the body to thought, that of the object to the eye. To illustrate these we could quote once more the stanza from "Le Cimetière marin" beginning "Stable trésor." Here are two other examples, from *La Jeune Parque*:

> Cette main, sur mes traits qu'elle rêve effleurer,
> Distraitement docile à quelque fin profonde.

(This hand, distracted and docile toward some profound end, on my features which it dreams of caressing.)

> Reptile, o vifs détours tout courus de caresses
>
> . . . .
> Coule vers d'autres lits tes robes successives.

(Reptile, o swift turnings ashiver with caresses. . . . let your successive robes flow toward other beds.)

In such verses movement is represented as complete though still in progress, the static position is noted before the motion, or there is an almost immediate dissociation of living, organic things, like the snake, into a pattern of discrete acts moved by a cause indistinguishable from movement. To such effects may be given the collective name of prolepsis or anticipation.

Prolepsis is difficult to define as a feature of style; in general practice it is used only to refer to a special use of the adjective, a famous instance being Keats's "So the two brothers and their *murder'd* man." No afterthought in Keats, prolepsis is used merely to heighten a narrative style. In Valéry, however, his frequent adjectival use—"Mais je sais ce que voit mon regard *disparu*"—is only an instance of a larger pattern. Extreme prolepsis may of course do away with a good deal of grammatical and logical subordination, the very effects peculiar to language. At times there is an obvious flaw, as when the poet causes an appositional phrase to precede the main clause solely because of metrical embarrassment. But most of the time, even though inversion and suspension be as great as

> Quel éclat sur mes cils aveuglément dorée,
> O paupières qu'opprime une nuit de trésor,
> Je priais à tâtons dans vos ténèbres d'or!
> (*La Jeune Parque*)

the various uses of prolepsis may be justified as an expression that the immediate object of perception is a visual surface, or more radically, that "substance," "essence," "soul" are but a succession of surfaces.

Now it is evident that this proposition stands close to painting, and especially modern painting, which recognizes plot, character, and movement only as a function of visual surfaces. And it may in general be said that prolepsis is the constitutive metaphor of painting, since painting is essentially anticipation: of action through positioned bodies, of these bodies through the effects of surface and light, of surface through the relations of line and color.

Yet the proposition "Substance is but a succession of surfaces" is evidently a paradox, the same one we find throughout the work of Valéry. Succession indicates a continuous series. How are surfaces continuous? Here is a girl: she moves, she has moved, she is about to move. What is at all times the line of her hands, feet, and face with that of her body, the line of her body with that of her surroundings? Is there one exhaustive line which, like a mathematical formula, could circumscribe the actual and implicit motion which all her surface makes with all other surfaces? "That woman who was just now there has been devoured by countless forms." *Painting* must seize this line, impossibly complex, but not by succession. It is given one moment only, one surface. It must render the essential by a simultaneity of surfaces. Poetry cannot pretend simultaneity, only succession; and then a succession not of *surfaces* but of *sounds* (which do not have a direct referent in sight), or *words* (which rarely have a complete referent in sight). To conceive substance as a succession of surfaces is so paradoxical that neither of these arts, nor music, may do it justice.

But Valéry does work toward an imaginative solution. In one of his books a figure appears which ends the race in which body is always swifter than thought or eyes, realizing an organic equation of infinite line, a total surfacing of the soul:

SOCRATES: It is the supreme attempt . . . She turns, and all that
is visible detaches itself from her soul . . . men and things
will form around her a shapeless and circular dough . . . She
turns . . . A body by its simple force, and by its act is strong
enough to alter more profoundly the nature of things than
the mind ever could in its thoughts and wildest dreams. . . .
She could die like this. . . .

ERYXIMACHUS: Sleep, perhaps, fall asleep with a magic sleep. . . .

SOCRATES: She will rest motionless at the very center of her movement. Isolated, isolated, like the axis of the world. . . .

ATHIKTÉ: Shelter, shelter, O my shelter, O Whirlwind—I was
within you, O movement, outside of all things.

The book is *L'Ame et la danse,* and the figure is Athikté the dancer.

The allusion to her magic sleep reminds us of "La Dormeuse," for the
sleeping woman of 1922 is probably an anticipation of the dancer of 1923.
Both figures result from speculation on the immediate objects of sense experience. Both present an imaginative victory over prolepsis, if prolepsis is
defined as that shortcoming in symbolic representation which forces us to
consider movement' or soul or understanding as a succession of discrete
events. But they are equally symbols for "metamorphosis overcome," if metamorphosis is defined as that shortcoming in symbolic representation which
forces us to show continuity (soul, movement, understanding) where there
is only a "diamant du Temps." In Athikté movement, soul, and body become
entirely surface, entirely visible, even though she rests at the still center of
motion; and in the sleeping woman the body and its secret dimension are
viewed only as visible surface, as form, while this form is neither a momentary and discontinuous apparition nor an enduring quality, but perpetually
virtual to the eyes.

Now Athikté acts as the explicit representative of the art of dance, even
as Eupalinos is a representative of architecture, and Amphion of music. But
what does the sleeper represent? The example of Athikté affirms the possibility that the body may be known in itself and with no intermediary other
than the act of dance. The example of Eupalinos affirms the possibility that
the mind may be known in itself without intermediary except the act of
construction. But the "Dormeuse" is an example of the "body of the world"
as poet and painter try to know it. The latter know it only in terms offered
by the object itself—conventional terms like color, line, concept, image, and
word—not, as dancer, musician, and architect know it, in terms almost
negligible as intermediates, terms which provide an almost direct intuition

of universal forms. "A beautiful body makes itself be looked at for its own sake" writes Valéry, and adds "But music and architecture make us think of something quite different from themselves. . . . It was the symphony itself that made me forget my sense of hearing. It changed so promptly, so exactly into souled truths and universal adventures or even into abstract combinations, that I no longer perceived the sensuous intermediary, sound [que je n'avais plus connaissance de l'intermédiaire sensible, le son]."

Poetry, then, perhaps painting also, differs from the other arts by a use of symbols which retain inevitable referents in conventional speech and image, and cannot therefore represent mind and body or consciousness of mind and body in a direct way. "La Dormeuse" tells us of the poet's impossible attempt to understand the body as if it did not need mediation; his desire to know reality without the aid of symbol and by sheer contemplation. And the last words of the poem, *mes yeux sont ouverts,* express this dilemma exactly, suggesting that the eyes are open by nature and necessity in endless anticipation and as a physical figure for an unrealized spiritual power. The intellectual pursuit of Valéry is to this end, that the body may be seen as what it virtually is, a magnificent revelation and instrument of the soul. Could it be viewed as such, the eyes would not be symbol, but reality.

IV

We have talked about the aesthetic consciousness, but Valéry makes no distinction between the aesthetic and other kinds of consciousness. In his very first essay, on the method of Leonardo da Vinci, he insists that artistic and scientific minds work toward the same end, the discovery of a fundamental law of continuity. Valéry is evidently oppressed by the modern multiplication of the modes of knowledge, and he would like to discover that method of intellectual construction which stands at the unitary base of mental endeavor. He even suggests in his essay on Poe's *Eureka* that the modern world needs a poet who would take his materials from the sciences: "We have no poets of Knowledge [poètes de la connaissance] among us, absolutely none. Perhaps this is because we have so strong a feeling for the distinction of genres, that is to say, for the independence of the divers movements of the mind, that we do not accept those works which combine them." Not only is Valéry haunted by the idea of a *mathesis universalis,* but he develops a highly conscious *method* of symbolic construction in order to unify various modes of apprehension, including the scientific. We shall now consider the character of this method and, finally, show it operative in his poetry.

At Valéry's appearance the concept of causality, criticized by Hume and

Kant, had lost much of its intellectual attractiveness, and had been put more and more on a par with metaphysical curiosities like radical heat, occult essence, etc. Knowledge and perception had become the inexplicable, central facts. For Valéry there is on the one hand consciousness, on the other, mere events governed by the "laws" of chance. Between consciousness and the fortuitous object lies perception and the mystery of perception. From the beginning he found himself attracted to two major phenomena, air and sea. The sea demonstrates most forcefully the operation of chance: "Foam lights up from *time to time,* on the field of the sea, and these *times* are created by chance." Or, "Here, the sea gathers, takes back into itself its innumerable dice, throws them once more." If the sea represents events governed by chance, air is the analogue of consciousness, the element of possibility, the luminous void. To cite here even one supporting quotation would belie the richness of all—"L'Air immense ouvre et referme mon livre." What under these conditions is the image for an act of perception or of knowledge? The answer is the fact of visibility, the action of one thing upon another from a distance, induction—"Could the inexplicable . . . have for its image *distance?* Action from a distance, induction, etc.?"

As early as the *Introduction à la méthode de Léonard de Vinci* Valéry is concerned with "action à distance." The essay holds that invention results from the discovery of a law of continuity for objects not yet subsumed under such a law. All speculation is said to have as its end the extension of continuity by means of metaphor, abstraction, and language. Action from the distance is an unimaginable thing. Great men of science like Faraday (discoverer of electromagnetic waves) came to their ideas through an attempt to fill the void, a purpose also evident in da Vinci, of whom the following passage is quoted:

> The air is full of an infinite number of straight and radiating lines
> that intersect and interlace without any one ever taking the tra-
> jectory of any other; and they represent for each object the true
> *form* of its being.

It is clear that the poet also thinks of continuity as visual in nature. If the concept of visual continuity is kept in mind, many obscure images are clarified. "Eté," for example, tells of the skin that gilds the vine-arbors of the air: "Toute la peau dore les treilles d'air." This surely refers to that network of visual or potential rays described by Leonardo, here represented as a luminous, life-giving, bacchic vine.

But the thoughts of the essay on Leonardo are still germinal. Two concepts touched upon, that of construction and that of substitution, receive fuller development in the poet's later work, and especially in *Eupalinos*. Both methods require a supreme play of ideas ("un jeu suprême d'idées") neglecting the material nature of the objects reflected on: "One order is substituted for another the initial one. ... Stones, colors, words, concepts, men, etc., their particular nature does not change the general condition of this sort of music in which they play only the role of timbre." Now these ideas, if taken seriously, must evidently derive from a theory of space and thought as homogeneous, i.e., uninterrupted by the bodies in it. And the imaginary space of Valéry is indeed a mathematical rather than a physical continuum, a locus of action which, though it does have three dimensions, is uninterrupted by the bodies it contains, and presents these as arabesques or as a succession of surfaces:

> Reptile, o vifs détours tout courus de caresses
>
> . . . .
>
> Coule vers d'autres lits tes robes successives.

If thought and space, then, are homogeneous, objects of thought (man, stone, word, color) are indifferent to the nature of thought, exerting no modifying influence; and the operations of the mind are reversible and indefinitely repeatable. The first proposition is already expressed in 1894 and the term "homogeneity" used, though the concept is best explained in a later addition to the Leonardo essay as "Color and pain; memories, expectation and surprise; this tree and the waving of its leaves, its annual variation, its shadow just like its substance, its accidents of shape and position, the faraway thoughts which it recalls to the distracted mind—*all this comes to the same*. ... All things are interchangeable—might not this be the definition of *things?*" The second proposition may be given the name which Valéry borrows from Henri Poincaré, reasoning by recurrence, but Valéry immediately lifts it from the sphere of pure intellect in order to make it a principle valid for all knowledge, whether through body or mind: "the conscious imitation of my act is a new act which comprises all the possible adaptations of the former."

Now Valéry's method of symbolic construction depends on a view of mind and space as homogeneous, together with the two consequences thereof, *the endless possibility of substitution and the indefinite repetition of the same act of knowledge.* To illustrate this method in operation we need only two verses, for Valéry has the power, a consequence of his method, to complete his entire thought over and over again in this short space.

Let us consider the following from "Eté":

> Et toi maison brûlante, Espace, cher Espace
> Tranquille, où l'arbre fume et perd quelques oiseaux.

(And you, burning House of Space, dear tranquil Space, where
the tree smokes and loses several birds.)

A first interpretation of this "tree that smokes and loses several birds" is
that the poet describes the mist around it, and some birds by chance flying
away. Valéry is far from insensitive to such moments of natural magic, especially when the event, as here, is of the essence of chance. Indeed, it is
necessary to understand it first as such. But the wonderful accent on *perd,*
the restraint of *quelques,* and the surrealistic touch of *fume,* may also suggest
much more. *Sfumato* or chiaroscuro is that condition which, according to
Leonardo, grants full visibility. *Perdre* returns a few stanzas later in description of the wave flowing onto sand, "Où sa puissance en pleurs perd tous
ses diamants." In both cases, of tree and wave, what is described is a yielding
of the materiality of matter to the brightness of burning space; and perhaps
the only pathos to be found in Valéry concerns a loss of visibility even in
the most ordinary circumstance—as here perhaps, where the poet tries to
render the impression of mist or leaves fading into the brightness of the air.
Whether bird or mist or leaf does not really matter, the impression on the
homogeneous mind remains the same—"this tree and the waving of its leaves,
its shadow just like its substance, its accidents of shape and position, the faraway thoughts which it recalls—*tout cela est égal.*"

The possibilities of such substitution (bird for leaf, leaf for bird) are, of
course, many; the charm of the verse results from its suggestion of a twilight
consciousness which perceives all things in terms of almost abstract motion
and proportion; and it needs no special effort to see that this couplet is also
a reflection on the nature of contour. What is the line that keeps this tree
from spreading over the air, or this air from burning the tree? In Leonardo's
notebooks, which Valéry knew very well, we find the following typical no-
tation:

> When the sun is in the east, the trees in that quarter are dark
> toward the center and their edges are in light.

Here then is another "arbre fumant"; it is evident that Valéry often borrows
the cleared vision of the painter, wishing, somewhat like the impressionists,
to see objects with the unprejudiced splendor of the eye.

Now the geometer, fundamentally, has the same problem as the painter;
he also speculates on contour, wanting to define a line without breadth and
a point without extension, so as to make "bodies" entirely intuitive. But

while the geometer must suppose a world of ideal and impermutable solids, a world of interior bodies, the painter works with exterior bodies, actual trees in real space. Valéry, like the painter, also thinks of exterior bodies; yet he is also in accord with the geometer, for he knows that however exterior objects are, they affect the mind only insofar as interior. And this is specifically expressed in a stanza from "Anne" (*Album de vers anciens*), where another house of burning space and another smoking tree and another bird appear:

> Mais suave, de l'arbre extérieur, la palme
> Vaporeuse remue au delà du remords,
> Et dans le feu, parmi trois feuilles, l'oiseau calme
> Commence le chant seul qui réprime les morts.

(But suave, the palm of the external tree stirs mistily beyond remorse, and in the fire, amidst three leaves, the calm bird begins its lonely, death-repressing song.)

The bright and inevitable calm opposed to the perceiving consciousness by whatever object is perceived has rarely been more perfectly rendered.

But after the painter and the geometer we may venture to add yet another view, that of the scientist. "Burning" and "smoking" are used in many ways by Valéry including that which signifies a change of state, the not quite explainable phenomenon in physics occurring when, increased energy being brought to bear on an object, not its temperature but its form changes. So ice becomes water and water, steam. It is in fact a kind of physical displacement that can be measured by the eyes; what is again important is the visibility of an object that changes its form—"The burning incense exhales an endless form" (*La Jeune Parque*). In Valéry, everything—flesh, time, soul—tends toward this change of state, going always from heavy to rarified, from less visible to more visible, finally to be lost in the overbright and burning house of space:

> De sa profonde mère, encore froide et fumante,
> Voici qu'au seuil battu de tempêtes, la chair
> Amèrement vomie au soleil par la mer,
> Se délivre des diamants de la tourmente.

(From its deep, still cold, and vaporous mother, look where on the threshold lashed by tempests, vomited bitterly by the sea into the sun, the flesh frees itself from diamonds of torment.)

(*Naissance de Vénus*)

> Aspire cet encens d'âme et de fumée.

(Inhale this incense of soul and smoke.)

>   (*Sémiramis*)

> Je hume ici ma future fumée.

(I breathe here my future's smoke.)

>   ("Le Cimetière marin")

This poetry is also an allegory on change of state, from heavy to rarified, all things seeking to reveal themselves by a change into light and air, but as they do, dying into the greater brilliance of the air (cf. "La Fileuse"). Therefore his apostrophe to space, full both of affection and of despair:

> Et toi, maison brûlante, Espace, cher Espace
> Tranquille, où l'arbre fume et perd quelques oiseaux.

Valéry's charm and logic are thus seen to depend on the substitutions of the homogeneous mind which perceives the outside world in terms of pure visibility, allowing no ideas of the reasoning reason and no impressions of materiality to stand between it and a direct visual effect. We would only add that such condensation of meaning in so small a space, thought being as complete almost in every couplet as in the whole poem, is due to the second quality of the homogeneous mind, its endless variation of the same act of knowledge, completed again and again in the shortest unit of sense.

V

The various interpretations here given center on one theme, *sheer visibility,* Valéry's desire to intuit the visible form and virtual idea of an object by a coincident movement of the naked eye and of the unconditioned, a priori consciousness. "La Dormeuse" is a meditation on how an image before the eye becomes an idea in the mind. It forms part of that incessant epistemological quest, common to poet and philosopher alike, which seeks the way from εἴδη to εἶδος.

Valéry completes the de-rationalization of sight begun by Hugo and furthered by the French symbolist poets. His vision dispenses with innate, sentimental, and acquired ideas, yet does not therefore admit the formative influence of the visible world. Sight, for him, is that luminous and perpetual limbo between perception and the unexplainably fixed idea: the gradual and endless inductions of the aesthetic consciousness. In his Leonardo essay of 1894 he has already formulated a theory of gradual induction:

The surest method of judging a painting is to recognize nothing at first, and to pursue step by step the series of inductions which a simultaneous presence of colored patches in a limited area makes necessary, in order to raise oneself from metaphor to metaphor, from supposition to supposition, and so to an intelligence of the subject.

This method parallels that of "substitution" which is operative in his poetry. His metaphors depend on it. In the Leonardo essay, again, Valéry gives a definition of metaphor as of imaginative logic in general: "All things move in the imagination from degree to degree." It is the function of metaphor and of analogy to extend to the utmost this continuous play of the visual and abstracting imagination, which we have previously characterized as the metamorphosis of metaphor, and, on the level of sound, as modulation. "Le Cimetière marin," for instance, is rather hard to explain without an understanding of Valéry's special use of metaphor. In Gustave Cohen's *Explication du Cimetière marin* one finds the following about the first line of the poem: "No one will doubt that the doves are the white sails of the fishermen of Sète," and when the word "doves" recurs in stanza nine, a note in fine print is added: "This no longer refers to the boats of stanza I." But one thought there was no doubt about the matter! What *do* the doves refer to? Cohen goes on to suggest that they are now the doves of the Holy Ghost, "a consolation which Faith offers to believers prostrate before their icons."

The critic is not absolutely wrong, but he has not understood that the concept of dove is in Valéry subordinate to a visual idea which never submits to complete conceptualization or, conversely, to an idea that desires but never attains visibility. This fact forces the poet to a continual change of metaphor. The sails are now doves and now sails, now perhaps the saucers of sunlight on the palpitating sea, now the whiteness of marble trembling in the shaded graveyard, now mysterious sheep, vain thoughts, inquisitive angels. It is the play that matters, "le jeu suprême" of a mind haunted by an inexhaustible visual desire.

If "Le Cimetière marin" renders the gradual process of induction that begins with sheer sight, then a poem like "Eté, roche d'air pur" may be said to render also the gradual process of induction starting in a modulated sound, the vowel-plus-*r*. In each case the true persistent subject is not originally or ultimately summer or a graveyard by the sea—themes more or less fortuitous—but induction and retroduction. "*Rendre purement possible ce qui existe; reduire ce qui se voit au purement visible,* telle est l'oeuvre profonde (*To return what exists to pure possibility; to reduce what is seen to pure visibility;* that is the deep, the hidden work)." "La Dormeuse" is the perfect representation of an act of knowledge, proceeding from sight and sound, proceeding from the imminent powers of consciousness, but always and truly virtual.

WALLACE STEVENS

Two Prefaces

CHOSE LÉGÈRE, AILÉE, SACRÉE

In 1930, Louis Séchan published a work on *La Danse grecque antique,* which contained a chapter on Valéry's *Dance and the Soul.* M. Séchan was Professor of Greek Language and Literature at the University of Montpellier. He sent a copy of this book to Valéry, who acknowledged it in a letter, which it seems worth while to copy at length, as follows:

> I thank you greatly for your attention in sending me your fine work on Greek dancing. I learn from it many things I ignored— and even ignored about myself. Your kind chapter on my little dialogue generously attributes to me much more erudition than I ever possessed. Neither Callimachus nor Lucian, Xenophon nor the Parthenia was known to me; and would not in any case have been of much use to me. Documents in general impede rather than help me. They result in difficulties for me, and consequently in peculiar solutions, in all those compositions in which history must play some part.
>
> In reality, I confined myself to dipping into Emmanuel at the Library, and I left open on my table the book of Marey which I have had for the last thirty years. Those outline drawings of jumping and walking, some memories of ballets were my essential

From *Paul Valéry: Dialogues.* © 1956, 1984 by Princeton University Press.

resources. The flutist does come from the Throne. The head compact like a pine cone from a living dancer.

The constant thought of the Dialogue is physiological—from the digestive troubles of the prelude-beginning to the final swoon. Man is slave to the sympathetic and pneumogastric nerves. Sumptuary sensations, the gestures of luxury, and spectacular thoughts exist only by the good favor of these tyrants of our vegetative life. Dance is the type of the runaway.

As for the form of the whole, I have tried to make of the Dialogue itself a sort of ballet of which the Image and the Idea are Coryphaeus in turn. The abstract and the sensible take the lead alternately and unite in the final vertigo.

To sum up: I in no degree strove for historic or technical rigor (and for very good reason). I freely introduced what I needed to maintain my Ballet and vary its figures. This extended to *the ideas themselves*. Here they are *means*. It is true that this idea (that ideas are means) is familiar to me, and perhaps *substantial*. It leads on, moreover, to wicked thoughts about philosophy (cf. "Leonardo and the Philosophers," which I published last year).

I should never have planned to write on the dance, to which I had never given serious thought. Moreover, I considered—and I still do—that Mallarmé had exhausted the subject in so far as it belongs to literature. This conviction made me first refuse the invitation of the *Revue musicale*. Other reasons made me resolve to accept it. What Mallarmé had prodigiously written then became a peculiar condition of my work. I must neither ignore him nor espouse his thought too closely. I adopted the line of introducing, amid the divers interpretations which the three characters give of the dance, the one whose formulation and incomparable demonstration through style are to be found in the *Divagations*.

I have explained myself at considerable length. But I feel I owe this to one who has been such an attentive and even fervent critic of my Dialogue. You have perfectly presented its spirit, which, in truth, is neither *this* nor *that*—neither with Plato, nor according to Nietzsche, but an act of transformation.

The nature of M. Séchan's book can be gathered from Valéry's comment on it. M. Séchan thought that Valéry's attitude toward *Dance and the Soul* as something fortuitous was typical of Valéry. He discussed Mallarmé's remarks in *Divagations* on the dance as corporeal writing or hieroglyphic, and he dwelt on the resemblance between the dance and the meditations of the spirit in moments of tension. He referred to the analysis of *Dance and the Soul* by Paul Souday in the latter's work on Valéry and, in particular, to the contrasting conceptions of the dance by the persons taking part in the present dialogue, thus: the conception of Eryximachus (the Eryximachus of Plato's *Symposium*) that the dance is purely sensory; the conception of Phaedrus (the Phaedrus of *Eupalinos*) that the dance is psychologically evocative; and the conception of Socrates, which reconciles the other two, that the dance is an interpretation of a secret and physical order. And finally M. Séchan speaks of the fact that both Schopenhauer and Nietzsche were influential forces at the time when Valéry was maturing. But he regards *Dance and the Soul* as Apollonian rather than Dionysian, because as Apollonian it corresponds better with the Greek genius. It is, in fact, possible, if only because Valéry published *Eupalinos* and *Dance and the Soul* together and because they seem to be inseparable companions, that Valéry had a sense that *Eupalinos* was Apollonian and that *Dance and the Soul* was Dionysian. On the other hand, it is certain that Valéry's own genius was Apollonian and that the Dionysian did not comport with it, and, with that, the subject may be dismissed.

Dance and the Soul is a lesser work than *Eupalinos,* since it does not contain the proliferation of ideas which characterizes *Eupalinos.* Socrates is always and everywhere proliferation. In this dialogue, however, he confines himself to the proliferation of a single idea. He asks repeatedly the question, "O my friends, what in truth is dance?" and again, "But what then is dance, and what can steps say?" and again, "O my friends, I am only asking you what is dance. . . ."

While these questions are being asked, a dance is going on, a ballet is being danced. The scene is a banqueting place with a banquet in course. There are servants serving food and no end of wine. The persons are Socrates, Phaedrus, and Eryximachus, great numbers of multicolored groups of smiling figures, whirling and dissolving in enchanted sequences, Athikté, the *première danseuse,* who is commencing, the *musiciennes,* one of whom, coral-rose, is blowing an enormous shell, another, a tall flute-player, who denotes the measure with her toe. Socrates is conscious of ideas that come to him as he watches Athikté and observes the majesty of her movements. Eryximachus exclaims: "Dear Socrates, she teaches us that which we do, showing clearly to our souls that which our bodies accomplish obscurely."

Phaedrus adds: "In which respect this dancer would, according to you, have something Socratic, teaching us, in the matter of walking, to know ourselves a little better."

These remarks illustrate the constant allusions to the dancers which keep the reader of the dialogue in the presence of the dancers. He hears the voices of the speakers and watches the movements of the dancers at one and the same time, without the least confusion, as he would do in reality; and as his interest in what is being said grows greater as the discussion approaches its resolutions, and as his absorption in the spectacle becomes deeper with his increased understanding of it and because of the momentum toward the ultimate climax, he realizes, for the first time, the excitement of a meaning as it is revealed at once in thought and in act.

The work is regenerative. M. Séchan quoted the words of Plato on the poet: *chose légère, ailée, sacrée.* These words apply equally to Valéry's text. Here again we have what we had in *Eupalinos,* the body as source and the act in relation to the body. Socrates says to Eryximachus:

> Do you not see then, Eryximachus, that among all intoxications the noblest, the one most inimical to that great tedium, is the intoxication due to acts? Our acts, and more particularly those of our acts which set our bodies in motion, may bring us into a strange and admirable state.

Still speaking to Eryximachus, he made a gesture in the direction of

> that ardent Athikte, who divides and gathers herself together again, who rises and falls, so promptly opening out and closing in, and who appears to belong to constellations other than ours— seems to live, completely at ease, in an element comparable to fire—in a most subtle essence of music and movement, wherein she breathes boundless energy, while she participates with all her being in the pure and immediate violence of extreme felicity.

As he continues, he says what sums up his argument and sums up the whole work:

> If we compare our grave and weighty condition with the state of that sparkling salamander, does it not seem to you that our or- dinary acts, begotten by our successive needs, and our gestures and incidental movements are like coarse materials, like an impure stuff of duration—whilst that exaltation and that vibration of life, that supremacy of tension, that transport into the highest agility one is capable of, have the virtues and the potencies of flame; and that the shames, the worries, the sillinesses, and the

monotonous foods of existence are consumed within it, making
what is divine in a mortal woman shine before our eyes?

There is a series of speeches by Socrates in the closing pages of the
dialogue which are full of the noble rhetoric of the truth. But they are still
rhetoric; and it is the presence of this rhetoric of the truth that makes the
work regenerative. It is rhetoric to say: "In a sonorous world, resonant and
rebounding, this intense festival of the body in the presence of our souls
offers light and joy. . . . All is more solemn, all more light, all more lively,
all stronger; all is possible in another way; all can begin again indefinitely."
So, too, it is rhetoric to say: "I hear the clash of all the glittering arms of
life! . . . The cymbals crush in our ears any utterance of secret thoughts.
They resound like kisses from lips of bronze." It is, however, this rhetoric,
the eloquent expression of that which is precisely true, that gives what it
expresses an irresistible compulsion as when Socrates says: "A body, by its
simple force, and its act, is powerful enough to alter the nature of things
more profoundly than ever the mind in its speculations and dreams was able
to do!"

While Socrates is pronouncing his subtle and solemn words, our eyes
remain fastened on Athikté, while she tries to make us see that which Socrates
is seeking to tell us. She moves through jewels, makes gestures like scintil-
lations, filches impossible attitudes from nature, so that Eryximachus says,
"Instant engenders form, and form makes the instant visible." She continues
to dance until she falls. When she has fallen and lies, white, on the ground,
she says something to herself, the simplest possible thing. Phaedrus asks what
it is and Eryximachus replies, "She said: 'How well I feel!' "—a remark
immense with everything that Socrates himself had been saying a moment
or two before. She has spoken in a rhetoric which achieves the pathetic
essential almost without speech. It is obvious that this degree of agitation
has been reached in what is, after all, an exegetical work, through the form
of the work. Valéry's slim and cadenced French adds its own vitality to the
original. It seems enough to present the work in this brief manner. André
Levinson said in relation to *Dance and the Soul:* "To explain a thing is to
deform it; to think is to substitute what is arbitrary for the unknowable
truth." What *Dance and the Soul* requires is not so much explanation as—
what Valéry called M. Séchan—attentive and fervent critics or, say, readers,
willing to experience the transformation which knowing a little about themselves brings about as by miracle or, say, by art.

Man has many ways to attain the divine, and the way of Eupalinos and the way of Athikté and the various ways of Paul Valéry are only a few of them.

GLOIRE DU LONG DÉSIR, IDÉES

Denis Saurat refers to *Eupalinos* as Valéry's "prose masterpiece," not meaning more, however, than that it was one of a number of masterpieces by Valéry in prose, not to speak of his masterpieces in verse. He cites a brief passage or two and then says, "You have to go back to Bossuet to find such writing in prose." It is easy to believe this of *Eupalinos* if you give yourself up to some of the more rhetorical episodes. There is, for example, the passage in which Socrates speaks of the chance that had placed in his hands an object which became, for him, the source of reflections on the difference between constructing and knowing. Phaedrus asked him to help him to see the object, and thereupon Socrates said:

> Well then, Phaedrus, this is how it was. I was walking on the very edge of the sea. I was following an endless shore. . . . This is not a dream I am telling you. I was going I know not whither, overflowing with life, half-intoxicated by my youth. The air, deliciously rude and pure, pressing against my face and limbs, confronted me—an impalpable hero that I must vanquish in order to advance. And this resistance, ever overcome, made of me, too, at every step an imaginary hero, victorious over the wind, and rich in energies that were ever reborn, ever equal to the power of the invisible adversary. . . . That is just what youth is. I trod firmly the winding beach, beaten and hardened by the waves. All things around me were simple and pure: the sky, the sand, the water.

Merely to share the balance and the imagery of these words is to share the particular exhilaration of the experience itself. Then, too, toward the close of the work, in the speech in which Socrates states the conclusions to which the speakers have been brought, he substitutes for oral exhilaration the exhilaration that comes from the progression of the mind. Only enough of this true apostrophe can be cited to identify it. Socrates says to Phaedrus:

> O coeternal with me in death, faultless friend, and diamond of sincerity, hear then:
> It served no purpose, I fear, to seek this God, whom I have tried all my life to discover, by pursuing him through the realm of thought alone; by demanding him of that most variable and

most ignoble sense of the just and the unjust, and by urging him to surrender to the solicitings of the most refined dialectic. The God that one so finds is but a word born of words, and returns to the word. For the reply we make to ourselves is assuredly never anything other than the question itself; and every question put by the mind to the mind is only, and can only be, a piece of simplicity. But on the contrary, it is in acts, and in the combination of acts, that we ought to find the most immediate feeling of the presence of the divine, and the best use for that part of our strength that is unnecessary for living, and seems to be reserved for the pursuits of an indefinable object that infinitely transcends us.

Valéry himself has commented on the work. In a letter to Paul Souday written in 1923, he said:

> I was asked to write a text for the album *Architectures,* which is a collection of engravings and plans. Since this text was to be magnificently printed in folio format and fitted in exactly with the decoration and pagination of the work, I was requested to limit its size quite precisely to 115,800 *letters* . . . 115,800 characters! It is true, the characters were to be sumptuous.
>
> I accepted. My dialogue was at first too long. I shortened it; and then a little too short—I lengthened it. I came to find these exigencies very interesting, though it is possible that the text itself may have suffered a little in consequence.
>
> After all, the sculptors never complained who were obliged to house their Olympian personages inside the obtuse triangle of pediments!

There is, also, a letter to Dontenville, *inspecteur d'Académie,* written in 1934. The letter to Paul Souday was written a few months after the composition of *Eupalinos.* The letter to Dontenville was written after the lapse of ten years. Valéry, referring again to the requirement of 115,800 characters, said:

> This rigor, at first astounding and repellent, albeit required of a man accustomed enough to the rigor of poems in fixed form, made this man wonder at first—but then find that the peculiar condition proposed to him might be easily enough satisfied by employing the very elastic form of the *dialogue.* (An insignificant rejoinder, introduced or cut out, allows us after a few fumblings

to conform with fixed requirements of measurement.) The adjustment was, in effect, easily made in the proofs.

The vast proof sheets I received gave me the strange impression that I had in my hands a work of the sixteenth century and was 400 years dead.

The name of Eupalinos was taken by me from the article "Architecture" in the *Encyclopédie Berthelot,* when I was looking for the name of an architect. I since learned, from a study by the learned Hellenist Bidez (of Ghent), that Eupalinos, an engineer more than an architect, dug canals and built scarcely any temples; I gave him my ideas, as I did Socrates and Phaedrus. Moreover, I have never been in Greece; and as for Greek, I have unfortunately remained the most indifferent of scholars, getting lost in the original text of Plato and finding him, in the translations, terribly long and often boring.

Since Valéry describes Eupalinos as of Megara, and since it was at Megara that the school of Euclid flourished, Valéry's ascription of the name of Eupalinos to the *Encyclopédie Berthelot* dispels the idea of any relation between Eupalinos and Euclid. Finally, to return to the letter to Paul Souday, Valéry said of "these dialogues":

They are works made to order, in which I have not managed or known how to establish a true thought in its most favorable light. I should have tried to show that pure thought and the search for truth in itself can only ever aspire to the discovery or the construction of some *form.*

What, then, are the ideas that Valéry has chosen to be discussed by the shades of Socrates and his friend Phaedrus, as they meet, in our time, in their "dim habitation" on the bank of Ilissus? They are alone and remain alone. Eupalinos does not appear and takes no part in the discussion, unless, as he is spoken of, an image of him passes, like the shade of a shade. The talk is prolonged, and during its course, one or the other speaker propounds ideas. If we attempt to group a number of the ideas propounded, we have something like the following:

There are no details in execution.

Nothing beautiful is separable from life, and life is that which dies.

We must now know what is truly beautiful, what is ugly; what befits man; what can fill him with wonder without confounding him, possess him without stupefying him. . . . It is that which puts him, without effort, above his own nature.

By dint of constructing, . . . I truly believe that I have constructed myself. . . . To construct oneself, to know oneself—are these two distinct acts or not?

What is important for me above all else is to obtain from *that which is going to be,* that it should with all the vigor of its newness satisfy the reasonable requirements of *that which has been.*

O body of mine . . . keep watch over my work. . . . Grant me to find in thy alliance the feeling of what is true; temper, strengthen, and confirm my thoughts.

No geometry without the word.

Nothing can beguile, nothing attract us, . . . nothing by us is chosen from among the multitude of things, and causes a stir in our souls, that was not in some sort pre-existent in our being or secretly awaited by our nature.

An artist is worth a thousand centuries.

Man . . . fabricates by abstraction.

Man can act only because he can ignore.

That which makes and that which is made are indivisible.

The greatest liberty is born of the greatest rigor.

Man's deepest glances are those that go out to the void. They converge beyond the All.

If, then, the universe is the effect of some act; that act itself, the effect of a Being, and of a need, a thought, a knowledge, and a power which belong to that Being, it is then only by an act that you can rejoin the grand design, and undertake the imitation of that which has made all things. And that is to put oneself in the most natural way in the very place of the God.

Now, of all acts the most complete is that of constructing.

But the constructor whom I am now bringing to the fore . . . takes as the starting point of his act, the very point where the

god had left off. . . . Here I am, says the Constructor, I am the
act.

Must I be silent, Phaedrus?—So you will never know what
temples, what theaters, I should have conceived in the pure Socratic style! . . . And exercising an ever stricter control over my
mind, at the highest point I should have realized the operation of
transforming a quarry and a forest into an edifice, into splendid
equilibriums! . . .
Then out of raw materials I was going to put together my
structures entirely ordained for the life and joy of the rosy race
of men. . . . But you shall learn no more. You can conceive only
the old Socrates, and your stubborn shade.

This is the substance of the dialogue between Socrates and Phaedrus,
or, at least, these sayings, taken from their talk, indicate what they have been
talking about. And what in fact have they been talking about? And why is
Valéry justified when, in his closing words, Socrates says: "all that we have
been saying is as much a natural sport of the silence of these nether regions
as the fantasy of some rhetorician of the other world who has used us as
puppets!" Have we been listening to the talk of men or of puppets? These
questions are parts of the fundamental question, What should the shades of
men talk about, or in any case what may they be expected, categorically, to
talk about, in the Elysian fields? Socrates answers this question in the following manner:

Think you not that we ought now to employ this boundless leisure
which death leaves us, in judging and rejudging ourselves un-
wearyingly, revising, correcting, attempting other answers to the
events that took place, seeking, in fine, to defend ourselves by
illusions against nonexistence, as the living do against their existence?

This Socratic question (and answer) seems empty. The Elysian fields would
be the merest penal habitude, if existence in them was not as absolute as it
is supposed to be eternal and if our disillusioned shades were dependent,
there, on some fresh illusion to be engendered by them for themselves in that
transparent realm. It cannot be said freely that Valéry himself fails to exhibit
Socrates and Phaedrus engaged in any such discussion, for as the talk begins
to reach its end, there emerges from it an Anti-Socrates, to whom an Anti-
Phaedrus is listening, as if their conversation had been, after all, a process
of judging and rejudging what they had done in the past, with the object of

arriving at a state of mind equivalent to an illusion. The dialogue does not create this impression. It does not seem to us, as we read it, that we are concerned with the fortunes of the selves of Socrates and Phaedrus, notwithstanding that that would be a great concern.

We might well expect an existence after death to consist of the revelation of the truth about life, whether the revelation was instantaneous, complete, and dazzling, or whether it was a continuity of discoveries made at will. Hence when a conversation between Socrates and Phaedrus after death occurs, we somehow expect it to consist of resolutions of our severest philosophical or religious difficulties, or of some of them. The present dialogue, however, is a discussion of aesthetics. It may even be said to be the apotheosis of aesthetics, which is not at all what we have had in mind as that which phantoms talk about. It makes the scene seem more like a place in provincial France than either an archaeological or poetic afterworld. In view of Valéry's reference to "the very admirable Stephanos," it is clear that the scene is the afterworld of today, since Mallarmé died in 1898. The trouble is that our sense of what ought to be discussed in the afterworld is derived from specimens that have fallen into disuse. Analysis of the point would be irrelevant. It seems enough to suppose that to the extent that the dead exist in the mind of the living, they discuss whatever the living discuss, although it cannot be said that they do it in quite the same way, since when Phaedrus told Socrates how Socrates, if he had been an architect, would have surpassed "our most famous builders," Eupalinos included, Socrates replied: "Phaedrus, I beg of you! . . . This subtle matter of which we are now made does not permit of our laughing. I feel I ought to laugh, but I cannot. . . . So refrain!"

This elevation of aesthetics is typical of Valéry's thought. It is itself an act of construction. It is not an imbalance attributable to his nature as a poet. It is a consequence of reasonable conviction on his part. His partiality for architecture was instinctive and declared itself in his youthful *Introduction to the Method of Leonardo da Vinci*. It was not an artificiality contrived to please the company of architects who had commanded *Eupalinos*. It seems most natural that a thinker who had traced so much of man's art to man's body should extend man's art itself to the place of God and in that way should relate man's body to God, in the manner in which this is done in *Eupalinos*. Socrates said: "I cannot think that there exists more than one Sovereign Good."

Phaedrus then spoke of what Eupalinos had said concerning forms and appearances. He repeated the words of Eupalinos:

Listen, Phaedrus . . . that little temple, which I built for Hermes,

a few steps from here, if you could know what it means to me!—
There where the passer-by sees but an elegant chapel—'t is but
a trifle: four columns, a very simple style—there I have enshrined
the memory of a bright day in my life. O sweet metamorphosis!
This delicate temple, none knows it, is the mathematical image
of a girl of Corinth, whom I happily loved. It reproduces faithfully
the proportions that were peculiarly hers. It lives for me! It gives
me back what I have given it.

Eupalinos had then spoken of buildings that are mute, of others that speak,
and of others that sing, for which he gave the reasons.

Socrates interrupted Phaedrus with a reference to his prison, which he
called "a drab and indifferent place in itself." But he added, "In truth, dear
Phaedrus, I never had a prison other than my body."

Eupalinos had gone on to speak to Phaedrus of the effect on the spirit
of the sites of ports: "the presence of the pure horizon, the waxing and the
waning of a sail, the emotion that comes of being severed from the earth,
the beginning of perils, the sparkling threshold of lands unknown." He did
not profess to be able to connect up an analysis with an ecstasy. He said:

I feel my need of beauty, proportionate to my unknown resources,
engendering of itself alone forms that give it satisfaction. I desire
with my whole being. . . . The powers assemble. The powers of
the soul, as you know, come strangely up out of the night. . . .
By force of illusion they advance to the very borders of the real.
I summon them, I adjure them by my silence.

He continued:

O Phaedrus, when I design a dwelling (whether it be for the gods,
or for a man), and when I lovingly seek its form, . . . I confess,
how strange soever it may appear to you, *that it seems to me my
body is playing its part in the game.*

Eupalinos ended with the prayer to his body, which Socrates called "an
unexampled prayer," when Phaedrus repeated it. It is Socrates himself—in
the apostrophe to Phaedrus, beginning "O coeternal with me in death," in
the closing pages of the dialogue—who says that man by his acts puts himself
in the place of God, not meaning that he becomes God but that he puts
himself in the very place of God: *la place même du Dieu.*

It follows that for Eupalinos and for men like him what they do is their
approach to the divine and that the true understanding of their craft and the

total need that they feel to try to arrive at a true understanding of it and also at an exact practice of it are immeasurably the most important things in the world, through which the world itself comes to the place of the divine. The present work has to be read with all this in mind. Any rigorous intellectual discipline in respect to something significant is a discipline in respect to everything significant. Valéry's own discipline appears in every page of the dialogue. The need to understand uncommon things and to manifest that understanding in common things shows itself constantly. The modeling of the cluster of roses is an instance. The comparison of the object found on the shore of the sea, a natural object, with an object made by man is another. The parable of the Phoenician and how he went about making a ship is a third. It is the parable of the artist. The image of the Phoenician's boat recalled to Socrates "the black, loose-flapping sails of the vessel with its load of priests, which as it labored back from Delos, dragging on its oars."

At this, Phaedrus exclaimed, "How little you seem to relish living your beautiful life over again!"

Socrates then asked, "Is there anything vainer than the shadow of a sage?"

And Phaedrus said, "A sage himself." The image of the man of action makes the shade of the man of thought regret his life. It is, in a way, the triumphant image of the constructor as it faces the image of the man of thought. Perhaps on his own grounds, it was Valéry, for all his life of study, full of the sea, watching the departure of the Phoenician's supreme boat on its maiden voyage: "Her scarlet cheeks took all the kisses that leapt up to meet her on her course; the well-stretched triangles of her full, hard sails held down her quarter to the wave."

Is it not possible that one of the most perceptive texts of modern times, although neither immense nor varied, and containing little of life and the nature of man, is yet a masterpiece? Within the limits of the work, Valéry expresses ideas relevant to the thought of his time as it came to consider, with an unprecedented interest, the problems of art. In the dialogue, Socrates speaks of these expatiations as if with a nuance of their triviality. As he continued to probe, his interest heightened to such an extent that he lost his own traditional character; and in this, he became part of the new time in which his shade comes close to us. The nuance of triviality had vanished by the time he reached the noble speech beginning "O coeternal with me in death," when he was ready to say:

> The Demiurge was pursuing his own designs, which do not concern his creatures. The converse of this must come to pass. He

was not concerned about the troubles that were bound to spring
from that very separation which he diverted or perhaps bored
himself with making. He has given you the means of living, and
even of enjoying many things, but not generally those which you
particularly want.

But I come after him. I am he who conceives what you desire
a trifle more exactly than you do yourselves. . . . I shall make
mistakes sometimes, and we shall have some ruins; but one can
always very profitably look upon a work that has failed as a step
which brings us nearer to the most beautiful.

In the end, Socrates had become the constructor, and if he had, then Valéry
had. The thinker had become the creator. Jean Wahl might have diminished
this to a defense mechanism. Perhaps it was an appearance of what Alain
called the inimitable visage of the artist. To be a little more exact in quoting
Alain, one should say that the creator had asserted its parentage of the
thinker, for Alain had spoken of thought as the daughter of poetry in a
passage peculiarly applicable to Valéry. He had said that of all the indicators
of thought the most sensitive were poets, first because they take risks a little
further than logic permits; also because the rule they adopt always carries
them a little beyond what they hoped for. Mallarmé and Valéry announce a
new climate of thought. They want clear enigmas, those that are developable,
that is to say, mathematical. Alain says:

And if it is true, as I believe, that Thought, daughter of Poetry,
resembles her mother, we shall see everywhere a clarity of details,
a clarity won by conquest, in the place of our vague aspirations;
and the young will make us see another manner of believing—
which will be a refusal to believe.

Eupalinos is a work of this "clarity of details." This is its precise description. In it Valéry made language itself a constructor, until Socrates
asked:

What is there more mysterious than clarity? . . . What more ca-
pricious than the way in which light and shade are distributed
over hours and over men? . . . Orpheuslike we build, by means
of the word, temples of wisdom and science that may suffice for
all reasonable creatures. This great art requires of us an admirably
exact language.

It has been said that Rilke, who translated so much of Valéry, including

Eupalinos, felt an intense interest, as a poet, in the language of the work. The page on music—"a mobile edifice, incessantly renewed and reconstructed within itself, and entirely dedicated to the transformations of a soul"; the page on the sea shore—"This frontier between Neptune and Earth"; the page on in the beginning—"In the beginning . . . there was what is: the mountains and the forests"—are pages of true poetry. It was natural for such pages to give Rilke pleasure. But what impressed him was what he called the composure and finality of Valéry's language. Rilke read *Eupalinos* when it came out in the *Nouvelle Revue Française,* and his translation of it was the last work he did before he died.

It seems sometimes, in the fluidity of the dialogue, as if the discussion was casual and fortuitous or, say, Socratic. But a discussion over which the mind of Socrates presides derives much of its vitality from this characteristic, so that when the talk is over, we have a sense of extended and noble unity, a sense of large and long-considered form.

OCTAVE NADAL

Introduction to Poems in the Rough

For a long time nothing about Valéry seemed to me more obvious than his predilection and his genius for the verse poem. To my mind, the intensity, the purity, the uniqueness of *La Jeune Parque,* "Le Cimetière marin," "Le Serpent," made this entirely clear. Rightly or not, it was in these poems that I found him most "changed into himself," for I have always thought of the invention of form as the essence of the creative act. The sign, too, of its authenticity, and in fact I know of no other. To me it is wholly apparent that every truly original stance of the mind, if it is to find expression, must have at its command a new language corresponding in form to the mystery that inhabits it, a language having a pace, a manner, a quality—a shape, as it were, or presence unlike any other. Which means that it must be created. Is it not remarkable, for example, that the phrase *Que sais-je?,* so perfectly expressing suspension of judgment and a particular intellectual temper, led Montaigne to discover the *essay,* which with the dialogue is still the literary form best adapted to the skeptical attitude? The *thoughts* of Pascal, those dark uninhabited meteors, bear inscribed in their riven structure the contours of an anguish that cannot be composed. Lamartine must be acknowledged as the creator of the *lyric of meditation;* Rimbaud, of the *illumination;* Alain, of the *propos.* Alain, for whom freedom of the mind was the fundamental law of man, could have formulated his thoughts in no other way than to "propose" them for deliberation. Consider also the various devices of style:

From *Paul Valéry: Poems in the Rough* (Bollingen Series 45, no. 2), translated by Hilary Corke. © 1969 by Princeton University Press.

nothing could be more revealing than their changing modes. It was Mallarmé's genius for allusion and "absence" that transformed the metaphor
into the symbol. It was likewise the profound powers of *vision* in Supervielle
which at last removed the shutters of concept from medieval allegory.

Several further considerations confirmed my earlier view. From his
grammar-school days at Sète in the 1880s until his "crisis of 1892," Valéry
had held to the practice of *verse* as the essential mode of poetry. Neither *The
Old Alleys,* a prose poem dedicated to Huysmans in 1889, nor the handful
of experimental prose pieces of about the same period were at all to be
compared with the profusion of sonnets and other poems in verse—some
two or three hundred that I know of—which he composed between the ages
of sixteen and nineteen and consigned wisely to a drawer. The former were
as yet merely fragments of "poetic prose," descriptive or decorative in nature; they in no way foreshadowed his later treatment of the prose poem,
the first published example of which was *Pure Dramas* (1892). This was the
moment when Valéry had just discovered Mallarmé, and Rimbaud's *Illuminations,* and was laying down the principles of his "method," the purpose
of which was to clarify the acts and functions of his own thought.

The silence or rather the half-silence that followed the "night in Genoa"
(1892) was not really a case of deserting poetry at all but rather of defining
its role in "the great game" of the mind; for, as we now know, the so-called
period of silence was frequently interrupted by an output both in prose and
verse, which was to remain unpublished and to which I shall return. It shows
beyond any doubt that the break with poetry—except, perhaps, with the
sort he called "literature"—was at no time decisive.

I was not unaware also that, after the period of *La Jeune Parque* and
Charmes, Valéry went on to the very end of his life writing in verse. This
indeed was his demon. Yet these later poems in no way recall his earlier
tireless pursuit of the perfectly realized pure poem. What is astonishing, in
fact, is their abundant natural flow of lyric feeling, coming at the end of a
poetic output brief in compass and even famous for the rejection of every
sort of looseness or indulgence. Neither had I forgotten the verse translation
of Virgil's *Eclogues* nor the rough drafts of poems here and there in the
Notebooks nor the *Carmina eroticissima* from nearly every period of his life.
Valéry had made a collection of the latter and thought briefly of having them
printed—in two copies, one for himself, the other for the "Enfer" of the
Bibliothèque Nationale. In an incisive preface, he spoke particularly of how
difficult it was to find a true poetic speech for so special a genre, where the
need for precision and for a degree of realism almost inevitably suggested
terms that were either vulgar or too technical—the vocabulary either of

anatomy or of the gutter. So far as I know, he never wrote poems of this kind except in verse, feeling perhaps that only the beauties of form and the transfiguring fire of poetry could purify the pudenda of the flesh.

Finally, I confess that I have been particularly struck by the fact that in his critical writings Valéry repeatedly proclaimed his poetic "revelation" and creed. For me, these were the proof of his vocation, which he himself sensed in the second of his given names, Ambroise: a name that to him irresistibly suggested *ambroisie* and *abeille*—"ambrosia" and "bee."

> O dieu démon démiurge ou destin
> Mon appétit comme une abeille vive
> Scintille et sonne environ le festin
> Duquel ta grâce a permis que je vive.
>
> (O god demon demiurge or destiny
> My appetite like a vivid bee
> Glitters and hums about the feast
> At which your grace has given me to live.)

Within the confines of formal verse, Valéry had tirelessly pursued the idea conceived in his early youth, of "poetry as music," in which "delightful movement" held sway over meaning and became the generating principle of the "charm"—i.e., poem. He was confirmed in this notion by some of his great predecessors. In numerous critical passages, and throughout the Notebooks with their almost daily inquiries into the nature of poetry, he constantly reaffirmed the creative supremacy of the verse poem over the prose poem. Actually his search for a language capable of producing "constellations of words," led him back time and again to the traditional meters as the only measure of time, the only control of rhythm that could manage a stop or a suspension of movement at the close of a rhyme. According to Valéry it is this decisive rest, partitioning off each line, which creates the inner play between the parts of a line as well as the mutual attraction of sounds forming clusters and connections out of the concrete elements of words.

To be sure, the definition of poetry which he proposed, "the kind of movement that transforms thought into harmonic figures," was equally valid, as we shall see, for the poem in prose. But I could not forget that Valéry himself had for a long time doubted this, insisting repeatedly on "the immortal difference" between the rhythmic structure of verse and that of prose. This difference resided in the fact that in *prose,* deprived as it is of the "whole rest" made possible by meter, each member *tends to go free of the others.*

Now I no longer believe—Valéry himself notwithstanding—that he is to be thought of solely as a poet in verse, nor that his poetic work is to be fully appreciated without his accomplishment in the genre of the prose poem. That would be to underestimate the ambition of his experiment and to see his poetic achievement in a mistaken perspective. For too long the perfection and purity of his verse, his fidelity to the restrictions of orthodox prosody (sometimes taken a bit foolishly as a revival of the classical models), have obscured that other register in which he was no less accomplished. It would have been surprising, in fact, if the possibility of extending the whole range of poetry, which (since Baudelaire) includes the poem in prose, had *not* occurred to a poet so concerned to exercise all the resources of poetic language.

That is not all. Baudelaire was the first in our literature not only to sense the autonomy of the poem in prose but, to say, in speaking of it, that poetry is to be defined not as the creation of beauty but as a form of art. The fact is that the prose poems in his *Spleen de Paris* led, thirty years later, to "the crisis in verse form" and the reaction against traditional prosody which Mallarmé and later on Valéry resisted, but to which both were more deeply sympathetic than anyone has realized. As a result the whole idea of style changed. Modern poetry, like painting and music, found its affirmation in those styles which no longer aimed at ideal beauty but meant to *live* by originality of invention. Just as the development from Manet to Cézanne, or from Monet and Kandinsky to Klee, tended to reduce painting to a world of objects (that is, to its *reality as painting*) and to consider its domain to be simply a number of individual styles, so modern poetry, with Rimbaud, ceased to be merely recitation, amusement, and idealization. The *Illuminations* marked a date of extraordinary importance in the history of French poetry. From that moment, our poets all but abandoned verse. Almost all were to practice a new poetics, no longer that of "poetic" prose nor of mere lyricism in prose, but a new form free of the old prosody, free too of those bastard genres derived from more or less happy combinations of prose and verse. They were all to be indifferent to the quest for "ideal beauty." At times, indeed, they were to show themselves suspicious or even contemptuous of it: "One evening I set Beauty on my knees. And I found her bitter. And I reviled her." They were quick to arrive at a kind of anti-poetry—that is, a poetry bent on rejecting everything that, before, had justified and defined it.

The poem in prose, picturesquely handled by Aloysius Bertrand, developed in depth by Baudelaire and carried to great heights by Rimbaud, has shown itself to be not at all a matter of the false lyricism of poetic prose, but in itself a new kind of poem, endowed with techniques of its own and as far from the verse poem as from pure prose.

The variety of styles it has brought with it must also be considered: each poet has given it his own particular turn. Nothing could be more fruitless than to propose a definition of the genre, pointing to its general structure, its typical features. The prose poems of Rimbaud, the *versets* of Péguy, Claudel, or St.-John Perse, the uphill deep-breathing strophes of Lautréamont, the cadences of Max Jacob or René Char, the *proèmes* of Francis Ponge, though they have in common the character of being neither verse nor poetic prose, are each marked by a tone, a contour, a manner so personal as to be unmistakable. On the shelves of our libraries, they represent as many styles as the canvases of today's painters do on the walls of our galleries, or the compositions heard in our concert halls. To take one example: Claudel's *versets,* instead of conforming to the external laws of traditional poetry, follow the natural measure of breathing, the respiratory rhythm that swells, lengthens, accentuates, heightens, or reduces the volume and speed of each line, according to the intensity, nature, and duration of feeling or thought. It is an art of inspiration and expiration brought back to its source in the rhythm of the breath, an art that in the time and space of the *verset,* inhales, then exhales the life we breathe: like the glass blower and his glass. It is an expressive form created by this poet; it is his own art. For Max Jacob, on the other hand, the poem in prose obeys what he calls laws of situation and transposition. In each of these individual cases, poetry is no longer to be found in modulation and the other devices of style—in the ornamentation which for three centuries had been habitual to French poets; here it is a language of its own, which is to say a language of forms. Its value, its very essence are determined by its style.

Before 1892, Valéry had gone no further than to employ in his prose pieces—lyrical, oratorical, or descriptive—the forms and practices peculiar to the verse poem. At the end of *Paradox on the Architect* (1891) he had used the extreme artifice of inserting, unchanged or almost, the whole of the prefabricated sonnet "Orpheus," with its flat surface of scarcely camouflaged alexandrines, into the two-dimensional fabric of the prose. Nothing could have been more rash than such a shift from exposition to metaphor, from walking to wings.

But Valéry was soon to give up writing verse in the manner of the Parnassians, and prose muddled with the mysticism of the Decadents. This was the moment of his discovery, about 1892, of the principles that were to govern his own fundamental attitude. At the same time, two events occurred which shook his new-found conviction: he often recalled the shock he had felt on first reading Mallarmé and only a few months later Rimbaud. He had been, so he said, "Intellectually thunderstruck by the sudden appearance of

these two extraordinary phenomena on the horizon of his mind." Yet he
managed to react against the main thrust of this discovery of "two such
highly offensive characters." On the one hand, against Mallarmé who had
taken poetry as the center of his universe, Valéry set up his own idol, the
Mind, as his principle and center; on the other hand, he found and exposed
at the heart of Rimbaud's intelligence a mysticism that tended to dazzle and
dissolve the mind in universal light—whereas Valéry, for his own part, was
seeking a more and more absolute intelligence, the equal of light itself.

Yet the language of those two creators was not to be disposed of so
quickly nor with such self-assurance; the perfection, the intensity of their
works drove young Valéry to despair. He believed that in these works he had
found "the limits of the art of expression." More particularly, the two cor-
ollary aspects of the *Illuminations,* the originality of their structure and their
meaning (that is to say, the universality of their theme embodied in the
greatest variety of sensory modes, and on the other hand the unprecedented
form of the poem in prose, at once *locus* and *formula* of the very vision of
the primal all) had astonished him profoundly. "These things were born,"
he wrote to Pierre Louÿs. Or again: "Only the supreme pages of the *Illuminations,* read at night in the most glacial of dreams, can shake me with
so unruly but firm a hand. Never before have I so penetrated, re-created,
and adored them." There can be no doubt that Valéry's meditations on these
crystalline forms of poetry in prose led him to reconsider what until then he
had believed, that it was impossible for prose to rise, as verse can, to a form
of expression in which all the phonetic and semantic elements chime together
and language loses its purely logical character. The *Illuminations* showed
him, in fact, the contrary: the creation of a poetic space that was a world
in itself, one that without quitting the realm of meaning, could enter the
sphere of *resonance.* This was the unforeseeable model. It gave him a sense
of the enormous distance as well as the unbreachable wall between poetic
prose and prose that is poetry. For Valéry there could no longer be any
question of writing prose poems as he had done before, using the resources
of prosody—rhythm, rhyme, alliteration, internal assonance and disso-
nance—nor even, more subtly, of setting up an interplay between these elements, as in verse.

Rimbaud had revealed to him the marvelous resources of prose as a
medium at once concrete and abstract, lifted beyond common sense by the
power of genius into an almost infinite variety of rhythmic combinations and
dissociations, even to the dissonances of primitive harmony. It was in this
"diamond-hard prose," more than in Mallarmé's *Divagations* or "Un Coup
de dés," I believe, that Valéry sensed the possibilities, as well as the advan-

tages for himself and his own discoveries, to be found in a unique form of poetic expression. But we must recognize how far such a temptation went.

It was precisely during the years of his intensive intellectual preparation in the Rue Gay-Lussac, when he was devoting himself to mathematics and physics and to the study of mental phenomena, that Valéry felt the need of a rigorous, abstract language that could express the actual functions and operations of the mind. The time had come when the passionate act of a mind pursuing its own secret was no longer satisfied by his interminable scribbling in his Notebooks, by the light of dawn. This could go on endlessly to no end. True, the very spirit of the enterprise meant rejecting any effort at literary production, even a contempt for books. The intellectual adventure was valid in itself, for its own potential and its *creux toujours futur;* its truth lay simply in going on. But in this kind of "absence" into which Valéry had voluntarily withdrawn there was a living paradox. On the one hand, certainly, was the overpowering drive of his mind, but on the other, the no-less-powerful destiny of his *genius,* which from early adolescence had drawn Valéry to poetry and literature. The stimulus of a method and a grasp of all its possibilities, even with the conviction that such an enterprise must not take the form of literature, could not finally quite stifle his desire to create. His innate creativity and sense of form never ceased, during his celibacies of thought, to visit him with a longing for the literary works he must write. Intellectual activity kept his creativity constantly on the alert. He came to the bold and altogether modern conclusion that *penser* is also *pouvoir: to think* is potentially *to do;* at times he even confused the two. Meanwhile, Valéry allowed himself to write *An Evening with Monsieur Teste* and the *Introduction to the Method of Leonardo da Vinci.*

It was at about the same time that the prose poem became the vehicle of his "return" to poetry. The more I reflect on the silence of those twenty years before *La Jeune Parque,* the more I am convinced that the poet was always there in Valéry, but a poet who had chosen another form than verse. *Pure Dramas* had given evidence as early as 1892 of his own kind of poem in prose, one that, beyond its intrinsic character, could be recognized in the harmony between its theme—*a thought traced back to its beginnings*—and the amplitude of its rhythmic form. This was the first of a series of more highly finished poems, all related structurally one to another through similarities in rhythm and syntax, musical continuity, and the particular tonal qualities of color and sound. The melodic and harmonic phrasing no longer followed the syntactical structure but the inflection of the voice.

In addition to *Pure Dramas,* there were some thirty poems in prose left unpublished, poems written under the influence of Rimbaud and of Mallarmé's *Divagations*. These were the first compositions in which Valéry had tried to transmute his theories into prose poems. He called them his *theoriorama*. In these poems his attempt was to bring together analytical thought and ecstasy, abstraction and sensuality, in *the mode and movement of prose*. Here the lift and undulation of the words, the powers of imagery and voice, create the unique space of poetry.

The importance that Valéry attached to *Pure Dramas* is obvious: he spoke of this poem repeatedly to Gide, Louÿs, and Fourment long before he sent it to them; he asked for their criticism and apologized for the ending, calling it mere *tautology*. Last of all, on one of those small scraps of paper on which he had the habit of recording for himself, and no doubt for his future scholiasts as well, his notes *In Memory of Myself*, he mentioned for the year 1892, along with his theories of coincidence, imagination, form, and ornament, his *Pure Dramas*.

The allusive arabesque of *Pure Dramas* traces the mind's desire as it returns to its source—to its very first look at the world. We may no doubt find in this poem a nostalgia for the primal light upon the first garden. And if we look further we may recognize the sort of angelism of the mind of which Valéry never entirely rid himself. The mystique of "pure mind" never ceased to evoke in him at moments of intellectual exaltation a dazzling sense of wings throughout all "intelligible space." From "The Angel at the Sepulchre," which he wrote as a boy, to "The Angel," written in 1922, a mysterious and faithful messenger of the imagination lighted the dawn skies of his mind and permeated the pure acts of his consciousness, which could never understand the suffering that was a part of its condition:

> *Je sens peser sur moi la fatigue d'un Ange.*

> I feel weighing upon me an Angel's weariness.

Even with these reservations, we must still recognize that in *Pure Dramas* the analogy is essentially intellectual. Behind the appearances in which things are caught, there is no miracle except the wonder of nature and the primeval order of her changes—that primal scene in which rhythm itself imparted to water its wave, to the stem its curve, to light its vibration. What the mind is able to imagine of the life of things—movement, reflections, echoes, endless lines—these do not exhaust its image-making powers. The marvel remains—uneasy, uncertain: "One could believe the shimmering garden is about to take flight—and if the moment's flowers sport wings to flee with, where shall we go, Ideas?"

The mind may dream "the pure Drama of a line drawn upon heaven-

colored or upon life-colored space! Only in beautiful movement can it exist."
Such are "the rarest and most harmonious forms of intelligence, and they
would replace all the others by their extraordinary beauty, which longs to
endure."

It was with the last of these observations that Valéry, eight years later
in *Agatha, or the Saint of Sleep,* was to resume his exploration of the literary
region of the mind. Here again he attempted to give the form of the poem
in prose to one of his boldest insights into language and the powers of
consciousness. Almost fifteen years separate this unfinished masterpiece from
his later one, *La Jeune Parque.* Yet a profound kinship joins the two. In fact,
the first panel of the diptych of *La Jeune Parque,* though woven of other
themes and a different fiction, traces the same anabasis of consciousness up
to "the limit of self-suspense." Consciousness in *Agatha,* contained as it
were in what has already been, moves back through time to gain access to
the "secrets of sleep." In the effort to reach into her own roots, she lets go
and drifts through herself as through a dream, observing with heightened
attention the successive shifts and variations of her own images and thoughts,
to the point of vertigo, where she herself is snuffed out in absolute dark. In
Agatha, the search for greater and greater "clarity" develops the other way
round from the way of light—that is, by the gradual darkening and letting
go, in controlled stages, of the functions of consciousness. The movement is
backward, tracing the willing effacement and regression of being, back to a
thought that has no beginning. "Our Lady of Sleep," lucidly descending as
if by stairs into the naked midnight of consciousness, watches over the nocturnal pole of thought. She is already her own "Jeune Parque" spinning the
thread of mind, no longer extinguished in light but at the heart of the "living
dark," unwinding and snipping the thread of her own destiny. This plunge
into the deep night of the mind is similar, though opposite in direction, to
the thinker's ascent to the mind's solstice in "Le Cimetière marin," where
consciousness desires to reach the still point of absolute radiance. From
midnight to noon, in the world and in the mind, from infinity to zero in
thought, between being and nothingness, consciousness attempts to expose
itself in turn to the twin splendors of sun and death.

It may be interesting in regard to Valéry's poetic work of that time to
consider how, in each case, he worked out the common theme of *Agatha*
and *La Jeune Parque.* He had originally written the latter as a prose poem
consisting simply of the framework of theory for an intellectual autobiography, with nothing of the fable and nothing of the whole "sexual" element,
which were added later on. *Agatha,* on the other hand, was from the first
to be constructed around a fiction, with scenes, characters, events, and ar-

gument. The idea for a tale came first. Valéry imagined Agatha at the moment before she sits down to dinner: lifting her arms to take hold of a platter, she falls, and her mother finds her stretched out asleep among the débris, etc. This projected fiction soon gave way to a strict study in "transcendental psychology" and along with it another prose poem "Plus je pense, plus je pense (The more I think, the more I think)" began to take shape. In the latter, nothing of the tale remained but its title.

During the years 1898–1903, intellectual and creative work went on together, but the products of the two remained separate—efforts to join them notwithstanding. A poem in progress would be staked out and attacked by means of a complex apparatus of analyses, notes, comments, and lists—on memory, dreams, sleep, the rise and eclipse of ideas, on pure sensation, etc.— the whole being an imaginary description or experimental projection of the functioning mind, under the sign of the famous adage: *Nihil est in intellectu quod prius non fuerit in sensu*. The mind observes the writer at work and circumscribes both his labor and what he creates. His intellectual probing seems at times to have come before, at other times after, the actual composition of his poems. Sometimes both activities must have gone on at once, or almost. However that may be, the most nearly finished work in this whole group of "documents" is the poem in prose *Agatha*.

Valéry left it unfinished; and therefore left unanswered, this time forever, one question which to my mind is important: what was his idea of the poem in prose—its structure, its technique, its function—during the period 1892–1912 when, thinking that he had turned his back on literature, he yet returned so irresistibly to the one literary form which he felt might "lift into song what has no need of song"—the motions and very acts of thought? He used to say to Gide, about words, that he had often wanted to throw his own boots at their heads, rather than polish theirs. But words were already taking their revenge on him, and were finally to subdue the rebel beyond all prediction. There can be no doubt that he attempted at that time "to construct a literary work in the manner of a vast mathematical operation." But what did he mean by that? "I once dreamed," he tells us, "of a piece of writing in which every thought that went into its making had been clarified— in which every nonessential element of meaning in the words had been removed. . . . More than that I wanted the reluctant reader to be absolutely gripped by those forms designed to take hold, suddenly, of the very mechanism of his thought and to think in his place, there where his thinking is done, just as a man who, if someone takes hold of the two parts of his arm and forces him to make certain gestures, is thus physically compelled to interpret and understand them."

   Does the published text of *Agatha* represent such an ambition? Is it one of those texts capable of reproducing in the reader the exact motions of the writer's mind? Does it have that formative power which Valéry dreamed of? It would be difficult to say. On the one hand, having no relation whatever in form to pure mathematics, and on the other, containing no fiction, the poem follows twin itineraries, the one analytical, the other metaphorical; and these develop at times separately, or again combine. The simplest, most abstract expressions quickly change into the full-bodied figures of a rhythmic prose charged with echoes and resonances of every kind. We see the world of the mind transposed into images, into plastic equivalents and the modulations of poetic language. The mechanisms and phenomena of the mind are expressed in analogies, its rhythms in ornament, its thought in reveries and visions.

   Baudelaire is known to have dealt with the various drafts of his *Spleen de Paris* in the same manner. He had known by intuition that the prose "poems in the rough," being artistically less finished than that of the verse poem, could adapt to the "fits and starts" of consciousness and bring back from its incursions into the labyrinths of sleep or dream or darkness the most uncommon wonders—or horrors—for its prize. Which would you have: a poetry tricked out with art, or a poetry drawn from life itself? Remember the poor child showing his toy to the rich child: a live rat in a cage! And both "laughing together like brothers, showing teeth of the *same* whiteness." Yet, in spite of his equally profound intuition of the scope and possibilities of the poem in prose, Baudelaire had continually revised the early drafts of his *Spleen de Paris* which, in their first form, their nudity, their raw immediacy, were the result of outbursts from the chaotic depths, the unfathomable terror of the abyss. He had been unable to refrain from revising them, bringing them, so he thought, nearer to perfection, introducing into their formlessness the strategies of music and imagery—in short, the resources and certainties of art.

   Valéry himself experienced a similar difficulty in handling form: how was knowledge to be turned into poetry, analytical thought into art? How bring together precise thinking and pleasure, pure consciousness and delight? Yet in that considerable undertaking which was *Agatha,* the only work in which Valéry actually attempted to join the thinker to the poet, his various efforts never quite came together, either from lack of time, or rather, as I think, because he never found the formula that would make them one.

   The fact that his "Orpheus" was left unfinished seems to me significant. Written and rewritten continuously from December 1897 to 1901, and again revised in 1920, it was to be a sort of tragic fairy-play. Valéry sketched out the plan, the principal scenes, the action, chose the characters, and then tried—in vain—to write a few fragments of dialogue. Nevertheless—and this bears on our point—two monologues, two islands of pure poetry in prose, emerged from the débris of this vast enterprise. Here again we may wonder about the failure of the projected drama and the perfection of these few pages, standing apart from a larger text in which they found no place. The characters created to exemplify the theater of the intellect remained, in "Orpheus" as elsewhere, ineffectual—pure allegories. Valéry never managed to give them either the reality or the illusion of "stage people," whether because he lacked the gift of losing himself to live again in a fictional self, or because the lucidity of his mind made him despise this kind of uncontrolled creativity, or again because his passion for intelligence blinded him to every other end than itself.

He seemed far more at ease with the form of the poem in prose. The fact that he came back to it so often, and compulsively, by way of so many experiments of every kind: "philosophical tales," "brief texts," "abstract poems," "poems in the rough," stories, and all sorts of compositions more or less related to these in form, or mixed (his taste for mixing the genres is well known) . . . his persistence in these practices seems to prove that he sensed in the prose poem, more than in any other literary form, the possibility of bringing into harmony both rigorous thought and the figurative means of expressing it. It is here perhaps that this poet's purest creative impulse is to be found. This at least is what we are beginning to perceive, with the gradual publication of the work of his famous "period of silence."

The *ABC* poems and *Calypso,* the latter (in contrast to "The Angel") standing proudly on the frontiers of sensual expression: these two show in retrospect the direction Valéry was taking from the moment he wrote *Pure Dramas.* The grand manner was to be recognized also, beyond the bounds of the verse poem, in certain pieces from *Mixture,* in one of the *Broken Stories,* or in some simple description (a tiger, a hand, a sunrise, a bird, a glance, a jewel, a tree, a seashell) in which we see and hear the clear diamond-hard crystal forming, giving us a prose poem specifically Valéry's.

One word more. It was at the moment when he was writing his "Fragments of the Narcissus" that the beautiful idea of "The Angel" came to him, not to be finished for nearly twenty-five years. The inclination, or rather the attraction away from the verse poem, is evident; we have only to consider the climate of the fiction and the theme of the incorporeal spirit in both. Narcissus' image in the pool—the reflected self, stripped of the opaque body—points to the analogy of pure mind to be embodied later on in "The Angel." By a moving conversion, the mind's reflection is made incarnate in a Being of diaphanous body. But the mind as Angel, having full knowledge of itself and all things—the darkness of "the darker half" now gone—looks into its own transparency and cannot understand how, always, it has been "a prey to infinite sadness." The tears of the mind flow at the very heart of light.

Here we come to the root of the mystery, the drama of thought in Valéry—that extreme point of consciousness where the mind's clarity still cannot understand its own "fatal cause." This tear-filled eye of the mind— the ineffable touchstone of all his poetic work—penetrates, like a secret and lustral water, even into the mind's proudest reaches. "So there is something else than light?" sighed the Angel. That an anguish so fundamental should have found perhaps its most perfect expression in this supreme poem, this alone would be enough, I believe, to alter the perspective in which Valéry's poetic work has so far been considered. We cannot henceforth confine it to a single register, the traditional modes of verse; his poetry has in fact another and no less authentic dimension of form, an entirely modern one, the prose poem.

LLOYD JAMES AUSTIN

Modulation and Movement
in Valéry's Verse

Hélas! ô roses, toute lyre
Contient la modulation!
—"La Pythie"

The central theme of *La Jeune Parque* and "Le Cimetière marin" was admirably defined by Marcel Raymond some thirty-five years ago, in one of the most penetrating and profound studies ever devoted to Valéry:

> In them, a struggle takes place between two contrary attitudes: the *pure* (absolute) attitude, that of consciousness entrenching itself in its isolation, and the opposite, or impure attitude, that of the mind accepting life, change, action, giving up its dream of perfect integrity and allowing itself to be beguiled by things and captivated by their changing forms.

These two attitudes are symbolised by the two figures who dominate Valéry's youth and age, respectively, and indeed coexist in conflict or consonance throughout his life and thought: Teste and Faust. Total detachment or total involvement are the opposite poles of human possibilities. The life of every human being is played out between them: both extremes may be conceived, but neither can be sustained. Valéry, like Gide, could well have said: "I am touched by extremes." But what makes Valéry's thought and art so rich in resonance is the fact that, like his most intimate enemy Pascal, he had the

From *Yale French Studies*, no. 44 (1970). © 1970 by *Yale French Studies*.

power to fill the *entre-deux*. He could have echoed Pascal's words, transposing them into the field of his own preoccupations:

> I have no admiration at all for the excess of one virtue, such as valor, if I do not see at the same time the excess of the opposite virtue. The sign of greatness is not to be at one extreme, but rather to touch both at once, and to fill all the intervening space (l'entre-deux).

Pascal characteristically goes on to say that this is perhaps impossible. The mind is but a point, a glowing ember: all it can do is to leap from one extreme to the other. He concludes: "Well and good; but at least this shows the soul's agility, if it does not show its breadth of grasp." "Agility of the soul," says Pascal. "Agility of the mind" would be Valéry's words. But while Valéry saw in mobility an essential feature of the mind, he explored in his poetry many modes of transition from one extreme or state to another, deliberate, stately, solemn, no less than swift and darting, *largo, andante* or *maestoso* no less than *allegro, presto* or *scherzando*. These brief notes will touch on a topic that calls for further discussion: Valéry's conception of modulation in poetry, itself part of a larger subject, his conception of poetic composition.

For Valéry, the writing of a poem meant the creation of a very remarkable form of discourse: a verbal structure in which certain properties of words are given the fullest possible application: their shape and form and colour, their precise denotations and their wide-ranging connotations, their sensuous qualities, felt no less in utterance than in apprehension, their powers of stark abstraction or richly satisfying concrete evocation. The kind of verbal structure he had in mind had analogies with his two favourite arts: architecture and music. This is not the place to discuss the excesses into which this notion of architecture has led some critics of Valéry. He certainly sought, in his poems, a subtle ordering of themes and elements, with effects of symmetries and contrasts, of balance of masses, of light and shade, closely allied to the aims and achievements of the architect. But as poetry depends for its effect upon succession, the analogy with music is closer. It is significant that Valéry should have combined the two notions in his early essay, *Paradoxe sur l'architecte,* which culminates in a sonnet where Orpheus becomes a builder of temples, the musician-poet becomes an architect. Much could be said on the relations between architecture and music, as on those between music and poetry. What matters here, as far as Valéry is concerned, is what he himself wished to borrow or recover from music. One fundamental point has often been made: the nonreferential character of music and architecture, the autonomous world each respectively composes of relations between visual or sonorous elements. Valéry's quest of *poésie pure* is linked to this admiration for, and envy of, the "purest" of the arts. This is familiar ground. What is perhaps a little less so is that the specific musical device which meant the most to Valéry was precisely that of modulation. This device is not only the source of some of his finest poetic achievements, but is also intimately linked with some of his central intellectual preoccupations. He frequently uses the term in describing his aims, particularly with reference to *La Jeune Parque;* it can be applied to many of his poems; and it goes to the centre of his world of thought and feeling.

Valéry defined the central theme of *La Jeune Parque* as: "the depiction of a sequence of psychological substitutions, and to sum up, the changes in a consciousness during the course of a night." He said again that he was trying to express "cette modulation d'une vie." And if modulation was the *motif* of the poem, it was also to be the main mode of expression. Indeed, Valéry claimed for both *La Jeune Parque* and "Le Cimetière marin" an origin in considerations of form, not substance. It is well known that "Le Cimetière marin," according to Valéry, owed its origin to the mysterious emergence in his mind of the decasyllabic rhythm in a given stanza form, and that this particular form seemed to him to have gradually led him to the sense of an appropriate content. *La Jeune Parque,* too, owed its origin to the challenge of a formal problem, that of achieving in poetry an effect similar to that of modulation in music: "*La Jeune Parque* was a quest, a literally boundless quest, for what could be achieved in poetry analogous to what is called 'modulation' in music." Valéry then characteristically generalises the notion of "modulation" and considers its applications to the wider spheres of artistic creation in its relation with natural processes. It is in such passages that the "universality" of Valéry, sometimes captiously called into question today, is triumphantly vindicated:

> Nothing, moreover interests me more in the arts than those transitions, which I see as the most difficult and skilled achievement, whereas contemporaries overlook or scorn them. I never weary of admiring the graduations of form through which the shape of a living body or of a plant imperceptibly follows out its own harmonious logic, or how the helix of a shell, after its several twists, opens out at last and is edged with a layer of its inner mother-of-pearl. The architecture of a great period used the most exquisite and carefully planned mouldings to link together the successive planes of its work.

So important was this notion for Valéry that he returned to it in 1944, in one of his last *Cahiers*. Here, after discussing details inserted in *Teste* and in "Le Cimetière marin" as a painter would insert touches to rectify the tonality, Valéry continues:

> If in this method of composition I can discern the influence of painting, in various things I have done I can discern even more clearly the influence of music; the vague idea (vague forme, uninformed as I am about music) and the magic of the word *Modulation* have played an important part in my poems. *La Jeune Parque* was obsessed by the desire of this *continuum*—doubly called for. First in the musical sequence of syllables and lines,— and then in the shifting and substitution of idea-images—themselves following the states of consciousness and sensibility of the *Speaker.*

Critics of *La Jeune Parque* in general refer to Valéry's intention to use modulation in his poem, and Jean Hytier in particular comments tellingly on the twofold aspect here defined by Valéry himself. Neither he nor any other has attempted to analyse this technique in detail. I shall later in this essay make some tentative suggestions concerning the role of modulation in *La Jeune Parque*. But first I wish to consider briefly its relevance to Valéry's poetry in general.

Modulation is a feature of form. For Valéry, the only reality in art was form, in literature no less than in the non-representational arts: "The only reality in literature is form; meaning is a shadow-show. Characters, objects, etc., all are suggested. But form is what is real—i.e., what can be handled and is involved in the author's real acts." For Valéry, in thought no less than in literature, it is not the statement or even the suggestion of a truth that counts, but the acts by which a form is shaped or moulded. In the arts that are deployed in a temporal sequence, in poetry no less than in music, one of the most essential formal elements is modulation: the passing from one key to another in music, the transition from one mood or dominant idea, emotion or sensation to another in poetry. Already Mallarmé, whose saying that poetry should "reclaim its essence from music" was taken up and amplified by Valéry, had said that in a poem the words should be merely "transitions of a musical scale." The idea, or rather the sensation, of flux and change and transition from one mood or state to another continually recurs in Valéry's poetry. The most privileged moment of all for Valéry is the moment of imminence, of poised expectancy.

The opening poem of *Charmes*, "Aurore," is appropriately built up of images of preparation and potentiality. The subtle webs of association spun by the poet's never-dormant ideas in the dark recesses of his unconscious mind as he slept are the prelude to creation:

> Ne seras-tu pas de joie
> Ivre! de voir de l'ombre issus
> Cent mille soleils de soie
> Sur tes énigmes tissus?
> Regarde ce que nous fîmes:
> Nous avons sur tes abîmes
> Tendu nos fils primitifs,
> Et pris la nature nue
> Dans une trame ténue
> De tremblants préparatifs.

But the poet breaks through the frail and quivering webs of ideas and swings from intellect to senses, as in the dramatic turning-point of "Le Cimetière marin" where, after the most "philosophical" of the stanzas, that invoking Zeno and his paradoxes, he cries out:

> Brisez, mon corps, cette forme pensive!
> Buvez, mon sein, la naissance du vent!

He then evokes the most precious moment of all, the moment of potentiality, of imminence, when the mind awaits the coming of "inspiration," as if it concentrated the hearing-power of the whole universe within itself:

> Etre! Universelle oreille!
> Toute l'âme s'appareille
> A l'extrême du désir . . .
> Elle s'écoute qui tremble
> Et parfois ma lèvre semble
> Son frémissement saisir.

In the final stanza of the poem, this expectancy is beautifully symbolised by the nymph of Hope, swimming through the invisible pool of time; and the same quivering of anticipation recurs, like a musical *leitmotif,* in the final image:

> J'approche la transparence
> De l'invisible bassin
> Où nage mon Espérance
> Que l'eau porte par le sein.

> Son col coupe le temps vague
> Et soulève cette vague
> Que fait un col sans pareil . . .
> Elle sent sous l'onde unie
> La profondeur infinie
> Et frémit depuis l'orteil.

There is a particular climax of expectancy in the "Ebauche d'un serpent," an expectancy involving the future of the whole human race, when the Serpent, after his seductive appeal, awaits the effect of his words. Valéry dwells on the moment of potentiality, when Eve is about to move:

> Génie! O longue impatience!
> A la fin, les temps sont venus,
> Qu'un pas vers la neuve Science
> Va donc jaillir de ces pieds nus!
> Le marbre aspire, l'or se cambre!
> Ces blondes bases d'ombre et d'ambre
> Tremblent au bord du mouvement!

And later, two splendid images evoke the pivotal moment: the quiver along Eve's spine, and the tumultuous tossing of the branches of the Tree of Knowledge.

One of the finest evocations of the moment of potentiality is the eighth stanza of "Le Cimetière marin," where the poet turns away from the brilliant space outside and, with a feeling of utter loneliness, looks like Narcissus into his own heart and awaits his own response to his experience, which will arise from "les sources du poème." The poet turns his gaze into his own inner depths, poised in eager expectancy over the void where the "événement pur" is about to appear: the moment is charged with infinite potentiality. The poet had been gazing over the vast expanse of the sea: now he awaits the echo that this experience is to arouse in the great, bitter, dark and resonant reservoir of the soul:

> O pour moi seul, à moi seul, en moi-même,
> Auprès d'un cœur, aux sources du poème,
> Entre le vide et l'événement pur,
> J'attends l'écho de ma grandeur interne,
> Amère, sombre et sonore citerne,
> Sonnant dans l'âme un creux toujours futur!

The inner immensity of the mind forever reverberates with the premonitory echoes of future events: images, emotions, ideas. For Valéry, coming events cast their echoes before. The mind is pure potentiality, a void forever filled with mental events, but forever resuming its hollow vacancy. In the Leonardo essay, Valéry remarks that the mind rarely lives in the present: "nine-tenths of its time are spent in what does not yet exist, in what no longer exists, in what cannot exist; so much so that our true *present* has nine chances out of ten of never existing." And in *Le Solitaire,* Faust asks the question: "And is not thought solitude itself and its echo?"

I shall come back to the finest example of the moment of potentiality at the end of this article. I turn now to examples of transition, revealing Valéry's skill in seizing certain moments when the present is permeated by all that is about to change. The lovely evocation of sunset in "Fragments du Narcisse" contains lines which Valéry considered "the most perfect" of all that he had written:

> O douceur de survivre à la force du jour,
> Quand elle se retire enfin rose d'amour,
> Encore un peu brûlante, et lasse, mais comblée,
> Et de tant de trésors tendrement accablée
> Par de tels souvenirs qu'ils empourprent sa mort,
> Et qu'ils la font heureuse agenouiller dans l'or,
> Puis s'étendre, se fondre, et perdre sa vendange,
> Et s'éteindre en un songe en qui le soir se change!

Valéry, explaining and elaborating his preference for these lines, affirmed that they were the result of prolonged effort, were most in conformity with his intentions, and being "completely devoid of ideas," could be considered to reach "that degree of purity which constitutes precisely what I call *pure poetry.*" Devoid of discursive "ideas" these lines may be: but they are charged with light and colour and emotion, being built on the tender personification of evening in the form of a loving and beloved woman. The play of assonance and alliteration, the subtle rhythms, and the placing of such pairs of words as "s'étendre" and "s'éteindre" make the passage not only "musical" in a loose sense, but more precisely illustrative of what Valéry meant by poetic "modulation."

The little poem "La Ceinture" gives a variation on the same theme. It is poised in the moment of loveliness before loss, and evokes it with extreme subtlety and delicacy.

La Ceinture

> Quand le ciel couleur d'une joue
> Laisse enfin les yeux le chérir

Et qu'au point doré de périr
Dans les roses le temps se joue,

Devant le muet de plaisir
Qu'enchaîne une telle peinture
Danse une Ombre à libre ceinture
Que le soir est près de saisir.

Cette ceinture vagabonde
Fait dans le souffle aérien
Frémir le suprême lien
De mon silence avec ce monde . . .

Absent, présent . . . Je suis bien seul,
Et sombre, ô suave linceul!

The sense of "La Ceinture," as Jacques Duchesne-Guillemin has remarked
in his perceptive commentary, is complete by the end of the third quatrain:
the final couplet is a kind of echo, but an echo which transposes the whole
theme into a new and poignant key. This structure allows for three stanzas
poised on the point at which the delicate beauty of the Western sky is en-
hanced by its approaching end, then for the final brief couplet where the
mood shifts and night and separation take over.

As in the passage from "Narcisse" quoted above, and as so often in
Valéry, sunset is evoked here once again as a woman. The moment is one
when the Western sky takes on the pink of a human cheek. The line "Laisse
enfin les yeux le chérir" subtly conveys that the sky by day is too dazzling
for the eyes to rest upon it: now at last they can linger almost with a caress.
Time is in momentary suspension. In the bold tmesis of the phrase "au point
doré de périr," abstraction is brought alive by the insertion of "doré" with
its touch of gold, into the prepositional phrase "au point de." A brief intensity is implied in "le muet de plaisir" and in "enchaîne," as the poet gazes
in silent fascination at a trailing band of clouds. This, in the fading light,
evokes the figure of an insubstantial, wraith-like being about to be ravished
by the darkness, dancing with a floating girdle, loosened before the moment
of possession by the night. The poet sees in the drifting clouds quivering
beneath the breeze the last link between himself and the world he is silently
contemplating. This quivering makes him waver between absence and presence, and feel a keen sense of loneliness in a world slipping away from his
ken. Darkness descends upon his mind as it spreads over the sky, and the
trailing clouds now evoke the image of a shroud.

"La Ceinture" uses the evocation of a sunset as a means of modulating the poet's changing moods, corresponding with the changing hues of the sky, moving from delight to distress and isolation as darkness falls. It symbolises, as J. Duchesne-Guillemin has shown, the frail, tenuous bond linking our minds to the world, and poignantly expresses a final complex feeling of both loneliness and lingering tenderness ("ô *suave* linceul"). This has something of the tone and imagery of the closing lines of Baudelaire's "Recueillement":

> Et, comme un long linceul traînant à l'Orient,
> Entends, ma chère, entends la douce Nuit qui marche.

Valéry's two major poems, *La Jeune Parque* and "Le Cimetière marin," are both built up on modulation between the two opposing attitudes evoked at the beginning of this essay. Of "Le Cimetière marin," Valéry said that its abstraction was "une abstraction motrice, bien plus que philosophique"; and this epithet "motrice," with its dynamic implications, admirably brings out the basic notion of movement and mobility and change which for Valéry was of the essence of human life and thought. The very condition of life as opposed to the absolute and its static perfection is precisely this flux and change. This sense of mobility is omnipresent in Valéry's poetry. It is significant that Valéry himself singled out among his lines, as falling the least short of his ideal, passages involving this kind of modulation: the passage from "Narcisse" quoted above, and the opening lines of the fifth stanza of "Le Cimetière marin":

> Comme le fruit se fond en jouissance,
> Comme en délice il change son absence,
> Dans une bouche où sa forme se meurt,
> Je hume ici ma future fumée,
> Et le ciel chante à l'âme consumée
> Le changement des rives en rumeur.

"Le Cimetière marin" as a whole leads us by subtle gradations, of which this pivotal passage is one, from what Valéry called "a state of sombre intensity, as it were complementary to the prevailing splendor," from the rapt contemplation of the sea lying spell-bound beneath "Midi le juste," from the meditation on death and mortality in the graveyard itself, to the dynamic evocation of a dash across the sand to plunge into the life-giving sea, whose waves now break against the rocks in flying clouds of spray beneath the rising wind of the finale, calling the poet to take up the challenge of time and change and transient life. The final mood of acceptance of life is no less correlative to the unleashed sea than was the initial state of aspiration to "le calme des dieux." Inner and outer change are balanced and combined, in a modulation between three moods: serenity, anguish and triumph. The line evoking: "Le changement des rives en rumeur," is followed immediately by the invocation to the sky: "Beau ciel, vrai ciel, regarde-moi qui change!" And this foreshadows the triumphant cry where man is seen as the principle of change within the whole universe itself: addressing the noonday sun, symbol of absolute perfection: "Midi là-haut, Midi sans mouvement," the poet proudly proclaims: "Je suis en toi le secret changement."

More detailed analysis of "Le Cimetière marin" would show how Valéry modulated his major themes of aspiration to immortality and acceptance of mortality, and how he interwove in his six-line stanzas the concrete symbols of his attitudes in such a way that each new theme is discreetly announced but gradually comes dominant, while the previously dominant theme continues in subordination to it.

La Jeune Parque, like "Le Cimetière marin," is built up on the central interplay between the vision of the absolute and the realisation of the limitations of human existence. Each of these attitudes is divided into two opposing extremes. The four themes interpenetrate with a crescendo of enriching modulations, precisely in the sense of transitions, each of which introduces a new emphasis but also recalls and modifies the previous themes.

The absolute (the urge to total "purity") takes the form of either positively, self-sufficient, un-self-questioning existence, or, negatively, the purity of non-existence. The first is represented by cosmic forces, such as "Midi le juste" in "Le Cimetière marin," or by a vision of a golden-age primitivism devoid of the sting of consciousness, as in "La Pythie" or more especially in La Jeune Parque, when the Parque associates herself with the heavens, or recalls despairing or proud memories of her life before the serpent's sting. Yet implicit in this is the unchanging monotony of ennui, and the sense of eternity is cut across by the shadow with its intimations of mortality:

> Vers mes sens lumineux nageait ma blonde argile,
> Et dans l'ardente paix des songes naturels,
> Tous ces pas infinis me semblaient éternels.
> Si ce n'est, ô Splendeur, qu'à mes pieds l'ennemie,
> Mon ombre! la mobile et souple momie,
> De mon absence peinte effleurait sans effort
> La terre où je fuyais cette légère mort.

The second or negative aspect is represented by the temptation of death, by the rejection of the cycle of life, by the refusal to create mortals doomed to suffer and die:

> Non, vous ne tiendrez pas de moi la vie! . . . Allez,
> Spectres, soupirs la nuit vainement exhalés,
> Allez joindre des morts les impalpables nombres!
> Je n'accorderai pas la lumière à des ombres,
> Je garde loin de vous, l'esprit sinistre et clair . . .
> Non! Vous ne tiendrez pas de mes lèvres l'éclair! . . .
> Et puis . . . mon cœur aussi vous refuse sa foudre.
> J'ai pitié de nous tous, ô tourbillons de poudre!

The realisation of human limitations also has positive and negative aspects. On the negative side there is the inability to sustain the dialogue with the absolute or to complete the act it logically demands, namely suicide. These human limitations are also given a physiological modulation. All these sides come together in the symbol of sleep, as in the stanzas added in 1942 to the early poem "Eté":

> Aux jeux universels tu préfères mortelle
> Tout d'ombre et d'amour, ton île de sommeil.

The sleep of the Parque is the pivotal point of the poem, catching up the four threads:

> Dans vos nappes, où lisse elle imitait sa mort
> L'idole malgré soi se dispose et s'endort,
> Lasse femme absolue, et les yeux dans les larmes,
> Quand, de ses secrets nus les antres et les charmes,
> Et ce reste d'amour que se gardait le corps
> Corrompirent sa perte et ses mortels accords.

On the positive side, the poem culminates in the acceptance of human limitations, with the Parque's rebirth to the bitter beauty of existence, symbolised by the sea: "Boire des yeux l'immense et riante amertume." This "âpre éveil" is the one possible form of human reflection of the absolute:

> Alors, malgré moi-même, il le faut, ô Soleil,
> Que j'adore mon cœur où tu te viens connaître.

Within the framework of these major modulations of theme, a number of other modulations are interwoven. There are modulations of the theme of self-contemplation as the unconscious, primitive joy of "l'égale et l'épouse du jour"; as the proud and bitter resource when consciousness dawns; as the shame of which death would rid us; and finally as the renewed and joyous (but still bitter) acceptance, culminating in a tender sense of necessities:

"Doux et puissant retour du délice de naître." There are modulations on the theme of the serpent: the Parque's rejection of his intervention because her own resources are sovereign:

> Va! je n'ai plus besoin de ta race naïve,
> Cher Serpent . . .
>
> . . . .
> Mon âme y peut suffire, ornement de ruine!

the serpent's return in sleep: "Abandonne-toi vive aux serpents." There are modulations on the theme of innocence, from the radiant evocation of primitive innocence to the echo in a darker key in the sleep passage just quoted: "Retourne dans le germe et la sombre innocence." The modulation from the absolute of self-sufficient existence to the absolute of "la pureté du Non-être" is powerfully recalled in the parallel:

> Je soutenais l'éclat de la nuit toute pure
> Telle j'avais jadis le soleil soutenu.

One of the most fundamental series of modulations concerns the tenderly sensuous contemplation of a human body (a central theme in Valéry's poetry: cf. "Anne," "La Dormeuse") with its sense of both delight and terror before all potentialities. To bring alive the extremes of physiological urges, and also the transitions between them; to give them their full sensuous and emotional value and yet unite them with a theme which plays out modulations on intellectual abstractions, is Valéry's avowed aim and his achievement. To do this through a meditation in the first person implies a special gift of both intensity and discretion that would need further analysis. More, too, could be said on the imperceptibility of the transitions, on the extreme richness of the fluctuations backwards and forwards, and on the sustained melodic line of musical expression in both "Le Cimetière marin" and, more especially, *La Jeune Parque.*

But I shall conclude this article with a glance at one of the loveliest of the shorter poems in *Charmes,* built up entirely on the *motif* of imminence, of poised expectancy.

Les Pas

> Tes pas, enfants de mon silence,
> Saintement, lentement placés,
> Vers le lit de ma vigilance
> Procèdent muets et glacés.

Personne pure, ombre divine,
Qu'ils sont doux, tes pas retenus!
Dieux! . . . tous les dons que je devine
Viennent à moi sur ces pieds nus!

Si, de tes lèvres avancées,
Tu prépares pour l'apaiser,
A l'habitant de mes pensées
La nourriture d'un baiser,

Ne hâte pas cet acte tendre,
Douceur d'être et de n'être pas,
Car j'ai vécu de vous attendre
Et mon cœur n'était que vos pas.

The theme is the joy of expectation, the symbol that of a lover awaiting his beloved in the silence of the night. Her footsteps are born of his silence: they can be heard only when there is no other sound. Their slow, restrained movement is described in terms of adoration: "saintement," "pure," "divine"; but the shadowy person thus approaching comes on human feet, bare and soundless, ready to bestow the gift of all her imagined beauty. The lover begs her not to break the spell too soon: if she is slowly shaping on her unseen proffered lips a kiss that will bring peace to him, the self within the thinker, let her not hasten this tender act, whose sweetness (like the poet between absence and presence in "La Ceinture") is poised between not-being and being.

Every detail of this poem is exquisite. The atmosphere of hushed expectancy and of deep but quiet joy is perfectly evoked. The symbol is fully realised and is self-sufficient. Its implications are wider than just an allegory of the coming of inspiration: it is the anticipation of the moment of experience in its own right, with a deep sense of promised peace ("apaiser"), that forms the essential theme. At a deeper level still, the line: "Douceur d'être et de n'être pas" is the miraculous resolution of the fundamental dilemma, the reconciliation of eternity and time. Here the two extremes touch and are momentarily and magically fused.

But only for a moment, and by the magic of art. Whether a source of delight or of pain, the world of time and change is the world of man, as opposed to the timeless, unchanging perfection of the absolute. In "Le Cimetière marin" the poet cries out defiantly to the noonday sun:

> Tu n'as que moi pour contenir tes craintes!
> Mes repentirs, mes doutes, mes contraintes
> Sont le défaut de ton grand diamant.

In "Ebauche d'un serpent," Valéry extends to cosmic proportions his preference for potentiality rather than actuality, where no longer the mind of man, but the universe itself is seen as a flaw in the pure and perfect void of the absolute:

> l'univers n'est qu'un défaut
> Dans la pureté du Non-être!

These Manichaean metaphysics are not, however, Valéry's last or only word. Like many others, he knew that the concept of perfection is in itself paradoxical, since there are qualities it by definition lacks, and so is itself imperfect and incomplete. The apostrophe of "Le Cimetière marin" is a proudly bitter affirmation from an "esprit clair" savouring an "amertume douce." It cannot but recall the closing lines of Voltaire's *Poème sur le désastre de Lisbonne:*

> Je t'apporte, ô seul roi, seul être illimité
> Tout ce que tu n'as point dans ton immensité
> Les défauts, les regrets, les maux et l'ignorance . . .
> Mais il pouvait encore ajouter *l'espérance.*

Here too a sense of imperfection and a sense of potentiality are combined.

Whatever Valéry's metaphysics were, he saw in art the realm of virtuality, of potentially infinite resonance. In his dialogue *L'Ame et la danse,* he evokes the movements of the little dancer Athikté; and Phaedrus asks: "Do you think she is portraying anything?" Socrates replies: "Nothing . . . But all things. Love no less than the sea, and life itself, and all thoughts . . . Can you not sense that she is the pure act of ever-changing forms?" Imminence, modulation and movement are different manifestations of "l'acte pur des métamorphoses." Valéry's poems are essentially composed of shifting, changing patterns of sensations, emotions and ideas, which he too constantly sought to "*moduler* . . . sur la lyre d'Orphée."

W. N. INCE

La Promenade avec Monsieur Teste

Among the writings concerning Monsieur Teste, *La Promenade avec Monsieur Teste* is one of the shortest and most fascinating. The effort required to understand it probably accounts in part for its fascination. Like much of what Valéry wrote, it is both very abstract and very concrete: abstraction and generality are entailed by the attempt to convey impersonally all things within the view of the narrator and Teste and to imply forms and structures while impressionistic notations communicate immediate involvement in the "pulpe enchantée" of the outside world. In the latter part of *La Promenade* we see the narrator touching on the question of the mysterious relationship between self and the outside world. The piece first appeared in 1946 (accompanied by four others that were also new) with the explanation: "Before his death, Paul Valéry had gathered a collection of notes and drafts with the intention of using them in a new edition of *M. Teste*. The following fragments which belong to very different periods have been chosen from this collection." I have consulted these notes and particularly the fifty-one fragments which are classified as belonging to *La Promenade*. Though Valéry's published piece is short, it would be beyond the scope of this short article to give a detailed examination of the manuscripts. I propose simply to offer what seem to me the most important points which emerge from studying them.

There are many variants, but most, especially in the first half of *La Promenade*, are slight—a word here, a phrase there, or details like the im-

From *Yale French Studies*, no. 44 (1970). © 1970 by *Yale French Studies*.

perfect tenses ("Nous nous rencontrions . . . Nous quittions . . . Nous écoutions") which preceded certain present tenses in the published version. In some early notes, *La Promenade* is envisaged as forming part of a larger composition: Valéry contemplated different possible developments which did not take final shape as far as *La Promenade* was concerned, though some were to be taken up in other writings concerning Teste. Thus, after clearly referring to the proposed beginning and early part of *La Promenade,* an early note explains:

> Faire un récit AVEC TROUS MARQUÉS *distractions* en insistant. Ce récit sera son histoire intellectuelle—la présenter avec le merveilleux voulu. histoire de femme—Amour[.] mélange d'amusant et de rigide et notations—accompagnement.

> (Write a story with interruptions marked as distractions, stressed. This story will be his intellectual history—present it with the desired enchantment: a woman—Love[.] a mixture of amusement and rigor, observations—with accompaniment.)

Something of the future letter by Madame Teste is here in germ. The manuscripts show that Valéry was not sure of the eventual tone of *La Promenade.* Thus one version involves direct speech from Teste to the narrator:

> M. Teste me dit: "Il n'y a au monde qu'une seule chose que je trouve sublime. C'est la matinée d'un homme qui pense, et qui se porte bien. Il se moque bien du soleil!—Et un amour bien réussi? lui demandai-je.—Mon cher, dit-il, soyons exacts: la femme sert à se passer de femme."

> M. Teste tells me: "There is only one thing in the world which I find sublime. It is the morning of a man who is used to thinking and is in good health. The sun does not bother him!" "—And a successful love affair?" I asked him. "—My dear chap, he said, let's be precise: a woman permits one to do without women.")

These astringent remarks of an intellectual monster who seeks to be autonomous are perfectly in keeping with others made by Teste in *La Soirée* and elsewhere, but the later versions of *La Promenade* exclude the more relaxed, less strongly abstract tone created by such direct speech. It is clear that Valéry played with various ideas and with his text. On one sheet we have the fourth paragraph ("Nous écoutons") partly in Italian and wholly in Latin and English: "We do hear, with delicate ears, the mixed noise of the large way, full with increasing nuances of steps of dense horses and interminable man, which animates vaguely the depth, doing it hurling [sic] as in a dream a kind of confuse [sic] number whose magnitude changes and imites [sic] the walking the opulent conversation of people, the transformation of indifferent ones in themselves, the general pesence [sic] of snob [sic]." The passage throws interesting light on Valéry's acquaintance with English as well as on the meaning and difficulty of his French text. For our present purpose, it constitutes a kind of superior doodle, revealing how he toys—*un peu en poète?*—with the substance of his text, perhaps waiting for further inspiration for *La Promenade.*

It is difficult if not impossible to date all the fragments (hence, presumably, the reference in the 1946 note to "des époques très différentes"). Some are almost certainly from 1897 or 1898 or near then, since they are on Ministry of War paper with printed figures and dates. The relative fading of the ink on some sheets, the possibility of relating Valéry's style of handwriting to certain periods of his life, can also be of some assistance. There is nevertheless little to help us date the fragments exactly: their numbering, effected since Valéry's death, does not follow chronology. But certain basic ideas run through them, either directly explained by Valéry or embodied in the variants. "Promenade . . . Poëme du PRÉSENT, de la netteté, de l'accommodation (Promenade . . . Poem of the *present,* of precision, of accommodation)" he writes, implying the central notion of the narrator and Teste on the pavement near the Madeleine, experiencing the numerous, immediate sensations of the passing crowd and the morning scene and moving through various states of awareness. This is confirmed by other explicit notes: "Un carrefour de Paris représente par son désordre et ses mille mobiles en directions différentes—l'état d'un être perpétuellement *surpris* (A Paris street corner with its disorder and a thousand bodies moving in every direction represents a being in a state of constant surprise)," and, alongside, "promenade de Teste dans la rue (Teste's walk in the street)."

His intention is first to describe the scene near the Madeleine as the published version does:

> Pour la Promenade (Teste) . . . Considération de la population mouvante sous les yeux—Ce carrefour avec les changements de sa population instantanée—la population d'une génération, le peuple statistique.

> (For [Teste's] walk . . . Reflection on the population moving before his eyes—This street corner with its crowd changing from moment to moment—the people of a generation, the statistical population.)

He adds at the bottom of the sheet: "quartiers centraux pleins de combi-naisons (the central quarters full of possible combinations)." The passers-by and the morning scene give rise to many immediate impressions which invade the onlooker. But Valéry's intention is to shift the perspective from dispersion to concentration so that what at first dominates becomes itself contained by something more powerful; the external scene is to be gradually encompassed by the onlooker's mind: "Promenade T. . . . Après description—faire de cet ensemble d'abord CONTENANT, un CONTENU et une partie . . . faire sentir la pensée envahissant le champ angulaire (Teste's walk. . . . After the descrip-tion—make out of this at first *all encompassing scene* a scene *contained* forming a part . . . show how the mind takes over the field of vision)." He clarifies his idea by drawing two interconnected circles, the first with "moi" written inside and "monde" outside, the second with "monde" inside and "moi" outside.

So far, we have encountered what could have been expected in the con-text of Monsieur Teste: a characteristic opposition between self and the "outside." *Corps* and *Esprit* on the one hand and *Monde* on the other. The contrast is explicitly noted by Valéry in the manuscripts:

> Prendre pour sujet de la promenade—la simple opposition de l'1 au multiple—La molécule essayant de se soustraire à la statis-tique—propriétés non statistiques, c'est M. Teste[.] Donc insister sur la foule.

> (Take as subject of the walk—the simple opposition between the one and the multiple—The molecule trying to escape statistics—non-statistical properties: M. Teste[.] Insist therefore on the crowd.)

In some of these notes, it is Monsieur Teste who is one term of the opposition, whereas in the published version of *La Promenade* the narrator fulfills the role (though his "nous" speaks for both of them).

> Le mouvement le changement . . . transformation des formes les unes dans les autres . . . foule—Sentiment . . . y opposer Teste parce qu'il en retire . . . apparition de ψ et de ϕ . . . formation ainsi d'un paysage (rue) puis portrait Teste . . . *foule* . . . opposer Teste à FOULE.

> (Movement, change . . . interchange of forms—crowd—Feeling . . . contrast Teste here since he withdraws . . . apparition of ψ and ϕ . . . thus formation of a setting (a street) then the portrait of Teste . . . *crowd* . . . oppose Teste to the CROWD.)

Valéry notes in one fragment: "Le retentissement [Le Bruit] debout de la meute[.] Etre chez moi (The resounding [the Noise] of the pack. To be myself)." This is very much the disdainful attitude of the Teste in *La Soirée*, who bids the audience at the Opéra surrender to the enjoyment of their spectacle and who affirms: "Eh! Monsieur! que m'importe le 'talent' de vos arbres—et des autres! . . . Je suis chez MOIS, je parle ma langue (Well Sir, what do I care about the beauty ['talent'] of your scenery, or of anyone's painted trees! . . . I am myself, I speak my own language)."

The relationship between the onlooker and the scene—"la pensée et le dehors dans leur jeu bizarre (thought and the world outside in their strange interplay)" as Valéry notes in one manuscript—occasions the greatest number of variants. He is undecided what development to follow. The published version shows the narrator and Teste as "anxieux de n'être pas un fragment de foule (fearful of being a part of the crowd)"; but the outside scene presses in on the narrator so that he is no longer sure what is strictly himself and what is the outside world ("Je ne sais où moi-même commence [I do not know where I myself begin]" says one manuscript). The last two paragraphs of the published version ("Ce qui me rend unique se mêle au vaste corps et au luxe passager d'ici [What makes me unique fuses with the vast body and the passing riches of this world]") give an impression of flux and indeterminacy as they fade out with a description of the interpenetration of two worlds, self and the outside. The manuscripts reveal other treatments of the theme which led to the published one. In one version, the thinking self is seen as being temporarily overwhelmed by the outside world and then reasserting itself:

> Une flamme d'air et d'hommes qui se remplace infiniment elle-même, m'anime,—déjoue, devance et constitue quelquefois précisément ma pensée . . . Puis, comme si un monde complet, roulant des morceaux d'êtres et d'incessants chevaux de couleur, ne l'avait pas interrompue avec son soleil et ses paroles,—une intention bien connue, fine plus que toute chose, ardente, inégale,—reprend.

> (A flame engulfing air and men, renewing itself constantly, quickens me, baffles me, anticipates and sometimes becomes my very thought. . . . Then a familiar intention, ultra-refined, ardent, constantly changing leaps up, as though a world in itself, spinning fragments of beings and tireless fiery horses, had not interrupted it with its blazing sun and its words.)

Now the onlooker is part of the outside world: "un mécanisme de soleil et de paroles, un monde complet contient ma tiédeur, ma chair personnelle (a mechanism of sun and words, a self-contained world encompassing my tepidness, my own flesh)" now the outside world is seen rather as depending on him, as being to some extent controlled by him:

> Mais moi, l'immense autrui me presse de toutes parts. Il respire, *où je veux,* dans sa propre substance impénétrable. Je souris: c'est un peu de lui qui, non loin de mes idées, se tord; et par ce change-ment dans mes lèvres, je me sens, tout à coup, subtil. (my italics)

> (But I, I am pressed on all sides by the external scene [l'immense autrui]. It breathes, where I will it to, in its own impenetrable substance. I smile, and something of it not far from my awareness twists and by this movement of my lips, I feel all of a sudden rarefied and subtle.)

The sense of superiority or control and the self-awareness here are echoed by the similar but not identical language of the fifth paragraph in the pub-lished version. But the paragraph in the manuscript immediately following the last sentences quoted leads on to the idea of the fusion of the two worlds first adumbrated in the published version in its short sixth paragraph:

> Il renferme, ce corps si extérieur, dans sa pulpe multiple, fait aussi de morceaux d'êtres et que [qui?] semblent mener d'incessants chevaux de couleur, ce qui me touche le plus et ce qui me touche le moins. Je ne sais ce qui est à moi.

> (This external scene in its multiple substance [pulpe], composed as well of fragmented beings, seemingly led by tireless horses, encompasses at the same time what moves me the most and the least. I do not know what is mine.)

"Ce corps si extérieur, dans sa pulpe multiple (This body so external to me in its multiple substance)" might at first sight be thought to refer to the narrator's own body. (One remembers La Jeune Parque's description of her own body as "cette blonde pulpe.") But in view of the "multiple" I think it must designate the external scene, "l'immense autrui" of Valéry's preceding paragraph (cf. "le corps de l'immense autrui" in my own next paragraph and the "vaste corps" of the published version's seventh paragraph).

The manuscripts show in much greater detail and more vividly than the published version of *La Promenade* how exercised Valéry was by the struggle involved in the relationship between self and the outside world. He gives powerful expression to the sense of being part of the external scene:

> De l'immense autrui qui a beau se varier et se changer je n'y verrais qu'un tas homogène. Le souffle et le corps de l'immense autrui nous touche. Les paroles et les gens palpitent. Je sens, un éclair, *l'ivresse du pouvoir*—Je me sens à la merci de la foule—Je pars à chaque moment avec le cocher qui roule à chaque fuite, je fuis. J'aime toute personne aimable.

> (In spite of the variations and changes in the external scene I see in it only a homogenous mass[.] The breath and the body of the external scene touches us. Words and people throb with life. I feel in a flash the headiness of power—I feel at the mercy of the crowd—I take flight, I depart at any moment with the coachman who sets off at a gallop with each escape. I like every amiable person I meet.)

"L'ivresse du pouvoir (The headiness of power)" may be the power of dominating the scene (the first sentence of the quotation expresses disdainful detachment) but in the context it more probably expresses the feeling of being overwhelmed by the imagination and empathy that, as we see here, can characterize Valéry no less than abstraction, preoccupation with self and desire for autonomy. Yet another version points up the struggle in question:

> De l'immense autrui les corps me touchent. Je suis peut-être plus fort peut-être plus faible. Jusqu'à quel point? Je me sens entre lui et moi—ne suis ni lui ni moi.

> (The elements of the external world touch me. Perhaps I am stronger, perhaps weaker. To what extent? I feel suspended between that world and myself—I am neither one nor the other.)

Other manuscripts show an opposition between the narrator's self and the outside world as well as his awareness that, paradoxically, he is neither "ceci" (the outside world) nor "cela" (self) and yet is both:

> Je ne sais ce qui est à moi,—pas même cette inquiétude ce sourire et même ce soleil. (With rather different language, this is as far as the published version goes in the same direction, in paragraph six.) Je ne suis pas cela où par milliers inutiles se répercute la forme humaine,—ni ceci où une puissance continuelle, dans un vide singulier, commence sans cesse sa propre démonstration. Il y a là deux.

(I do not know what belongs to me,—not even this disquiet, this smile nor even this sun. [Cf. paragraph six of published version] I am neither that [the outside world] where useless thousands of human forms bounce off each other,—nor this [the self] where a continuous force, in a strange void, manifests itself again and again. Both are present.)

Another version describes again the sense the narrator has of being in various forms and places and also of providing the means whereby the world, including himself, reaches awareness:

Je me sens en plusieurs endroits, là où se répand par milliers d'échos la forme humaine et ici que les mots et les sensations contemplent. Le monde regarde en moi. *Toutes ces voitures* (yeux) *des centaines, etc., regardent en moi—la Pensée.*

(I am aware of being in many different places, there where by the thousands of echos the human form disperses and here where words and sensations look on. The world looks through me. All these carriages [these eyes], hundreds of them, etc. look through me—Thought.)

At this point, in several versions, a crisis is reached. Valéry tries to explore it but his attempts must not have satisfied him, hence, no doubt, the absence of any explicit reference to it in the version his family published. The crisis can be explained thus: the narrator has expressed very strongly not only the opposition between the external scene and a certain self but also the distinction between both and the observing self. When he tries to fathom the external scene, its reality eludes him; in one version, the cross-roads and "le peuple statistique (the statistical population)" are described as "image *d'un degré plus élevé* ... etc. *Mais on ne sait pas de quoi.* On sent que c'est une image mais le réel qu'elle représente échappe, résiste à la pensée (an image of a *higher level* ... etc. *But one does not know of what.* We feel that it is an image, but the reality which it represents escapes us, resists formulation as thought)." In most characteristic Testian fashion, he tries to reach truth or certainty by concentrating on his inmost self. He tries to call up all his thoughts, all his powers of awareness:

Alors, invinciblement, je veux penser à toutes mes pensées, je détourne quelque chose vers quelque chose vers toutes mes choses internes (possibles, cachées) (La pensée est une chose non existante dont on est sûr qu'elle aura lieu)—j'appelle enfin pour une résistance l'ensemble de toutes mes idées. Celles venues et celles nées et celles à naître.

(Then invincibly, I want to take up all my thoughts, turning one thing toward another, toward all my internal [possible and hidden] things [thought is a non-existing entity which is certain to take place].—Finally, in order to resist, I call upon the whole of all my ideas. Those past, those present and those to come.)

In this and other versions the narrator seems to experience the hopeful imminence of an escape from his difficulties through "cette magnifique pluralité: l'ensemble de mes idées (this magnificent plurality: the whole of my ideas)." But the hope or expectation is soon dashed: "mais, au lieu, je ne sens venir qu'une formule," says one version; in another: "Non—signe seul. La notion qu'il est permis de concevoir le total de mes idées—et ce signe fait équilibre à la terrible vue (but, instead, only a formula takes shape," says one version; in another: "No—only a sign. The notion that I might conceive my ideas as a whole, and the sign sets off the terrible sight)." A kind of failure is encountered in both spheres, the external and the internal. One of the fullest and clearest versions of this crisis brings together all the aspects not found together in other, shorter, notes: he is neither the outside world nor a unique self; external and internal reality, usually perceived as "signes," really merge in a higher consciousness which he will now try to evoke and fully grasp; the attempt fails and he is left with mere clichés or linguistic symbols:

> Je ne suis ni cela où par milliers d'exemples inutiles se répercute l'humaine forme—ni ceci, unique, dont tous les moments regardent.
>
> Je m'approche un peu plus de ma difficulté: les roues chaudes, le vent simple, les facettes de la foule (population), les palpitations de robes, touchent—mais où?—d'autres créations mobiles—une parole toute silencieuse juge et les spectacles du (au) soleil sont singulièrement *vus* par quelques signes et ils sont accueillis de suite par quelques grandeurs changeantes de fatigue et de plaisir. converse avec elle-même et oppose entre eux (qui échange entre elle-même) des mots également favoris.
>
> Alors, je veux enfin connaître toute mon étendue, je veux penser à toutes mes pensées, je les appelle; la plus petite, la plus ancienne . . . la future, la niaise, la folle, l'immonde—pour noyer tout ce qui passe dans ce qui a passé, et fondre le retentissement

robuste de la bande vivante—dans tout ce que je sais. Je crois
tenir cette magnifique pluralité: l'ensemble de mes idées . . . mais,
au lieu, je ne fais monter du néant qu'une sorte de formule ou de
symbole et je me dois borner à concevoir avec ivresse—quelque
chose comme une quantité qui me serait très chère. C'était une
sensation spéciale d'indéfini et de possible comme le moment du
départ ou un sourire au fond d'un puits.

(I am neither that [the outside world] where by thousands of
useless examples human forms bounce off each other—nor this,
a unique self observed by all his moments.

I am coming now somewhat closer to my problem: the hot
wheels, the mere wind, the faceted crowd [population], the flutter
of dresses, touch—but where?—for other moving creations—a
quite silent word judges and the spectacles of [in] the sun are
strangely *seen* by some signs and they are immediately received
by some varying extents of fatigue and pleasure. [?] converses
with itself [interplays with itself] and compares equally favored
words.

Then, I want to know at last my true extent, I want to think
all my thoughts, I invoke them; the smallest, the most remote in
time . . . , the ones to come, the foolish, the mad, the filthy, in
order to drown all that is happening in what has already happened, and to melt the vital resounding of the living mob—in
everything I know. I seem to hold that magnificent plurality: the
whole of my thoughts . . . but, instead, I only call up from nothing
a kind of formula or symbol and I have to limit myself to heady
imagining—something like a quantity which would be very dear
to me. It was a special sensation, indefinite and possible, like the
moment of parting or the smile at the bottom of a well.)

I have left the most interesting manuscript to the last, because, though
syntactically a little incoherent and certainly not brought to the perfection
of expression Valéry required for publication, it perhaps goes some way
towards elucidating either "cette magnifique pluralité: l'ensemble de mes
idées (this magnificent plurality: the whole of my ideas)" or the mysterious
"sensation spéciale d'indéfini et de possible (special sensation, indefinite and
possible)" which remains after the narrator's failure to summon all his
thoughts:

Et dans la rue, soudain écoutant à travers le bruit, à travers toutes

choses, par une coupure pour lui entr'ouverte dans LE SIÈCLE—
la musique des Sphères, le fleuve d'éther—comme s'il s'arrêtait
dans l'être (opposer au charroi réel), divisant le monde, à la division du courant—La canne dans le ruisseau courant qui peigne
l'eau et le sable,—et, passant et repassant en un instant une in-
finité de fois, le même fleuve—appartenant à deux-n mondes.—
bruissement éternel, brise infiniment profonde, détachement doux
mais si important, et dont on revient (semble-t-il en cet instant
même) tout autre et confirmé dans sa puissance, dans sa sagesse,
dans sa modestie, dans son mépris, dans son ironie, dans tout ce
qui affirme et nie, donne et retient, nie l'affirmation et affirme la
négation.

Comme si—quelque chose étrangement simple et niable et né-
gligeable, simplement traversée ou nous traversant, ayant été ajou-
tée à la mémoire du sujet, et à sa connaissance ou expérience du
monde,—ce monde et ce sujet en étaient profondément trans-
formés.

Leçon reçue tout à coup dans la rue et par un incident *ineffable*.
—jusqu'à ce que la rue et les choses deviennent abîme, au-delà,
ultra-monde—monde où sont les secrets et les âmes des morts.

(And back in the street, he finds himself suddenly listening in
spite of the noise, in spite of everything, through a slit barely
opened for him in this *world below,* to the music of the Spheres,
to the ethereal flow—as though he had brought being to a halt
["contrast with the flow of reality"] his walking stick in the gutter, dividing the world at the parting of the waters—streaking
running water and sand—and crossing over again and again in
one instant the same stream, belonging at the same time to two
worlds . . . The eternal rustling, steady endless breeze, tender but
so important detachment from which one returns (it seems in
that same instant) all together different and yet reassured of one's
force, of one's wisdom, modesty, disdain, irony, reassured of all
that affirms and negates, gives and retains, denies affirmation,
and affirms negation.

As if—world and this subject were profoundly transformed by
something strangely simple, deniable, and negligible, just crossed
or passing through us, having been added to the memory of the
subject and to his knowledge or experience of the world.

A lesson suddenly learned in the street by an *ineffable* incident

... until the street and everyday things become abyss, the beyond, the world beyond, a world where the secrets and the souls of the dead are found.)

The adjective "ineffable" is scarcely accurate. Valéry movingly describes his attempt to penetrate to the depth of his experience and of his own being in terms of a mystical departure from ordinary time and an apprehension of the bliss of the eternal present; the crudeness of much language and conceptualization is left behind, self and the outside world are less naively separate (despite the "opposer au charroi réel"), opposites are mystically reconciled ("tout ce qui affirme et nie, donne et retient, nie l'affirmation et affirme la négation [all that affirms and negates, gives and retains, denies affirmation, and affirms negation]"), detachment and participation come together ("détachement doux [tender detachment]") in a state approaching the lucid tenderness more fully and beautifully expressed by his Faust. Consciousness, and especially consciousness of relationships, is one of Valéry's major interests and themes. Though he often shows it causing bitterness or anguish through a sense of separation, he also sees it as man's greatest faculty, deepening and enriching his experience of everything, giving him not just intellectual knowledge but contact that is both sensuous and abstract with himself and the outside world. In the last manuscript given, the everyday scenes of the street "deviennent abîme, au-delà, ultra-monde (becomes abyss, the beyond, the world beyond)": the penetrating experience of the simplest reality can lead Valéry to glimpse the essential if fragile equilibrium that can be reached between thought, feeling and self-observation, between self and the rest, between the individual and the universal. "Quelle merveille qu'un instant universel s'édifie au moyen d'un homme et que la vie d'une personne exhale ce peu d'éternel (How marvelous it is that a universal instant is created by means of a man and the life of a person emanates this bit of the eternal)." As I have tried to show in greater detail elsewhere, Valéry's passionate, jusqu'auboutiste nature and the intensity of both his intellectual and affective life can cause him to go beyond mere "signes" to explore the tension between être and connaître and to express the wonder of existence, the sense of integration, conscious and sensuous, with reality. The manuscripts of La Promenade suggest something of all this. Readers familiar with Valéry's writings will from time to time have been reminded by these manuscripts of other works by him. The collocation of "puissance," "sagesse," "modestie," "mépris" and "ironie" makes one think perhaps of "Le Cimetière marin" where the human mind and its perceptions come into a comparable reciprocal relationship which embraces intellectual and emotional values such as I have indicated.

The manuscripts of *La Promenade avec Monsieur Teste* help to clarify Valéry's intentions and give us a better understanding of the published version. They are interesting and valuable in themselves, for what they reveal that is not in the published version. They show that *La Promenade* was potentially a more ambitious composition than the published version proved to be. Behind the short published piece lay many tentative versions and much probing enquiry that takes us to the heart of some of Valéry's most constant preoccupations.

CHARLES G. WHITING

La Jeune Parque

In early 1912, André Gide and Gaston Gallimard came to Valéry and attempted to persuade him to publish a collection of his early verse and prose. Valéry resisted the idea, although he was preoccupied with his future and with what he would do after the death of Edouard Lebey, for whom he was working as a sort of secretary. Gallimard had a typescript prepared, and Valéry, weary of abstract thought, amused himself by making changes in his early poems, trying to improve musical continuity and to correct their unevenness. The old desire to write poetry, which he had never completely abandoned, grew stronger in him, and he began speculations on the problems poetry created in his mind. Speculation required in turn verification, and he started writing what he considered to be a final farewell poem to poetry which would run to some forty lines. In April 1917, after more than four years of work on some 800 pages of manuscript, this became the 512 lines of *La Jeune Parque,* one of the really great poems in French twentieth century literature. Writing it, Valéry had fortified his mind against the anguish of the war communiqués.

Valéry has emphasized that what interested him, as he turned seriously to poetry once again, was the degree of critical intelligence and will power he could exert in the creative process. It was an opportunity to use the scientific rigour, in which he had been training himself for twenty years, in something which would become a finished construction, a completed poem. In turn, this effort governed by *self-awareness* provided the poet with a

From *Paul Valéry.* © 1978 by Charles G. Whiting. Athlone Press, 1978.

constant series of illuminations on the functioning of the mind, and Valéry
has affirmed that this was the greatest benefit he drew from four years of
work. Valéry also placed in his poem the results of twenty years study of
the living and functioning human being, modes of thinking and of feeling.
He saw *La Jeune Parque* as a series of psychological states and said that the
general subject of the poem was "la Conscience de soi-même," awareness of
these states. But this intellectual surveillance, this awareness and curiosity
in the Parque is always completed by imagery of the body. "J'ai même été
forcé, pour *attendrir* un peu le poème, d'y introduire des morceaux non
prévus et faits après coup. Tout ce qui est sexuel est surajouté. Tel, le passage
central sur le Printemps qui semble maintenant d'importance essentielle."
This is no doubt an extreme statement, since at least part of the Serpent
passage was written in 1913, and the lines "Quel repli de désirs, sa traîne!
Quel désordre / De trésors s'arrachant à mon avidité" appear in the "first
state" of the poem, as well as the sexual "soirée" passage:

> Souviens-toi de toi-même! O chaste joue, affronte
> L'innocente, coupable, et belle que je fus,
> Celle qui se fondant par les fluides fûts,
> Ennoblissait l'azur de la sainte distance!
> Ranime de ton sang la pâle circonstance,
> Le trouble transparent qui baigne dans les bois,
> Où tu te parlais seule, où j'écoutais ma voix
> Que j'ignorais si rauque et d'amour si voilée . . .
> Le col charmant cherchait la chasseresse ailée.

It is likely, however, that the major theme of the poem unfolded for Valéry
with the poem's development. That theme can perhaps best be described as
a dramatic struggle between a desire for intellectual purity, for a god-like
state, and the exigencies of life of a human being seen as a part of nature,
and obeying inevitable laws of physiological functioning, development, re-
production, and self-conservation.

Valéry, however, also affirmed that the content of the poem was made
up of nothing but "lieux communs." This rather startling observation, as
well as Valéry's revelation that the character of the poem appeared in its
final stages, only serves to demonstrate that if one major aspect of poetic
activity for Valéry was the exercise and discovery of his mind, the second
was the achievement of the perfection of form. Telling how he began his
poem, Valéry said: "Je voyais quelque récitatif d'opéra à la Gluck; presque
une seule phrase, longue, et pour contralto." Still another well-known comment by the poet stresses the importance of continuity: "*La Jeune Parque*

fut une recherche, littéralement indéfinie, de ce qu'on pourrait tenter en poésie qui fût analogue à ce qu'on nomme 'modulation' en musique. Les 'passages' m'ont donné beaucoup de mal." Wagner, as well as Gluck, inspired Valéry. The musical continuity of Racine's dramatic poetry was another model, particularly in such fragments as the "songe d'Athalie" and the "prière d'Esther." In "Le Prince et la Jeune Parque," Valéry has told how an article of reminiscences in *Le Temps* of 1 December 1913 revealed to him precise details of the diction of the great tragedian Rachel (1812–58) in the part of Hermione in *Andromaque,* and how these details on her breathing, rhythm, accents, and the use of a voice which ranged over two octaves helped in a difficult moment of his work on *La Jeune Parque.*

Such an approach to poetry meant that Valéry was using words as a painter uses colours or a composer works with sounds, and in this attention to words, their musical and suggestive qualities, he carries on the tradition of the nineteenth century symbolists while combining it with the strict rules of classical prosody. A quotation from a notebook of 1914 proves how important words and formal considerations were in the creation of the content of the poem: "Tout le développement (du Serpent) est sorti de la rime à *ordre.*" Words, sounds, accents and rhythms are the substance of this poetry, as we can see so well in these two lines from Valéry's favourite passage:

> Pâle, qui se résigne et saigne sans regret?
> Que lui fait tout le sang qui n'est plus son secret?
>
> (ll. 387–88)

Who cannot be sensitive to the strong accent on "Pâle," to the succession of slightly plaintive *i* sounds, to the soft music of the sibilants and the *gne* endings, as well as to the interplay of sound between *sans* and *sang* and the enriched rhyming words (*sans regret / son secret*)? While attentive to such details, Valéry also constantly interested himself in the formal structure of the whole poem. At one time he envisaged the "Larme" and "Suicide" sections as a conclusion to the poem. This was in the "fourth state" of *La Jeune Parque,* which ran to 337 lines and was finished in May 1916, less than a year before publication. But finally these two sections were shifted to the end of the first part of the poem (ll. 280–324) while, as Duchesne-Guillemin has noted, other formal considerations created the conclusion. Valéry confided to Emilie Noulet that he had to *finish* the poem, and it is likely that consideration of what would create a satisfying equilibrium with the previous passages devoted to reflections, death, night, sleep, defeat and regret weighed as heavily in the poet's mind as any intentions derived from his philosophy of life. Once again this implies that only through a study of its form can *La Jeune Parque* be truly appreciated.

Title, Epigraph, and Dedication. A number of possible titles were considered by Valéry as he wrote the poem before *La Jeune Parque* was decided on. These included: *Hélène, Larme, Pandore, Alpha de la Lyre, Ebauche, Etude Ancienne, Discours, La Seule Parque, l'Aurore, Ile,* and *Psyché.* The title *La Jeune Parque* was found early in 1916, at least a year before being finally selected. It suggests the idea of a "young destiny," and like some of the other titles Valéry considered, it helps give a discreet colouration of antiquity to this poem written by a man born on the shores of the Mediterranean. Other allusions to antiquity appear in the reference to the Cygne-Dieu (l. 429), the image of the doves of Aphrodite (l. 186), the idea of the self or the world as a prison (l. 72, l. 331), and no doubt in the images of nudity and the occasional body-metaphor of the statue (l. 158). The epigraph ("Le Ciel a-t-il formé cet amas de merveilles / Pour la demeure d'un serpent?") comes from *Psyché* by Pierre Corneille, and contains an error. Corneille had written: "Le Ciel aurait-il." As Duchesne-Guillemin has pointed out, already the epigraph suggests an erotic metaphor, since the serpent in Corneille's play was nothing else than a disguise for Eros. The dedication is to André Gide where Valéry refers to his poem as an "exercice." Once more he is emphasizing the formal considerations, the laws of prosody, the importance of willpower, effort, conscious awareness, critical alertness, and finally that benefit to which he gave such importance, the intellectual training obtained from four years of difficult work.

Lines 1–49. The poem begins with the Parque as a lone tragic figure in the vast grandiose scene of night sky, remote stars ("diamants extrêmes"), sea and rocky coast. Two poles: the remote heavens with their constellations, and the tormented intimacy of the self. The first two alexandrines are irregular, expressing by their rhythm the distress of the young girl. The broken rhythm is accompanied by sounds of lament, but this lament is neither declamatory nor lacking dignity. It is restrained and moving. Then in the third and the following lines, the Parque takes hold of herself, and the rhythm of the verses becomes regular.

The Parque now addresses her hand, pressed to her face and ready to console her, and which waits for a tear to fall and for an illumination of her broken heart. Once more the decor is evoked, now the sea (ll. 9–12) and it is particularly clear here how the decor will be used throughout the poem. At all times it will be intimately linked with the Parque herself. Here the sounds of the sea obviously reflect her own self-reproaching, disappointment and bitterness. In lines 9 and 10, sibilants, the murmur of *me murmure,* and the dark vowels of *houle* and *ombre* make the presence of the sea very real, a sea already announced by the sibilant of *proche* in line 3. Onomatopoetic effects, however, are very infrequent in Valéry's poetry, and usually the relation between sound and sense is more subtle, as in the acute vowels and nasals of lines 10–12, expressive of the Parque's pain and lament.

Again in lines 13–17, she turns to herself, to her cold hand and trembling breast, perhaps the first image in the poem which makes us powerfully aware of the physiological dimension of *La Jeune Parque,* an originality of which Valéry was particularly aware and justly proud. Line 13 in an early manuscript began with "Que fais-je" which Valéry later altered to "Que fais-tu," vastly improving the dramatic quality of the dialogue with the self. Then in lines 14 and 15, we have the effective yet integrated metaphors, *feuille* and *îles,* for unlike the surrealists of the 1920s, Valéry was intent on not breaking the continuity of the poem. In line 16 the Parque begins turning toward the constellations above, with which she is *liée,* because they are symbols of purity, symbols of the Absolute, and soon she will tell how she turned toward the Absolute upon discovering that she was a mere mortal being. "Soif de désastres" in line 17 probably refers to her curiosity, to her desire to explore her painful duality, a need in her which constantly gives dynamism to the poem. The sky is *inconnu* (l. 16), because *she* has been changed by the powerful manifestation just now of her sexual nature.

Now the Parque begins an apostrophe to the pure and remote stars, in a discourse reminiscent of biblical style which once again elevates the tone of the poem. The Parque questions herself, seeking what caused her present pain. Was it because of a dream? The poem now moves into the very recent past in line 32 as the Parque tells how she reacted to that dream, dominating her body, discovering its strange extent, strange because she had just awakened, but strange also, no doubt, because she was discovering its sexual nature. Then comes the famous line 35 with its imagery of body, awareness of the body, and awareness of awareness: "Je me voyais me voir." In 1896, Monsieur Teste had already declared: "Je suis étant, et me voyant; me voyant me voir, et ainsi de suite." The Parque gazed into the mysteries of her *profondes forêts* (l. 36), an image of the body and the world of the senses (cf. "forêt sensuelle," l. 53 of "Aurore" in *Charmes*). There her gaze followed the serpent who had just bitten her. There is a suggestion, of course, of the serpent in Genesis, but as [Octave] Nadal has pointed out, the theological suggestions of *La Jeune Parque,* like the atmosphere of antiquity, are only superficial colourations.

The serpent and its bite symbolize here the sexual nature of the Parque as well as her conscious awareness of herself, and not "evil" or awareness of good and evil. She is "sinueuse" (l. 35), because she contains this serpent within herself. In lines 38–40, the rhythm of the verses reveals once again her emotion. She is aware not only of sexual feelings (*désirs, désordre, trésors*), but also of her dark thirst for clarity. "Sombre" in line 40 appears to be polyvalent, referring at the same time perhaps to the Parque's darkly mysterious inner life, her sexual nature, and her sorrow. Coiled around herself like a serpent, *she* is her "seul possesseur" (l. 47), and within her a secret sister burns who prefers herself to that other part of the Parque which is "extremely attentive."

Lines 50–101. In a long passage, the Parque now quotes herself, repeating the words she used to dismiss the serpent, that "ornement de ruine" (l. 54), "bras de pierreries" (l. 58), who appears here again with emphasis on his sexual significance. The Parque is proud and strong, self-controlled, as her serpentine mind dominates herself ("je m'enlace," l. 51), and the passage is filled with imperatives. She explores her mind, realizes her limits (l. 68), although admitting that the weary mind can create illusions of power (ll. 69–72). Imagery of imprisonment and escape announce already passages evoking her ardour for the Absolute. Other inclinations can bring the return of the serpent, who now reappears with imagery of caresses, languor and drunken passion. "Thyrse" evokes the bacchantes, and this word again discreetly recalls classical antiquity. But once more she dismisses the serpent, and the alert, proud intellect triumphs. She emerges from an "absence" (l. 92) (Valéry uses a word from Mallarmé's vocabulary), an absence whose mortal contours were soothed only by herself—and not by a lover. Duchesne-Guillemin raises a pertinent objection at this point in the poem, asserting that Valéry's method of working on separate fragments resulted occasionally in contradictions of sense: "Mais alors, si elle vient d'avoir si bien conscience d'elle-même avant de commencer devant nous son chant, comment se fait-il que nous la voyions s'interroger et sembler à peine se réveiller?" In lines 97–101, which still evoke the Parque in the moments *preceding* lines 1–27, she is lucid, aware of what has happened, and eager to preserve this new revelation about herself, this "douleur divine" (l. 97), although the serpent has been dismissed. At the same time, this passage leads into an account of more distant memories, those of a "mortelle sœur," a "mensonge," an "antique corps insensible."

Lines 102–48. But this time of ignorance when she lived happily beneath the sun and by the sea was also a moment of unity of being and of union with the world. Valéry renews the image of the *chevelure*. Her flowing, wind-blown hair was no delight for men and lovers, but a symbol of freedom and of union with this seaside, sun-bathed decor. The rhythm is regular in the passage beginning with line 110, reflecting the tranquillity and regularity of this life of pagan pleasures. It is one of the great sensual passages in Valéry's poetry with imagery of the soft pulp of blond flesh penetrated and devoured by the sun. In this distant past, however, she knew neither her sexual nature nor her eventual death, that "amère saveur" (l. 117), which prolongs the fruit image of line 114. "Captive" (l. 122) with its seventeenth-century suggestion (*captive par amour*), she strode through banks of flowers which were bent over by a simple and virginal dress discreetly apparent on the "vivantes couleurs" (l. 131) of her nude body. Valéry is far from the orna-mented women of Baudelaire.

The Parque half regrets those innocent happy days of the harmonious self when there was no hesitation between wish and action. Everything seemed unchanging and eternal until one day when watching her shadow glide over the earth, she realized that she was mortal and that she would finally die. Acute *i* sounds accent the anxiety of this realization in lines 141–42 and again in 145–48.

Lines 148–221. She was "captive" (l. 156) then of the perfume of orange flowers (l. 151), and the evaporation of these perfumes symbolizes the pass-ing of all things and time. She lost interest in her surroundings, and if her body trembled beneath the sun's rays, it had become a statue (l. 158), no longer "Poreuse" (l. 113). Then once again she passes to present time in lines 153–55, as she penetrates deeper into the mysteries of the self beneath the night sky. Her eye, dark with astonishment, contemplated her desire for death (l. 161), and from the beginning of the passage she was "armed" (l. 149) by the idea of death. Her response to mortality was a death chosen by her, and in lines 165–66 she thinks of the death wish of the Pythia, and acute vowels again appear in the verses. (There is an allusion here no doubt to Valéry's "La Pythie" in *Charmes*.) Then in line 170 she watched a bird in the sky, its "miroir d'aile" (constructed from "miroir aux alouettes") and saw it disappear and die in the dark gaze of her eye.

Line 173 is elliptical, and "j'étais" should be understood after the word "regard." It was dangerous (for her) to be the prey of her eye with its dreams of death, because that eye, from its soft lids ("plages de soie," l. 174), had already seen too many identical days. Because she knew she would die, life lost its savour and nothing had value any more (l. 179). Thus she was no longer existing in time, but was half-dead, or half-immortal (ll. 180–81), and her future history was "cold," without interest, and the self detached ("feux absolus") from any participation in life. Will Time dare from various past days ("diverses tombes," l. 185), recall an evening favoured by the doves of Aphrodite? (cf. "Episode" in *Album de vers anciens*). This evening brings with it a blush of shame attached to this fragment ("lambeau voyageur") of her childhood, and mixes a rose colour with the emerald tones of sunset.

Now the Parque tells how on this particular evening she experienced her first sexual feelings, which she recognizes now, but did not recognize then. She asks her memory to bring a blush to her face as a sign of refusal of that other self (ll. 190–92). Then she orders her blood to give life to the remote memory ("pâle circonstance") and to the innocent self of the old happy days (l. 195). Finally that blood will be a fire consuming the pale memory (l. 196). She wants to recognize and hate that child and "ce silence complice," and in this phrase the sounds become soft and caressing. Let her voice cry out again, with its cry of love, love she had not recognized because she was seeking *death:* "Le col charmant cherchant la chasseresse ailée" (l. 202). The image suggests a swan's neck and the swan's legendary song at the moment of death, while "la chasseresse" is a winged arrow and no doubt also Artemis, "a huntress and a 'lion unto women,' because their sudden and painless deaths are ascribed to her" (*Oxford Classical Dictionary*). Vines brushed her cheek, "grands cils," lashes of an imagined lover, and the light of evening was criss-crossed with lashes and fluid tree-trunks communicating a sense of confusion, disorder and movement created by the powerful sexual desires of the Parque. The hypallages of line 208 suggest that it was she who was "broken" and "confused."

In line 209 she again quotes words she spoke in the past. The ardour she didn't recognize at the time as a sexual reaction was an élan toward death—not an ordinary accidental or normal one, but a chosen death which she saw as the attainment of an absolute, immortality, a divine state. Her eyes would be like stars (cf. ll. 18–23) tracing the *templum* (Latin: space marked out by the augur's baton) in the sky, while her body would become the object of a cult. The imperfect tense of line 211 glides into the present tense of line 212 as the Parque is again seized by desire for death. Vertigo confuses her vision and piercing *i* sounds reappear beginning with line 213. She implores death to deliver her, and the Platonic theme of man as slave or prisoner of the body (cf. ll. 331, 482) occurs in lines 219–20. Then with a skilful modulation through the rhyme, we pass to the famous "springtime" passage in line 222, originally a separate poem, "Renaissance," and added in the final stages of the writing of *La Jeune Parque*.

Lines 222–372. The originality of the magnificent "springtime" passage, so forceful and lyrical, lies in its attention to the real elements and actions of springtime rather than in simply the feelings of the poet:

> Demain, sur un soupir des Bontés constellées,
> Le printemps vient briser les fontaines scellées:
> L'étonnant printemps rit, viole . . . On ne sait d'où
> Venu? Mais la candeur ruisselle à mots si doux
> Qu'une tendresse prend la terre à ses entrailles.
>
> (ll. 225–29)

Just as it is the blood of the Parque which is affected by the coming of spring, we have the action of the winds, the breaking-up of ice, the flowing of water, sap rising in the trunks, and leaves bursting out on the branches. The physiology of springtime is linked with the physiology of the Parque. "Bontés constellées" in line 225 are the winds and stars of spring. "Etonnant" in line 227 should be understood in its old sense of "provoking a strong reaction," "Ecailles" in line 230 are the leaves of the trees, and in line 238 "ramer" is a play on words implying both "rames" and "rameaux." According to Lucienne Cain, lines 230–32 were written in 1897!

The Parque herself experiences a powerful sexual response to this arrival of springtime, asking with a pathetic repetition of "Quelle" (l. 243), who could resist such an appeal? Sighs lift her breasts (l. 248) (cf. "L'Abeille" in *Charmes* for the same rhyme abeille / corbeille), and the image of the bee (l. 250), always linked with the mind in both *La Jeune Parque* and *Charmes*, signifies a critical moment of choice between the "Lumière" (l. 253) of life, or death and purity. Typical physiological imagery is continued in lines 254–55 where we sense the beating of her heart, and where her breast, captive of its network of veins, burns and swells. Then in line 257 the theme of sexual response shifts to the theme of maternity. Again the image of the "autel" recurs (cf. l. 210) with its discreet coloration of Antiquity, but here the Parque would be sacrificed to life and its cycles, "éternels retours" (l. 263). Furthermore, giving life implies another eventual death like the one she discovered (ll. 141–48). She cries out her refusal in an exclamatory passage (l. 269), where Valéry uses a series of negatives and substantives, a rhetorical device unusual in his poetry: "Non, souffles! Non, regards, tendresses . . . mes convives." The passage ends with a concern for others (l. 278), surprising in this poem centred on the Parque.

Then this pity for others becomes an admission of her own defeat, in an extraordinary physiological passage which traces the progress of tears along their paths from secret inner grottos until they obscure her vision.

"Envieuse" in line 281 is an archaism meaning "desirous." "Orgueil" in line 285 refers to the tear itself, proud product of this labyrinth and now forced outward: "contrainte," (l. 286). "Sacrifier" and "libation" (ll. 288–89) again suggest Antiquity. Then the theme of tears modulates into the theme of suicide as the Parque wanders closer to the precipice overlooking the sea. "Cygne" in line 307 is an image of her own body, rather than some prospective lover (cf. "col charmant," l. 202). Her "pact" (l. 311) with the earth implies that she too is earth. At the end of the passage, however, she hesitates. "Celui" should be understood before "qui" in line 322, and line 324, although repeating line 304, indicates that she is turning back from the edge of the cliff.

Lines 325–60. Between line 324 and line 325 the Parque again sleeps and then re-awakens as dawn appears. Valéry himself said: "Je vois, par exemple, un commencement d'*acte* à ce vers." The apostrophe to herself, "Mystérieuse MOI" (l. 325) is intended, of course, to recall another apostrophe, "Harmonieuse MOI" (l. 102), communicating to the reader their contrast as well as a sense of all that has occurred between the two moments in the poem. There is a significant contrast also between the black night and heaving sea of lines 316–21 and the bright dawn and calm sea of this new episode, but for the Parque nothing seems changed. The sun ("un miroir," l. 327) rises from the sea, the stars ("signes," l. 329) fade away, but the Parque is still the same, still a prisoner of life (l. 331), "victime inachevée" (l. 335), "impérissable hostie" (l. 338) (again allusions to Antiquity). The calm waves wash her body ("seuil," "écueil," ll. 335–36), but it is a body ready to turn again to desires and tormented by memories. Then this theme of sameness and ennui modulates to one of renewal, purity and laughter, radically changing "la tombe enthousiaste" (l. 346), that burial place where her élan towards death was a divinely inspired frenzy. Now she eagerly greets the islands, not yet visible, and this image recalls that "Ile" was once considered as a title for the poem, symbol of the isolated inner drama of the Parque. Here they are "jouets de la jeune lumière" (l. 349), and the expression suggests childhood, gaiety, activity. Soon they will be beehives of action (ll. 350–55), and the image resembles a stanza of "Air de Sémiramis":

> Soleil, soleil, regarde en toi rire mes ruches!
> L'intense et sans repos Babylone bruit,
> Toute rumeurs de chars, clairons, chaînes de cruches
> Et plaintes de la pierre au mortel qui construit.

Finally, the Parque calls the islands "merveilleuses Parques," because they are like human destinies, participating in life, creating flowers in the air, but in the depths of the sea cold and dead.

Lines 361–80. The word "glacés" (l. 360) brings back thoughts of death, and the Parque recounts recent memories now, nocturnal memories evoked in daylight, whereas the first part of the poem contained daylight memories recounted at night. Moreover, the second part is far more an account, and even at times an account of what *might* have been, while the first part had a larger proportion of lines devoted to present action. Beginning with line 361, the Parque tells what happened in the hours between line 324 and line 325. She left the precipice and went back home, in a calmer state, still, however, seeking death and listening to the final beats of her heart (again a physiological detail). But with an image which recalls Mallarmé's Hérodiade looking into her mirror (l. 380), she realizes that she had experienced no real movement toward death.

Lines 381–405. Valéry wrote of this passage of *La Jeune Parque:* "De ces morceaux, il en est un qui, seul, représente pour moi le poème que j'aurais voulu faire. Ce sont les quelques vers qui commencent ainsi: 'O n'aurait-il fallu, folle, etc.'" It is a dynamic, suggestive passage culminating in a magnificent image of the rising, expanding smoke of a funeral pyre mingling with the constellations in the heavens, but despite its emotional moments, the whole passage has an extraordinary continuity. In the opening lines, the Parque regrets her last chance for a proud refusal of life, a "transparente mort" (l. 384) identified with purity. Beginning with line 386, the third person is used to evoke a powerful vision of what might have been. Then lines 395–96 are slowed by punctuation as she begins to identify with the vision, and the first person is used again. After this, in the concluding third of the passage, the verses become more rapid and emphatic. The rhyme *fumée / consumée* significantly recalls the fifth stanza of "Le Cimetière marin," and the word "s'abandonne" in line 402 recalls line 34 of the same poem: "Je m'abandonne à ce brillant espace." Dentals accent the expansion of line 402, and there is a shift to the present tense recalling the movement in lines 211–12, as her "essence" mingles with the stars.

Lines 406–64. But in line 406, the Parque stops short, and refuses to undergo again the élan toward death of lines 211–17. "Sombre lys," "dark allusion" (cf. "Le Cimetière marin," ll. 42, 47), she couldn't conquer the desire of the body to *live,* and always curious, always searching within herself, she seeks to discover that thread of instinct (an allusion to Theseus and Ariadne) which brought her back to life and the new day. The image of the serpent recurs in line 423, interestingly polyvalent, called forth by the sensuality of the perfumed breast, the idea of a sinuous return to life, and finally by the dark and sad animality of line 424 which perhaps borrows from an image of Rimbaud's "Le Bateau ivre":

> Echouages hideux au fond des golfes bruns
> Où les serpents géants dévorés des punaises
> Choient, des arbres tordus, avec de noirs parfums!
>
> (ll. 54–56)

She was betrayed by the "chair profonde" (l. 425) and the nasal suggests the deep mysteries of the flesh. But there was no sexual dream—the first of several allusions to the beginning of the poem—she simply fell asleep. Several details remind us of the seaside decor, "conque" (l. 440) and "reflux" (l. 441). Sorensen has commented on the moving simplicity of the comparison (rarely used by Valéry in La Jeune Parque) with the bird alighting in order to rest. She descends to a sort of death, commanded by mysteriously dominating shades, and she is a victim offered to the night, "bras suppliciés" (l. 455), cf. "mains abandonnées" (l. 449). She returns to "le germe," to the original and fertile beginning of beings, and to a "sombre innocence" (l. 458) which calls forth again the image of the serpent and the word "trésors" (cf. l. 39). Then this magnificent "physiological" passage closes with a seemingly endless alexandrine, slowed by six accents, and the only remaining italicized lines of the poem, a passage of pure surrealism:

> (La porte basse c'est une bague ... où la gaze
> Passe ... Tout meurt, tout rit dans la gorge qui jase ...
> L'oiseau boit sur ta bouche et tu ne peux le voir ...
> Viens plus bas, parle bas ... Le noir n'est pas si noir ...)
>
> (ll. 461–64)

Lines 465–512. All her pride was mingled with lowly dreams, uncontrolled by the highest faculties of the intellect, when her body spread itself upon the bed, freeing her in sleep: "lasse femme absolue" (l. 477). It is a sleep like death, a mystical fusion with the universe (l. 469), but it is not the exalted death of lines 395–405. The mysterious ark of the body (l. 481), its contours and charms (l. 478), and desire for love (l. 479), prevented her suicide, and her violent emotions became nothing more than lamentations.

The "jeune soleil" (l. 487), and the adjective is an hypallage here, suggesting not only the freshness of morning, but also the youth and vigour of the Parque, sweeps away remorse, and the young girl watches without emotion the disappearance of the star of inhuman purity (l. 486). She offers herself once more to the sun, recalling the imagery of lines 107–14, but the image is an ambiguous one in both passages. If in lines 107–14 she was innocent, yet already unconsciously yielding to sexual inclinations, here at the end of the poem she is offering herself to more than a mere sexual destiny. This superb ending is an eager acceptance by the Parque, and by Valéry himself, of the totality of life and all its possibilities:

> Le pas le plus difficile que l'homme aura à franchir, si son développement se poursuit, sera l'acceptation—et surtout l'accoutumance à—ou *l'assimilation de l'acceptation* de la "vie" telle quelle—sans illusions.
>
> Ressentir, en somme, comme naturel ce qui est naturel.
>
> Ne pas demander une vie éternelle—comme un enfant demande la lune.
>
> (*Cahiers*)

The powerful, brilliant finale, after an initial question, occupies a long period of seventeen lines. As in the first lines of the poem, the Parque again approaches the sea, but here her body is no longer filled with a weak trembling. It is thoroughly alive, roused by a sharp awakening, and the bitter, reproachful sea of line 11 is now a "riante amertume" (l. 498). The whole ending is filled with imagery of vivacity and expansion. The wind, "âme intense" (l. 501), whips the waves, destroying a monster of purity (l. 503). "Une vierge de sang" (l. 511), a living virgin with golden breasts, lifts herself in sacrifice toward the rising sun (cf. l. 118). The affirmation of the final line is powerfully reinforced by a bold borrowing from Catholic ritual: ("sous les espèces du pain et du vin").

GÉRARD GENETTE

Valéry and the Poetics of Language

In writing of Valéry and the *poetics of language,* I use that deliberately
Bachelardian phrase (quite legitimately, since there is a poetics of space and
a poetics of reverie, as well as, by implication, a poetics of fire, air, earth,
and water) to mean the human imagination applied to language, as it is
applied elsewhere to space or the elements, and also to mean the poetic or,
more generally, literary investiture of those images and that reverie. It seems
to me that one major—if not *the* major—axis of the linguistic imagination
is the idea of, the desire for, and, provisionally, the *myth* of a *motivation* of
the linguistic sign or (quite properly in this particular context) the *word.* In
an even more specific sense, what is involved here is the idea of motivation
by *analogy*—a relation of resemblance, a mimetic relation—between "the
word" and "the thing."

   In our European literary and philosophical tradition, this idea was first
presented and examined in Plato's *Cratylus.* I say "in Plato's *Cratylus*"
instead of "by Cratylus in Plato's dialogue" because Cratylus' affirmation
of the so-called "fitness of signs" [*justesse des noms*] is seconded by Socrates
when he argues against Hermogenes in the first part of the dialogue. Though
he does not really articulate it, Hermogenes argues for what we would call
in Saussurian terms, the *arbitrariness* of language, or more precisely, its
conventional nature. And it is this position which Socrates, in a sort of
palinode, ends up at least partially defending against Cratylus. As a result,

From *Textual Strategies: Perspectives in Post-Structuralist Criticism,* edited by Josué V.
Harari. © 1979 by Cornell University. Cornell University Press, 1979.

Plato's own position on the matter remains partly unknown or obscure. But that is of little importance for my subject here: I have referred to Plato only so that I could borrow from him the eponymous figures of Cratylus and Hermogenes to symbolize the two opposing—but not contradictory—theses of the mimetic motivation and the conventionality of language.

In general, modern linguistics seems to have decided in favor of Hermogenes: this is one of the principal emphases of Saussure's *Course in General Linguistics;* and, even earlier, it was the opinion of W. D. Whitney and William James, who picturesquely expressed it by stating that "the word *dog* does not bite." To go back still further, the idea can be found in the *Encyclopedia:* "Words have no necessary relationship with that which they express."

Let me make it clear that, in reviewing these opinions, I do not pretend to oppose "knowledge" to "ignorance" or "truth" to "error." That would be all the more improper in view of the fact that Saussure's affirmation of the *arbitrariness of the sign* has always been a matter of controversy, even among his own followers. Furthermore, linguists such as Otto Jespersen, Edward Sapir, Roman Jakobson, and Ivan Fónagy have made numerous attempts to identify as precisely as possible what Jakobson calls—using a vocabulary borrowed from C. S. Peirce—the "ironic" elements of language: at the very least, this shows that in their view such elements are not totally nonexistent.

Still, the fact remains that the so-called scientific position is to a certain extent and by its very nature a *deceiving* position, a position which frustrates human desire insofar as this desire is invested in myths. Linguistics states quite flatly that language is essentially conventional, though it admits certain traits of mimetic motivation that must be located and analyzed (a task that is not always easy). In opposition to this flat and purely empirical position, we will call *Cratylism* (as Roland Barthes proposes) "that great secular myth which wants language to imitate ideas and, contrary to the precisions of linguistic science, wants signs to be motivated."

In calling Cratylism a myth, as does Barthes, I do not mean to designate it as an error in opposition to a truth, but rather as a thought oriented, to use Freudian terminology, more by the pleasure principle than by the reality principle. It is a thought, be it true or false (or more-or-less true or more-or-less false), that is first and foremost the expression of a desire. The mimetic interpretation of language, it seems evident to me, corresponds to an almost universal (this does not necessarily mean "natural") desire whose cause remains unknown but whose force and drive each of us can feel within himself. Whether true or false, Cratylism is a myth: it is above all a *seductive* thought.

I shall make no attempt here to sketch the history of Cratylism from Plato's time to our own. My intention is merely to situate Valéry's position in this secular debate. Doing so requires a brief review of the stage in Cratylism's history which immediately preceded Valéry himself. This brings us obviously to Mallarmé.

In order to appreciate the shift brought about by Mallarmé in the history of the "linguistic imaginary," one must establish a distinction between what I shall call, for lack of better terms and without any connotation of value, primary and secondary Cratylism. Primary Cratylism, that of Cratylus himself, consists in simply positing linguistic signification as a mimesis of the object by the noun (here language is almost always reduced to a collection of words, most often nouns, to the exclusion of verbs and tool-words, and it thus becomes what Saussure disdainfully called a "nomenclature"). One can try to explain this mimesis by an elementary symbolism of phonemes and/or graphemes. Such symbolism is most often supported by a simple list of words containing those phonemes or graphemes and expressing the idea supposedly evoked by each. Thus it is said that the sound *T* evokes stopping or stability, and that this capacity for evocation is demonstrated by the number of words, such as *table, top,* or *tomb,* that contain the consonant and express this idea or some similar one. Obviously, it is enough to choose one's examples well, to ignore contrary examples, and to be able to count on the compliance of one's audience (reader or interlocutor). Thus Socrates, after having posited that *R* is the phoneme of movement, is able to devote a digression to the Greek word *kinesis* without Hermogenes' interrupting him to point out the surprising absence of that phoneme in the very word that signifies "movement."

I would also include within primary Cratylism the somewhat more difficult attempts to base the expressive value of phonemes on articulatory physical considerations, as when Socrates explains the symbolism of the sliding of *L* by the sliding of the tongue over the palate, or the size symbolism of *A* and *E* by the fact that both are long vowels. This is still primary Cratylism in the sense that it concerns what certain linguists call "natural" language, a language which is presented as equipped with a mimetic aptitude that is in some way *native*.

Anyone who has read *Les Mots anglais,* published in 1877, can see that Mallarmé practiced this form of Cratylism. The first chapter fits into a long line of previous speculations that runs from the end of the eighteenth century and even includes the idea, which had been dear to President Charles de Brosses, that a word's entire signification—what Mallarmé calls its "radical virtue"—lies in its consonants, and particularly in its initial or "attack" consonant. This leads to lists of words grouped by "families" according to their first letter, as well as to those symbolic values such as: B = production, giving birth, fecundity; C = prompt and decisive attack; D = continuous action without variation, stagnation, heaviness, obscurity; GL = joy and light; and so on.

One may object here that *Les Mots anglais* is a marginal work, of which Mallarmé himself wrote to Verlaine that "it would be better not to mention it." Yet just because the work's intention and object were purely pedagogical and/or commercial does not mean that profound dreams were not invested in it, and since my topic of discussion is Mallarmé's influence on Valéry, I need only quote the latter's opinion: "*Les Mots anglais* is perhaps the most revealing document that we possess regarding the private work practices of Mallarmé."

From the outset one trait distinguishes Mallarmé's Cratylism from that maintained by his predecessors; for perhaps the first time, the "demon" of analogical motivation exerts itself on a *foreign* language. Before Mallarmé, Cratylian tradition involved either treating one's mother tongue as if it were the only one in existence, as Socrates did, or else, like de Brosses and Court de Gébelin, positing in principle that one speaks of the universal originating language, and then, in fact, reasoning on the basis of material furnished by one's native language, which is always treated as "supreme" (to borrow a word from Mallarmé himself).

For Mallarmé, on the contrary, the object of Cratylian reverie is not only a foreign language (English), but, very specifically, the most foreign element in this language of dual origin, what he calls its Gothic or Anglo-Saxon heritage—to the exclusion of all vocabulary imported from France at the time of the Norman invasion. The privilege of foreignness, if not of ethnographic *estrangement,* is clearly marked in the last sentence of the first book: "One seldom sees a word so surely as from the outside, from where we are—in other words, from a foreign land."

Primary Cratylism in *Les Mots anglais* does not therefore function as an analogic motivation of the language (French) that Mallarmé "normally" used as speaker and poet. Quite to the contrary, English appears here, from the exterior and at a distance, as some sort of almost inaccessible linguistic paradise, and therefore as the image of a *lost* linguistic paradise or *linguistic utopia* recognized and assumed as such. It is the image of a hypothetically or mythically original language, ideally and miraculously expressive, such as everyday language *is not*. English, therefore, becomes the locus and object not of enjoyment, but of *regret*: it is the inverted reflection of a lack, or of what Mallarmé calls a "defect," which is the nonexpressive, or nonmimetic character of the (French) language.

This regret, which is both the disavowal of primary Cratylism as a belief in language's motivation and the maintenance of a nostalgic preference with regard to that nonexistent or lost motivation—something like: "I would be delighted if language were mimetic, but I am forced to recognize that it is not"—is clearly and strongly expressed in a famous page from "Crise de vers," which was written at least ten years after *Les Mots anglais*:

> Imperfect languages in that they are several, the supreme one is missing. . . . But, at once, turned toward the aesthetic, my sense regrets that discourse fails to express objects by strokes that correspond to them in coloring or in aspect, these [strokes] exist in the instrument of the voice, in [various] languages and sometimes within one [alone]. Compared to *ombre* (shadow), [which is] opaque, *ténèbres* (darkness) seems only slightly dark; what disillusionment in the face of a perversity which confers contradictorily a dark timbre on *jour* (day) and a bright one on *nuit* (night).

I discontinue the quotation here in order to close the subject of primary Cratylism: discourse *fails* to coordinate the signifier and the signified, or as Mallarmé and then Valéry called them, the *sound* and the *meaning*. The word *ténèbres* is lighter than the word *ombre,* and the word *nuit* lighter than the word *jour.* The Cratylian coincidence exists "sometimes within one" language (English for example), but not in French. The "perfect" or "supreme" language does not exist, or if it exists, it is elsewhere; perhaps the "good language" is always that of our neighbors. The end of the quotation shows a most unexpected reversal, however, a switch to what I call secondary, poetic Cratylism: "—*Only,* let us know that *verse would not exist:* verse, philosophically, remunerates the defect (*défaut*) of languages [being] the superior complement."

The nonmimetic character of language is thus, in a certain way, the opportunity and the condition for poetry to exist. Poetry exists only to "remunerate," in other words, to repair and compensate for the "defect of languages." If a language were perfect, poetry would have no reason for being, since it would have nothing to repair. Language itself would be a poem and poetry would be everywhere, which obviously means that it would be nowhere. Mallarmé's conversation with Francis Vielé-Griffin in which he lends his interlocutor a thought already his own confirms this even more clearly: "If I follow you correctly, you base the creative privilege of the poet on the imperfection of the instrument that he must use; a language hypothetically adequate [*adéquate*] to translate his thought would suppress the literary man [*littérateur*], who would thereby become Mr. Everybody."

Secondary Cratylism inaugurated here by Mallarmé is therefore no longer a Cratylism of language, but a Cratylism of the poem—or, as Mallarmé said, of *verse*—which finds support in an anti-Cratylism or Hermogenism of language. For the first time in such a clear way, the idea of a *double language*—or, to use Mallarmé's own term, a "double state of the word, raw and immediate on one hand and essential on the other"—is articulated here. The raw and immediate state is that of everyday language, the language of simple communication and conventional, or even commercial, exchange: "it would suffice, in order to exchange human thought, for each person to take, or to put in the hand of another, silently, a bit of change." The "essential" state is obviously that of poetic language:

> Verse which remakes from several vocables one total, new word, foreign to language and seemingly incantatory, completes this isolation of the word, denying, in one sovereign stroke, the element of chance remaining in the terms [the arbitrariness of the sign] despite the artifice of their alternate immersion [*retrempe*] in meaning and sonority, and provokes in one the surprise of hearing [for the first time] such an ordinary fragment of elocution, at the same time that the recollection of the object named basks in a new atmosphere.

In this way appears the familiar and almost obvious notion of *poetic language,* or the *poetic state of language,* which creates a decisive division in the linguistic substance. Henceforth there are two languages in language, one of which (everyday language) is left to arbitrariness and convention, while the other (poetic language) is the refuge of mimetic virtue, the locus of the miraculous survival of the primitive verb in all its "incantatory" power. I will not follow this theory further in Mallarmé, nor deal with the much more difficult question of determining to what extent it works in his poetry. It is now time to return to Valéry.

Valéry's thoughts on poetry were, of course, at first a prolongation of Mallarmé's, meditations on the *exemplum* offered by Valéry's one-time mentor. Valéry admired above all in Mallarmé what he called "the identification of 'poetic' meditation with the possession of language, and the careful study in himself [Mallarmé] of their reciprocal relations." Valéry says elsewhere, and the metaphor is revealing, "Mallarmé understood language as if he had invented it." One can say that Valéry's own poetics of language is articulated as a resumption and a new elaboration of Mallarmé's idea of double language.

To begin with, Valéry still shows some fast fading traces of primary Cratylism. In a letter of July 1891 to André Gide, one finds a "word reverie" as Bachelard calls it, or rather, a name reverie—the name of a country—somewhat comparable to those that Proust will give his hero some twenty years later in the last part of *Swann's Way*. Gide writes Valéry that he will travel to Antwerp, and this name inspires in the latter what almost amounts to a short prose poem:

> ANTWERP: A wild and black Baudelaire lies in that word. A word full of spices and pearls, unloaded, under a rainy sky, by a drunken sailor, at the door of a tavern. . . . The pink lantern draws the blacks to the sad streets where the *enchemisée* stomps in the mud. And songs of a distant tongue, aboard ships sunk in silence, continue in the background. As you see, I let myself stroll on these foreign words until I am near you.

It may be characteristic that this reverie, a kind of derision or caricature of Cratylian reverie, permits one to see without much difficulty that everything which seems to be in a word comes from elsewhere—in this case, from what one already knew, or believed one knew, about the place which the word designates, but which one no longer dares quite say it *resembles*. An important comment on this subject appears in *Tel Quel:* "The power of verse stems from an *indefinable* harmony between what it *says* and what it *is*. 'Indefinable' enters into the definition. This harmony must not be definable. When it is, it becomes imitative, and that is not good. The impossibility of defining this relationship, together with the impossibility of denying it, constitutes the essence of verse."

It is not an exaggeration to say that Valéry's entire theory of poetic language is contained in this brief passage, as long as it is clarified by other passages. One can now see what I meant by fading traces of primary Cratylism in Valéry's writing: *imitative harmony* is rejected here, not as impossible, following Mallarmé, but as too simple. The author of the line "L'insecte net gratte la sécheresse" from "The Graveyard by the Sea," was in a position to know that imitative harmony is possible. He rejects it not because it is impossible, but because it is too *simple* and especially too univocal. The harmony between what verses *say* and what they *are*, between their signified and their signifier, "must not be definable."

One would be tempted to conclude, from this insistence on the indefin-

able and this rejection of the traditional resource of imitative harmony, that
the harmony at which Valéry aims is *not* imitative, and that consequently
his secondary Cratylism, abandoning the value of mimesis, is *no longer* a
Cratylism. Such a conclusion would miss the inevitable sense of the word
harmony, however. To say harmony is to say, necessarily, echo and consonance, affinity in co-presence. The idea of *harmony between sound and
meaning* is a more subtle version of Cratylism, but still a version. We must
now ask of what this version consists.

As I have said, Valéry takes up and prolongs Mallarmé's idea of the two
states of language. The most straightforward formulation of this concept is
found in the text entitled "Je disais quelquefois à Stéphane Mallarmé":

> One must choose: either to confine language to the simple tran-
> sitive function [which is everyday language] of a system of signals;
> or else to allow some [these are obviously poets] to speculate on
> its sensory properties by developing its *concrete* effects, its formal
> and musical combinations.

Or perhaps, in this other formulation:

> A poet makes simultaneous use of everyday speech—which sat-
> isfies only by being understood and which is therefore purely
> transitive—and of that language which contrasts with it, as a
> garden carefully planted with selected species contrasts with the
> wild countryside in which all species grow.

This opposition figures elsewhere in the famous parallel of walking and
dancing, in which ordinary language is clearly designated by Prose, and the
other, of course, by Poetry:

> Walking, like prose, aims at a precise object. It is an act directed
> toward something which we want to reach. Circumstances of the
> moment, such as the need of an object, the impulse of one's
> desire, the state of one's body, one's sight, and the terrain, etc.,
> make walking what it *is,* prescribe its direction and its speed, and
> give it an *end.* All the characteristics of walking derive from these
> instantaneous conditions, which combine *in a different way* each
> time. There are no movements in walking which are not special
> adaptations and which are not abolished each time and seemingly
> absorbed by the completion of the act, by the reached goal.
>
> Dance is something else altogether. It is doubtless a system of
> acts, but they have their end in themselves. It goes nowhere. . . .

Here we rejoin prose and poetry in their contrast. Prose and poetry make use of the same words, the same syntax, the same forms, and the same sounds or timbres, but they are coordinated and stimulated in different ways. . . . Here is, however, the great and decisive difference. When the man who walks has reached his goal—as I have said—when he has reached the place, the book, the fruit, the object that formed his desire, this possession promptly annuls, definitively, his entire act; the effect devours the cause, the end has absorbed the means; and whatever the act may have been, only its result remains. It is exactly the same with "utilitarian" language: the language that just helped me to express my plan, my desire, my command, my opinion, this language which has fulfilled its duty, collapses and disappears upon arrival. I emitted it so that it might perish, so that it might become radically transformed into something else within your mind; and I will know that I was *understood* by the remarkable fact that my discourse no longer exists: it is entirely replaced by its *meaning*—that is, by images, impulses, reactions, or acts which belong to you: in short, by an interior modification of yourself. . . .

The poem, on the contrary, does not die for having lived: it is made expressly to be reborn from its ashes and to become again, indefinitely, that which it just was. Poetry is recognizable by the fact that it tends to reproduce itself within its form: it stimulates us to reconstitute it identically. . . .

As a result, between form and content, between sound and meaning, between the poem and the state of poetry, a symmetry is manifested, an equality of importance, value and power, that is not in prose; it is opposed to the law of prose—which decrees the inequality of language's two constituents. The essential principle of the poetic process—that is, of the conditions of production of the poetic state by the word [*parole*]—is, to my mind, this harmonic exchange between expression and impression.

As can be seen in this last sentence, the essentially intransitive, or *autotelic*, character of poetic discourse comes from a *harmony* between sound and meaning, which is the central idea of Cratylism. Utilitarian language, that kind which is at work when I ask you for a light and you answer by giving me one (in other words, by converting language into something), disappears upon being comprehended. Poetic discourse, on the other hand, activates itself and is conserved in its form because this form is necessary.

Furthermore, this form is necessary because it is in harmony with its own meaning: in a way, poetic discourse somewhat artificially recreates Cratylus' dream of a natural "fitness of signs."

Here, immediately, Valéry's poetic neo-Cratylism clashes with a difficulty that he knew well and always kept in mind: the arbitrariness of the sign, the "defect of languages." How can one create within conventional language a nonconventional state of language? How can one create within "arbitrary" language a harmonic state of language?

> That [Valéry says lucidly] is to ask for *a miracle*. We realize that there is hardly an instance in which the connection between our ideas and the groups of sounds that suggest them each in turn is anything more than arbitrary or purely fortuitous.

Or again:

> Each word is an instantaneous assemblage of a *sound* and a *meaning* that have no relationship to each other.

And again:

> It follows from this analysis, that a poem's value resides in the indissolubility of sound and meaning. This condition seems to require the impossible. There is no relationship whatsoever between the sound and the meaning of a word. The same thing is called HORSE in English, IPPOS in Greek, EQVVS in Latin, and CHEVAL in French; but no operation whatever on any of these terms will give me the idea of the animal in question; no operation whatever on this idea will give me any of these words—or else we would easily know all languages, beginning with our own.

One must admit that Saussure's principle of the arbitrariness of the sign has never been so forcefully contrasted to the secular dream of a harmonic language. This is the strangest, indeed the hardest part of the contradiction. And yet. . . .

And yet, we are exactly at the edge of what is, for Valéry, the solution of the enigma. The following sentence seems to contain the key word: "And yet it is the poet's task to give us the *sensation* of intimate union between word [*parole*] and mind [*esprit*]."

The key word is obviously "sensation," which one can safely interpret, *in this context,* as signifier or, even more radically, as *illusion.* The indissolubility of sound and meaning, the harmony between word and idea is, *language being what it is,* only an *illusory sensation.* The poet's task is to create this illusion; this task is magical, but magical in the most devalued, doubtless the most *critical* meaning of the term. In performing this task, the magician is only an illusionist, even if he were to become the first victim of his own illusion. The following lines from "Poésie et pensée abstraite" suggest this idea quite well:

> One must consider that this is a totally marvelous result. I say *marvelous* although it is not excessively rare. I say *marvelous* in the sense that we give to this term when we think about the marvels and wonders of ancient magic. One must not forget that poetic form was for many centuries enlisted in the service of magic. Those who devoted themselves to these strange operations had to believe, of necessity, in the power of the spoken word, and even more in the efficacy of this word's sound than in its signi-fication. . . . The *momentary being* who made this verse could not have made it if he had been in a state where form and content appeared separately to his mind. On the contrary, he was in a special phase of his domain of psychic existence, a phase during which the word's sound and meaning take on or retain an equal importance—something which is excluded from everyday lan-guage, as from the needs of abstract language.

The verse in which the mimetic necessity of the verbal sign is realized, in a fleeting and therefore illusory way, is the work of a *momentary being,* the poet in a *poetic state.* Once created, however, the work aims at another, not momentary, being, in whom the poetic state or Cratylian illusion will be maintained and reproduced each time that he enters and re-enters into contact with the poetic word. This being is the reader, and of course it is he, and not the poet, who is, for Valéry, the essential locus of the poetic happening:

> A poet's . . . function is not to feel the poetic state: that is a private matter. One recognizes the poet—or at least, each person recognizes his own—by the simple fact that he turns the reader into an "inspired being." Inspiration is, positively speaking, a gracious attribution which the reader makes to his poet: the reader offers us the transcendent merits of the powers and graces that develop within him. He searches for and finds in the poet the marvelous cause of his amazement.

The amazed reader, the reader in the poetic state is therefore the reader to whom the "verse," in other words the fragment of language before him, appears as necessary, definitive, forever completed and unchangeable, sealed by the indissoluble harmony of sound and meaning. No one is more intimately persuaded than Valéry that this amazement is, in a sense, a fortunate illusion; for Valéry, a "completed sonnet" signified only an "abandoned sonnet," and the notion of a completed work—in other words, the notion of the work itself—could have proceeded only "from fatigue or superstition." Seen from another angle, this same situation also implies that the poet abandons the poem, which for him is never completed. The reader then completes it, and in so doing, turns it into a work. The completed work is the work (being) read; the Cratylian thaumaturge is the reader.

Such is, in general terms, Valéry's neo-Cratylism or poetics of language, which we have traced both in its development and in its conceptual specificity. Of course, the history of Cratylism does not stop with Valéry, and it might be interesting to follow up the simultaneous and subsequent echoes of the idea of poetic language. There is, for example, Claudel's opposition between ordinary language—which *designates* rather than *signifies* objects, giving us "a sort of practical and rough reduction of this language, its value, which is as banal as change (*monnaie*)"—and the language of the poet, who does not use words "for utilitarian ends, but to constitute from all these sonorous phantoms . . . a picture that is both intelligible and enjoyable." There is also Proust's antithesis between *words* (common nouns), which "give us a clear and banal little picture of things like those hung on school walls" and *names* (proper nouns), which "give . . . a confused image of persons and towns which draws out from their brilliant or somber sonority, the color with which the image is uniformly painted." In addition, there is Sartre's distinction between prosaic, conventional, and exterior *signification,* and poetic *meaning:* "*Signification* is conferred upon an object from the outside by a signifying intention, but [poetic] *meaning* is a natural quality of things."

Finally, there is Jakobson's definition of *poetic function* as an autotelic message centered on itself, and his use, in the essay entitled "Linguistics and Poetics," of Valéry's formula: "the poem is a prolonged hesitation between sound and meaning." (We might mention in passing that Jakobson also quotes another formula, this one by Pope, which is a perfect anticipation of Valéry's theory: "The sound must *seem* an echo of the sense."

All these resonances are sufficient proof that Valéry's (Mallarmé-Valéry's) version of Cratylism—the mimetic virtue of language as a real or illusory privilege of the poem or of poetic language—and therefore the poetic function as a compensation for and a defiance of the arbitrariness of the sign, have become our Vulgate, the implicit fundamental article of our literary aesthetic. It is so familiar, so natural, so transparent to us that, for all intents and purposes, we do not see it any more; we have some difficulty in conceiving that it has not always existed, and perhaps will not always exist. It is not self-evident, however, and in a certain way—which I wanted to show while developing my main thesis—this conception of the poetic function is a historical fact: it already belongs to history—which means, perhaps, to the past.

RENÉ WELLEK

Paul Valéry's Poetic Theory

The poetic theory of Paul Valéry can be seen as almost the direct opposite of that of Croce: in Croce we find the most complete identification of the author's creative act with the work of art and the response of the reader, the most emphatic devaluation of what ordinarily is called for in favor of sentiment, the strongest feeling for the historicity of literature. In Valéry we are confronted with a theory that asserts the discontinuity between author, work, and reader, emphasizes a most extreme regard for form and nothing but form divorced from emotion, and takes poetry completely out of history into a realm of the pure and the absolute.

Valéry expounded his poetics in a systematic fashion only once: in the course on poetics he gave at the Collège de France from 1937 to 1945. He published only the introductory lecture, and the meager notes published in *Ygdrassil* by George Le Breton covering eighteen lectures between 25 December 1937 and 25 February 1939 add little. The lecture moves in the confines of preliminary philosophical considerations. A study of the mass of notes accumulated by Valéry during his so-called silence (from 1892 to 1917) and a complete transcript of the course hardly changes what we already know from Valéry's considered pronouncements in the published essays, collected mainly in the five volumes of *Variété* (1924–44) and in *Pièces sur l'art* (1931), in the essays in *Poësie* (1928), in "Réflexions sur l'art" (1935), in scattered prefaces, addresses, and in the great number of aphor-

From *Four Critics: Croce, Valéry, Lukács, and Ingarden.* © 1981 by the University of Washington Press.

isms throughout volumes such as *Mélange* (1941) and *Tel Quel* (2 vols.,
1941–42). Valéry is not a systematic philosopher or aesthetician: he propounds a number of insights which are sometimes, at least, superficially
contradictory; he is, within a very limited range, a practical critic and above
all a practicing poet who examines the creative process or speculates about
his craft. He implicitly raises fundamental questions without often claiming
or attempting to solve them within a consistent framework.

Much of the interest of Valéry's thought lies precisely in its tentativeness,
in its suggestiveness, in its extremism which, however, is held only provisionally, often for the sake of a specific argument or as a contradiction to
accepted opinions, in order to surprise or shock, to experiment with a
thought, to see where it will lead.

Valéry, like many other theorists, sharply distinguishes between the author, the work, and the reader, but he goes further than any other writer I
know in doubting the continuity and even the desirability of continuity
among the three. He complains that in most aesthetics one finds "a confusion
of considerations some of which make sense only for the author, others are
valid only for the work, and yet others only for the person who experiences
the work. Any proposition which brings together these three entities is illusory." He would assert more positively that "producer and consumer are
two essentially separate systems," and most boldly that the "art, as value,
depends essentially on this nonidentification (of producer and consumer),
this need for an intermediary between producer and consumer." Valéry sum-
marizes:

> In short, a work of art is an object, a human product [*fabrication*],
> made with a view to affecting certain individuals in a certain way.
> The phenomenon Art can be represented by two perfectly distinct
> transformations (It is the same relation as that in economics be-
> tween production and consumption). What is extremely impor-
> tant to note is that the two transformations—the one which goes
> from the author to the *manufactured object* and the one which
> expresses the fact that the object or the work modifies the con-
> sumer—are entirely independent. It follows that one should al-
> ways consider them separately.

Thus, art is *not* communication, certainly not direct communication
between authors and readers. "If what has happened in the one person were
communicated directly to the other, all art would collapse, all the effects of
art would disappear." Art would become rhetoric, persuasion. Thus, "the
mutual independence of the producer and the consumer, their ignorance of

each other's thoughts and needs is almost essential to the effect of a work."
But it is hard to see how such a theory can be upheld in its extreme formulation: if the gulf between creator, work, and reader were unbridgeable,
there would be no works and the works (if existent) would be completely
incomprehensible. But although Valéry tries out the theory without quite
seeing its consequences, he is right when he emphasizes the difficulties of
these relationships: Has the work anything to do with the author? Has the
reader's interpretation of a work anything to do with its supposed "real"
meaning? He answers "very little," but to my mind he can hardly answer
"nothing at all."

If we isolate the three factors and begin with the author, we can see
that Valéry has the courage of his conviction and is really not so much or
not primarily interested in the product, the work of art, as in the process of
production, the creative process independent of its result. As a matter of
fact, if one wanted to explain the psychological or genetic origin of Valéry's
theory, one would probably find that it started with his interest in the creative
process and was motivated by it. Valéry is interested in this activity in itself
and has thus created the somewhat monstrous self-caricature, Monsieur
Teste: he has written elaborately about Leonardo da Vinci, the universal
man. When, in a formal, rather empty anniversary speech, he praised Goethe
in the terms he had used for Leonardo, he implicitly praised himself or rather
the ideal he had set up for himself. Goethe is the potential creator, who has
the genius of transformation, of metamorphosis; he is Orpheus, Proteus.
Goethe's speculations on metamorphosis and evolution attract Valéry more
than his poetry. He admires the combination of scientist and poet. Valéry's
thought moves so much on this very general level of human creativeness that
he can assimilate artistic creativeness to scientific creativeness by some general term such as *speculation*. The essay on Edgar Allan Poe's *Eureka* is
inspired by such an identification (or by the hope for such an identification)
of science and poetry through the common element of imagination, though
Valéry avoids the term.

If one is interested in the creative process as such, one will disparage
the work of art. This is what Valéry does, both in words and in deeds.
During his many years of silence, he obviously felt that he was elaborating
his ideas and his personality, and that expression and especially publication
were purely secondary to this inner activity. "The Great Work for me is
knowing work as such—knowing the most general transformation, of which
the works are only local applications, particular problems." Thus the work
of art is conceived as existing only in the act. "Poetry is essentially *in actu*."

A work of mind exists only in action. Outside of that act, nothing is left but an object which has no particular relation to the mind. Transport a statue which you admire to a country sufficiently different from ours and it turns into a meaningless stone, a Parthenon into nothing more than a small marble quarry. And when a piece of poetry is used as a collection of grammatical difficulties or examples, it ceases immediately to be a work of the mind, since the use that is made of it is utterly alien to the conditions under which it came into being, while, at the same time, it is denied the consumption value that gives it meaning.

Implicitly, of course, the discontinuity is here deplored or considered as a condition to be overcome under ideal circumstances, but the emphasis remains on the act of composing, not on its result. Thus Valéry could tell an interviewer that a work of art is never finished, that we deliver it to the public only under the pressure of external circumstances. We can only abandon it. Valéry always assumes that there is first a thought and then its artistic dress, or rather shape or form. Too ready communication of the thought would prejudice the artistic process.

It is not surprising that Valéry has given us several minute introspective accounts of the composition of his poems and that he excels in this analysis. But whatever the specific interest of these "marvels of introspection," as T. S. Eliot calls them, Valéry arrives, of necessity, at very little for theory, since his introspection leads to the conclusion that there is no direct relationship between a specific state of mind of the author and the work itself. Indeed, there might be a very considerable distance between the original idea, the germ of the work, and the finished product. The organic analogy of begetting, growing, and being born is rejected: there is no continuity between the act of conception and the work produced. The germ of a work of art can be anything: "Sometimes a certain subject, sometimes a group of words, sometimes a simple rhythm, sometimes (even) a prosodic scheme. . . . It is important to remember that one germ may be as good as another. . . . An empty sheet of paper; an idle moment; a slip of the tongue; a misreading; a pen that is pleasant to hold." Anything might suggest the germ of the poem. The poetic state is "perfectly irregular, inconstant, involuntary, fragile . . . we lose it, as we obtain it, *by accident*." One could call this a theory of inspiration, but Valéry is very reluctant to admit inspiration. "I believed and still believe that it is ignoble to write from enthusiasm alone. Enthusiasm is not a state of mind for a writer." Inspiration is no guarantee of the value of the product. "The spirit blows where it listeth: one sees it blow on fools."

If poetry or art in general is not inspiration, it is obviously not dream.

In an age in which *surréalisme,* Freudianism, and symbolism asserted the kinship of poetry and dream, Valéry repudiates it emphatically, though he recognizes that "the poetic universe bears strong analogies to the universe of dreams," and that as an historical fact, this confusion between poetry and dream has been understandable since the time of romanticism. But, "the true condition of a true poet is as distinct as possible from the state of dreaming. In the former I can see nothing but voluntary efforts, suppleness of thought, a submission of the mind to exquisite constraints, and the perpetual triumph of sacrifice. . . . Whoever speaks of exactness of style invokes the opposite of dream."

Though Valéry recognizes some initial irrational suggestion such as two rhythms insisting on being heard, as he describes it in "Mémoires d'un poème," all the practical emphasis falls on the share of rational speculation after the moment of conception, on the poetic calculus, on the poet's exercise of choice among possibilities, his clairvoyant, highly conscious pursuit of a sport or game. Valéry loves to think of the art of poetry as "a sport of people insensitive to the conventional values of common language." He says, in slightly different terms, that a poem is "a game, but a solemn, regulated, significant game" or "a kind of calculus" or an algebra. Thus "every true poet is necessarily a critic of the first order," but, of course, this criticism by no means makes the poet a philosopher. Valéry, surprisingly enough in view of his intellectualism, sharply divorces poetry from philosophy, not as an act, but in its result. "Every true poet," he admits, "is much more capable than is generally known of right reasoning and abstract thinking." Still, philosophical poetry is impossible, is not even a possible idea. Valéry disparages poet-philosophers such as Alfred de Vigny. He can say that "to philosophize in verse, was and still is the same as if one wanted to play chess by the rules of the game of checkers."

What Valéry demands of poetry is always something pure, something *sui generis,* and thus poetry cannot be continuous with the personality of the author; it is and must be impersonal to be perfect. "Perfection eliminates the person of the author," or even more strongly: "I don't see what something that keeps reminding me of the man behind it has to do with art. . . . The writer's duty, his proper function, is to fade out of the picture, to obliterate himself, his face, his personal concerns, his love affairs. . . . What makes a work is not the man who signs it. What makes a work has no name." What Valéry admires in poetry is the effort of men such as Victor Hugo and Stéphane Mallarmé (one is surprised at this pairing) "to form non-human ways of discourse, absolute discourse, in a sense—discourse which suggests a certain being independent of any person—a divinity of language."

The continuity between author and work is minimized and especially the emotions of ordinary life are resented or rejected as themes of art. "Our most important thoughts are those which contradict our feelings," says Valéry repeatedly; and, "All emotion, all sentiment indicates a defect in adaptation." Valéry resents the emotional effect of art: e.g., he complains that in reading Stendhal's *Lucien Leuwen* as a young man he felt the illusion so strongly that he could "no longer distinguish clearly between my own feelings and those which the artifice of the author communicated to me. . . . *Lucien Leuwen* brought about in me the miracle of a confusion which I detest." We hardly need to say that Valéry has no use for confessional literature and looks very coldly at the criterion of "sincerity" or "good intention":

> Everything that aims at sensibility . . . romances, Musset, beggars, the poor of Victor Hugo, Jean Valjean arouses disgust if not anger in me. Pascal playing with death, Hugo with poverty, though they be virtuosos on their instruments, are basically repugnant to me. The calculated effort to draw tears, to break hearts, to excite by something too beautiful or too sad, makes me merciless. Emotion seems to me a forbidden means. It is an ignoble act to make anybody weak.

Thus nothing seems to him more absurd than "to confide one's sorrow to paper. . . . What a quaint idea! That's the origin of many bad books, and of all the worst ones." The essay on Stendhal, though not without sympathy, sees him as an exploiter of sincerity. "The will to be sincere with oneself is inevitably a principle of falsification." Such an author is an actor who arrives at cynicism out of desperate ambition. "When we no longer know what to do in order to create a stir and to survive, we prostitute ourselves, we expose our *pudenda,* we offer them to public view." In telling the history of his return to poetry, Valéry somewhat ruefully admits that "the majority of writers have tried, and the greatest poets have miraculously succeeded in the task of reproducing the immediate emotions of life." But he always resented literature which tried to convert and persuade him. "I dislike picturing, across the page I read, a flushed or derisive face, on which is painted the intention to make me love what I hate or hate what I love." This is the task of politics and eloquence but not of poetry and certainly not of the poetry Valéry wants to write. He wanted to go a different way and did so. He has a clear conception of a work of art constructed by the intellect, free from personal and emotional admixtures, pure, or as he sometimes says, absolute poetry.

The phrase *pure poetry,* old as such, is first used by Valéry in the preface to Lucien Fabre's *Connaissance de la déesse* (1920) to suggest the ideal of the symbolists, which will always remain an ideal, though Valéry recognizes that it is only an abstract ideal. It is a tendency toward the utmost rigor in art, "toward a beauty ever more conscious of its genesis, ever more independent of all *subjects,* and free from the vulgar attractions of sentiment as well as from the blatant effects of eloquence." It is "the perfect vacuum and the absolute zero of temperature—ideals neither of which can be attained, and only approached at the price of an exhausting series of efforts." It is "pure in the sense in which a physicist speaks of pure water." Pure poetry is a "poetry which results, by a kind of *exhaustion,* from the progressive suppression of the prosaic elements of a poem. By prosaic elements we mean everything that *without damage* can be said also in prose; everything, history, legend, anecdote, morality, even philosophy, which exists by itself without the necessary co-operation of song." The purity of poetry is obviously for Valéry a standard of judgment. "A poem is worth as much as it contains of pure poetry." At times, Valéry thinks of it as a kind of admixture of pure gold among foreign matter. "What one calls a poem is in practice composed of fragments of pure poetry embedded in the substance of a discourse."

But what is this pure gold, how can it be distinguished from prose? Poetry, first of all, cannot be paraphrased, cannot be reduced to its prose content. Valéry condemns in strongest terms the heresy of paraphrase. "Nothing beautiful can be summarized. . . . Homer and Lucretius were not yet pure. Epic poets, didactic poets, and their like, are impure." The "absurd school exercise which consists of putting verse into prose . . . implies the belief that poetry is an *accident* of the *substance* prose. But poetry exists only for those in whose eyes such an operation is impossible and who recognize poetry by this very impossibility." The impossibility of paraphrase logically implies the impossibility of translating poetry. "Translations of the great foreign poets are architectural blueprints which may well be admirable; only they make the edifices themselves, palaces, temples, and the rest disappear."

But why cannot poetry be reduced to prose, or to thought or theme? Valéry has several answers: one which he repeats many times is that prose language perishes when it is understood, while poetry demands repetition, demands and suggests a universe. Prose is practical, it presupposes a realm of ends. "As soon as the aim is reached, the word expires." But the universe of poetry is "a universe of reciprocal relations analogous to the universe of sounds within which the musical thought is born and moves. In this poetic universe, resonance triumphs over causality." The poem must "maintain itself in a condition as remote as possible from that of prose." "The poetic

universe arises from the number, or rather from the density of images, figures, consonances, dissonances, by the linking of turns of speech and
rhythms—the essential being continually to avoid anything that would lead
back to prose." Valéry here resumes old motifs of aesthetics: the contemplative isolation of poetry, its divorce from the world of ends, its creation of a
new world that can be achieved only by exploiting the resources of language
to the utmost, by removing its world from that of ordinary speech by use
of sound and meter and all the devices of metaphorics.

Valéry stresses the poet's intimate relation to language: he has told
several times the famous anecdote about Edgar Degas, who complained that
he could not write although he was full of ideas for writing poetry, to which
Mallarmé answered: "My dear Degas, poetry is not written with ideas. It is
made with words." For Valéry, the poet has a kind of "verbal materialism":
"You know that only the words and the forms are the real discourse." Poets
are combiners and arrangers of words. "One must adjust these complex
words like irregular blocks, speculating about the chances and surprises
which such arrangements prepare for us, and give the name of 'poets' to
those whom fortune favors in this work." The real greatness of poets is that
they are able to "grasp strongly with their words things of which they have
had but fleeting glimpses in their minds." Literature, apparently all literature,
"is in truth only a kind of speculation, a development of certain properties
of language." The poet creates his own special language, a language within
a language. "Like a political power [he] mints his own money." "The problem is how to extract from this practical instrument [everyday language] the
means of realizing an essentially nonpractical work."

If poetry is words, it is, of course, not words in isolation, but words in
a pattern, words formalized. One could collect from Valéry the most extreme
formalist statements. He quotes Frédéric Mistral with approval: "*There is
nothing but form* . . . form alone preserves the works of the mind." He
approves of Mallarmé, with whom "the material is no longer the *cause* of
the 'Form': it is one of the effects." Content is "*nothing but an impure
form*—that is to say a *confused* form." Valéry praises Hugo because with
him "the form is always master. . . . Thought becomes with him a means
and not the end of expression." And he says of himself: "I subordinate
'content' to 'form' (the nearer I am to my *best* state)—I am always inclined
to sacrifice the *former* to the *latter.*"

Valéry complains that "the philosopher does not easily understand that
the artist passes almost without distinction from *form* to *content* as from
content to *form.*" The form, he says with an inversion of usual imagery, is
"the skeleton of works: but some works have none. All works die, but those

that have a skeleton last much longer than those that were soft all through."
This formalism extends to the origin of the poem. "A delightful, touching,
'profoundly human' (as the dunces say) idea sometimes arises from the need
to link up two stanzas, two developments of a theme." Once Valéry even
said that "the principal personages of a poem are always the smoothness and
the vigor of the verse." But on the whole Valéry rarely goes to such extremes
of formalism, which could be matched only by that of the Russian group.

Much more frequently Valéry thinks of poetry as a collaboration of
sound and sense, a compromise between the two. He conceives of sound
and sense as "two independent variables," between which there is absolutely
no relation. Words are arbitrary signs: there is no natural relation between
sound and sense. The doctrine of the *mot juste* has no justification. "Flaubert
was convinced that for every idea there exists a single form. . . . This fine
doctrine unfortunately makes no sense." Thus the union of sound and sense
established by the poet is arbitrary but indissoluble: "The value of a poem
resides in the indissolubility of sound and sense. Now this is a condition
which seems to demand the impossible. There is no relation between the
sound and meaning of a word. . . . Yet is it the business of the poet to give
us the feeling of an intimate union between the word and the mind." This
union must resist dissolution. "If the sense and the sound (or the content
and the form) can be easily dissociated the poem *decomposes*." This union
of sound and meaning is song, but not quite song. We must remember that
Valéry also said that poetry is calculus, sport, exercise, even a game. But
apparently song (*chant*) in Valéry's mind is not literally song (*carmen*); it is
also enchantment, incantation, charm, magic. Valéry called a collection of
his poems *Charmes;* and he means it also as a suggestion of the original
function of poetry. "There is a very ancient man in every true poet; he still
drinks from the very springs of language." But this primitivism is reconcil-
able with the greatest refinement. Mallarmé, "the least primitive of poets,
gave . . . the magic formula." The poet is the Orpheus who brings all nature
to life, who has the animizing power of ancient man. Thus all poetry will
be and must be metaphorical. "The poet who multiplies figures is only re-
discovering within himself language in its *nascent state*."

Poetry is thus figurative and incantatory and, of course, metrical. Valéry
has little use for free verse. He always praises the merits of strict metrical
schemes and of all poetic conventions. "The demands of a strict prosody are
the artifice that confers on natural language the qualities of a resistant
matter." In verse, as Valéry interprets it, there must always be a clash between
speech and metrical pattern and even the most artificial rules of French
metrics are good (though arbitrary) just as any kind of restraint is good.

Even a small vocabulary is considered a good thing: "A restricted vocabulary, from which one knows how to form numerous combinations, is worth more than thirty thousand words which do nothing but embarrass the acts of the mind." Valéry defends stanzaic forms and is enraptured by the sonnet. He would want to encounter its inventor in the underworld. However bad his sonnets might have been, Valéry would like to tell him: "I set you in my heart above all the poets of the earth and the underworld. . . . You have invented a *form,* and the greatest have accommodated themselves to this form." The constant argument is the value of convention, of restriction, even of chains. "Restriction can be achieved only by the arbitrary." Valéry can thus revive one of the oldest doctrines of poetics, that of difficulties overcome. This "difficulty overcome" is for Valéry a criterion of value. "Every judgment which one wants to make of a work of art must first of all take into account the difficulties which the author has set up for himself to overcome." We hardly need to say that Valéry prefers classicism to romanticism: classicism is superior because of its set conventions.

All these elaborate conventions, the dance, even the dance in fetters, are there for a purpose: to achieve that ideal artwork, unified, antirelative, non-temporal, imperishable, eternal, something beyond the decay of nature and man, something absolute. The poem, Valéry says, is "a closed system of all parts in which nothing can be modified." Beauty, Valéry defines, is precisely "the sentiment of the impossibility of variation." "What is finished, what is complete gives us the feeling of our being powerless to modify it." "What is not entirely finished does not yet exist," he says paradoxically, especially in view of his constant insistence on poetry as an act, as a continuous activity and on the impossibility of finishing. But this is precisely the distant ideal of perfection for which Valéry finally has to give up finding words. Beauty is ultimately inexpressible. It implies an effect of ineffability, indescribability, it signifies "inexpressibility." "Literature attempts by words to create the state of a lack of words." Thus a central obscurity in poetry is justified. "What is clear and comprehensible and corresponds to a precise idea does not produce the effect of the divine." "Everything that is beautiful, generous, heroic is in essence obscure, incomprehensible. . . . Whoever swears faithfulness to clarity, renounces thereby being a hero."

This curious criterion of resistance to transformation is very central to Valéry's ideal of poetry. Racine's *Phèdre,* he discovered, resisted attempts to change it. "I learned by direct experience and immediate sensation what is perfection in a work." A lack of this resistance is what Valéry considers the main objection to the novel:

As a reader of novels and histories I could not help observing all the freedom which these writings left me to modify [them] at my pleasure. . . . Novels demand passivity. They claim to make you take them at their word. They should be careful not to awaken the faculty of invention which, as to details, is in all of us at least equal to that of the author, and which can be, at every moment, exercised diabolically and can amuse itself with modifying the text, with bringing in an infinite number of possible substitutions which every narrative allows without noticeable alterations of its theme. . . . That is why I admire those novelists who tell us that they live (as one says) their characters and live them to the point of being rather lived by them than living them. I am convinced that they speak the truth as I myself have once or twice in my life experienced something analogous, I think, to such a sort of incarnation. But how can one gloss over the fact that everything ends on paper, that however intense and intimate the illusion of the author may be, it is translated into words, into phrases fixed once for all for everybody, exposed to our view, to the reactions and maneuvers of a mind which may be an active mind?

Valéry can rewrite a novel, in imagination, and that is why it is "a naive genre," ultimately inferior to poetry. But this is not the only reason for Valéry's depreciation of the novel. The novel is also "historical," based on truth and memory, and neither truth nor memory means anything in art for Valéry. He does not care for memories. "I certainly shall not search for lost time," he says, alluding to his difference from Proust. Just as he does not care to remember his own past, so he does not care for history. "I am antihistorical," he says bluntly, and he often regrets the effects of historiography: the inciting of national passions, the keeping alive of old grievances and illusions.

His other objection to the novel is its claim to "truth": "Whereas the world of poetry is essentially closed and complete in itself, being purely a system of ornaments and accidents of language, the universe of the novel, even of the fantastic novel, is joined to the real world—just as a painted background merges imperceptibly into real objects, among which a spectator comes and goes." Valéry finds this appeal to truth puzzling. How is it that "a collection of details which are insignificant in themselves, and valueless one by one should produce a passionate interest and the impression of life?" "The novel," he says elsewhere, slightly varying the thought, "is possible because of the fact that this truth costs nothing . . . like air or sunlight. It lends itself to an infinity of compositions of equal probability." Besides, the novel is, of course, prose in Valéry's sense. "Unlike poems, a novel can be summarized; in other words, its plot can be told. It can be shortened without materially changing the story; . . . it can also be translated without losing its value. It can be developed internally and prolonged indefinitely." The same is true of epic poetry, of any long poem. It "can be summarized. . . . A melody cannot be summarized," says Valéry, crushingly to his mind, as statement and truth are excluded *a priori* from his definition of poetry.

It is merely consistent that Valéry does not know what to do with drama although he himself wrote dramatic scenes, dialogues, and what he calls "mélodrames." "Everything that is dramatic in life, in history, etc., seems to me of secondary interest. . . . This indifference to violent and spectacular incidents explains to me why I am not a novelist, a historian, or a dramatist." He is frankly puzzled as to why man finds pleasure in tragedy. He recognizes that

> man likes to feed on the sight of the misfortune of others. Two centuries ago, ladies went to see people put to torture. In any case it seems that the tragic genre is completely opposed to the production, in the soul, of the highest state which art can create in it: the contemplative state—the state of sensuous knowledge in which all the notions and emotions which cannot enter into the composition of a harmonious, though momentary life are abolished at the same time.

Still, surprisingly, Valéry recognizes that Greek tragedy has accomplished the impossible:

> In putting on the stage the most atrocious stories in the world, they have imposed upon them all the purity and perfection of a form which insensibly communicates to the spectator of crimes and evils an indefinable feeling which makes him regard these horrible disorders with a divine eye. . . . [He can] always come back from the emotion to comprehension, from excess to measure, from the exceptional to the norm, and from nature overthrown to the unchangeable presence of the profound order of the world.

One cannot help reflecting that Valéry might have admitted the same transforming power of art in other cases: even in the epic or the social novel, as he himself admits that there is, "in the order of the arts, no theme and no model which execution cannot ennoble or degrade, make a cause of disgust or pretext for enthusiasm." Actually, Valéry appreciated the poetic power of

Zola. But in his own practice he more and more insisted on only one theme of poetry: that of "the life of intelligence [which] constitutes an incomparable lyrical universe. . . . There is an immense realm of the intellectual sensibility," hitherto neglected by poetry. It was Valéry's right to insist on this discovery; every artist recommends the art he himself practices. Every artist is an apologist for his own art, and that is, in part, the interest of his criticism. But as a general theory of literature it seems an extremely narrow, exclusive, puristic view, a specialty hardly applicable beyond that unique closed system of Valéry's civilized mind.

Valéry's ideal of poetry remains absolute, almost frozen into the grandeur of a "pure form." One would imagine that such a hard structure would have to be apprehended by its audience as purely as it was conceived, as impersonally as it was created. But here Valéry's strong sense of the discontinuity of author and reader interferes. A work of art to his mind is open to many interpretations, is only in a loose relationship to its audience. A work of art is essentially ambiguous. "It is an error contrary to the nature of poetry and which could even be fatal to it, to claim that to a poem corresponds one single, true meaning which conforms to or is identical with some thought of the author." Valéry, with a sort of mischievous courtesy, has written introductions to Gustave Cohen's commentary on "Le Cimetière marin" and to Alain's commentaries on *Charmes,* which manage to praise the authors without committing himself to the acceptance of a single one of their interpretations. "My verses have the meaning which one gives to them," he says bluntly. "There is no true sense of a text. The author has no authority. Whatever he wanted to say, he has written what he has written." The last part of this pronouncement is entirely defensible: it reasserts his suspicion of good intentions. "Bad verses are made of good intentions." Valéry is quite right to say, "when a work has appeared, its interpretation by the author has no more value than its interpretation by someone else. . . . My intention is only my intention and the work is the work."

This insight into the detachment of the work from the author, into the "intentional fallacy," does not dispose of the problem of interpretation. All interpretations are not equal: there remains the problem of correctness. Valéry seems nearer the truth when he says: "There is no very fine work which is not susceptible of a great variety of equally plausible interpretations. The richness of a work is the number of senses or values which it can receive while still remaining itself." The accretion of meaning in the process of history is a fact: great works of art have proved their vitality by this variety of appeal. Valéry recognizes the effects of history on the meaning of a work of art. "The change of an era, which is a change of reader, is comparable to a change in the text itself, a change which is always unforeseeable and in-calculable." Valéry echoes a phrase used by Coleridge when he says that "certain works are created by their public. Certain other works create their public." But Valéry indulges in dangerous paradoxes when he asserts the role of "creative misunderstanding" or gives us this little dialogue: "I understand this text badly. . . . Don't bother. I find fine things. It draws them out of me. It matters little that I know what the author said. My error becomes the author." Here the way would be opened to extreme caprice and anarchy. The break between work and audience would be complete.

But we must not make too much of irreconcilable contradictions and paradoxes in Valéry's thought. In discussing Descartes he has warned us that "every system is an enterprise of the mind against itself. . . . If one tries to reconstruct a thinking being from an examination of the texts alone, one is led to the invention of monsters who are incapable of life in direct proportion to the strict carefulness that one has devoted to the elaboration of the study." We must not try to force unity on Valéry's thought, we must not invent a logical monster. Let us be content to have shown the main motifs of his thought on poetry.

JEFFREY MEHLMAN

Craniometry and Criticism:
Notes on a Valéryan Criss-Cross

A man of intelligence (lato et stricto sensu) *is a man who has good*
series. Wins often. We don't know why. Nor does he.
                                    —PAUL VALÉRY, *Mauvaises pensées*

First series, Poetry. Valéry, during World War I, undertakes, at Gide's
suggestion, to consolidate his farewell to poetry by preparing an edition of
the *vers anciens* of his youth, the remains of a vocation he had abandoned
during his crisis of 1892 as ultimately deleterious to mind. That farewell, in
one of the hoariest episodes of modern literary history, turned into a paradoxical return. Valéry soon found himself embarked in spite of himself on
his major poem, *La Jeune Parque,* the "involuntary *Aeneid*" he completed
in 1917. A virgin awakens to find her virginity threatened by the tear she
can no longer quite remember having shed during a dream: Who indeed
could be crying, she asks, beside(s) herself ("Mais qui pleure, / Si proche de
moi-même au moment de pleurer?"). As the tear writes (or "marks") its way
through the Parque's body, provoking its host to flight, it comes to figure
the poem itself, the apparently unwanted issue of Valéry's reawakening to
poetry. For the subsequent volume *Charmes,* I have attempted to demonstrate
elsewhere, is readable as a transformation of the complex "tear-work" of *La
Jeune Parque.* From which demonstration, two examples: "Le Cimetière marin" begins with a meditation on the sparkling surface of the sea ("La mer,
la mer toujours recommencée"), and modulates into an evocation of the sea
as a retentive eye:

From *boundary 2* 11, no. 1 (Fall 1982). © 1982 by *boundary 2.*

> Stable trésor, temple simple à Minerve,
> Masse de calme, et visible réserve,
> Eau sourcilleuse, Oeil qui gardes en toi
> Tant de sommeil sous un voile de flamme,
> O mon silence!

(Stable treasure, simple temple to Minerva, / Calm mass and visible reserve, / Supercilious water, Eye keeping in yourself / So much sleep beneath a veil of flame, / Oh my silence!)

Valéry's "silence," the cult of intelligence (Minerva), the eye closed with slumber. . . . A minimal solicitation of the text, and we find the awakening of the Jeune Parque and the scintillation of the Mediterranean surface (LA MER, LA MER) rebegun anagramatically as LARME. A redistribution to which we shall return.

A second recurrence of the tear, in summary of my earlier demonstration, is afforded by "Le Vin perdu." The poet finds himself gratuitously casting a bit of wine ("tout un peu de vin précieux") into the ocean. The sea resumes its transparency, but the poet becomes witness thereafter to a kind of intoxication of the waves as "the deepest of figures" spring into the air. Now the poem's second quatrain begins by asking who desired that loss or waste ("Qui voulut ta perte, ô liqueur?"). It repeats, that is, the Jeune Parque's mystification concerning her tear: "Qui pleure là?" True, the (transformed) tear here is emitted unimaginably *into* the "eye" (i.e., the sea of our previous example, "Le Cimetière marin"). But it is precisely the threat to both visual imagination and the distinction within/without that is at stake in Valéry's tear-work. A final line we shall quote from "Le Vin perdu" ("Songeant au sang, versant le vin") has the poet dreaming—un-Eucharistically—blood for wine. Let us retain it as an index of the extent to which the repetition of the tear is inseparable from its transformation as difference.

Second series, Politics. Toward the end of World War I, then, Valéry emerged with his poetic "maturity," but as well with a political formula, which he himself was inclined to repeat as a kind of shorthand for his own presumably profound sense of the political state of the world: "We civilizations (*nous autres, civilisations*), we now know that we are mortal." The line served as something of a signature for Valéry after its initial appearance in "La Crise de l'esprit" (1919), to which we shall presently turn. From that text, consider first Valéry's evocation of Europe during the years of the War, the period, that is, during which he was composing *La Jeune Parque:* "An extraordinary tremor went coursing through the marrow of Europe. She felt through every one of her centers of thought (*noyaux de pensée*) that she no longer recognized herself, no longer resembled herself, that she was about to lose consciousness. . . . Then, as in a desperate defence of her whole physiological being, the whole of her memory was suddenly—and confusedly—restored to her. . . . And in the same mental disorder, beckoned by the same anxiety, European culture underwent the rapid revivification of her innumerable modes of thought." Above and beyond the accuracy of Valéry's suggestions about the intellectual intoxication of the war years, one is hard put not to relate the threateningly intense return of Europe's intellectual memory to the return of Valéry's abandoned poetic vocation in the near-convulsions of *La Jeune Parque*. Whence, moreover, the interest of Valéry's meditation on Europe in the second "letter" of his essay, for it culminates in an elaborate recurrence of an image we have already encountered. The poet argues that the crisis of European intelligence is less a function of the havoc wreaked by the war than of the random diffusion of the treasure of European inventiveness into areas of the world more populated than itself. The inequality among regions of the globe, the improbable superiority of Europe, will thus disappear, or rather superiority will henceforth be based no longer on intelligence but on the "statistical" realities of population, area, raw materials, etc. Whereupon Valéry, forgetting the national argument, poses a class analogy: the current crisis of Europe recalls the effects of the diffusion of culture within each nation midst progressively larger sections of the population. Is there a fated degradation of mental life concomitant with such diffusion? He comments:

> The attractiveness (*charme*) of the problem for a speculative mind stems first of all from its resemblance with the physical fact of diffusion,—and then from the abrupt change of that resemblance into a profound difference, as soon as the thinker returns to his initial object, which is *men* and not *molecules*.
>
> A drop of wine fallen into water (*une goutte de vin tombée dans l'eau*) barely colors it and tends to disappear after a pinkish mist (*après une rose fumée*). Such is the physical fact. But suppose now that a short while after that dissipation and return to limpidity, we saw, here and there (*çà et là*) in the vase which seemed to have become *pure* water again, drops of *pure* dark wine forming—imagine our astonishment. . . . This phenomenon of Cana is not impossible in the physics of the intellect and of society. In such cases, we speak of *genius* and oppose it to diffusion.

Not the least of the problem's incipient "charms," it will be seen, is that it is centered on an image that will appear three years later in *Charmes* as "Le

Vin perdu." We are, then, to all appearances, at one of those crossroads—between poetry and politics—with which thought, in Monsieur Teste's phrase, is paved. For the expenditure of wine in the poem is part of the tear-work series. The intersection, moreover, is sufficiently ample to accommodate an entire line of verse: "Après une rose fumée." An interpretation? Let us first underscore the dimensions of the parallel. From 1913 to 1917, Valéry re-emerges, in spite of himself, as a poet in the figure of the awakening Jeune Parque, traumatized to observe what is no longer quite her own substance, a tear, spent in the world. During the same years, Valéry's Europe knows a comparably intense reactivation of its intellectual capital only to see it spent—as a liquid emission—outside itself. The political problem of the essay is the retrieval of that initial inequality, in the precise form of the return of that emission. But the poetry—as tear-work—is thinkable as nothing so much as the logic—or graphics—of that return . . .

Third series, Physics. The image which Valéry uses in "Le Vin perdu" and "La Crise de l'esprit" was borrowed from Henri Poincaré's discussion of the second principle of thermodynamics ("Carnot's Principle") in *La Valeur de la Science*: "Should a drop of wine fall into a glass of water (*qu'une goutte de vin tombe dans un verre d'eau*); whatever the law of the internal movement of the liquid, we will soon see it colored with a uniform pinkish tint (*une teinte rosée*), and from that moment on, we will shake the vase in vain, the wine and the water will no longer appear able to separate out." It is precisely the irreversibility of such processes—ultimately of physical time itself—which is posited by Carnot: in Poincaré's formulation: "heat can pass from the warm body on to the cold body, and it is impossible thereafter to follow the reverse path, and establish differences of temperature which have been effaced." Time is the obliteration of difference. But Valéry's excursion into "intellectual physics" was predicated on the suddenly perceived possibility of a "différence profonde," the reconstitution of the wine-drops. Such was the task assigned in Poincaré's text to Maxwell's imaginary demon, "who can sort out molecules one by one, and would be able to constrain the world to return into the past." The dilemma of the tear, then, is the condition of (im)possibility of reestablishing European superiority.

J. C. Maxwell introduced the demon in his *Theory of Heat* (1871). Observing that the second law of thermodynamics posits the impossibility of producing "any inequality of temperature or of pressure without the expenditure of work," he continued:

> Now let us suppose that . . . a vessel is divided into two portions,
> A and B, by a division in which there is a small hole, and that a

being, who can see the individual molecules, opens and closes
this hole, so as to allow only the swifter molecules to pass from
A to B, and only the slower ones to pass from B to A. He will
thus without expenditure of work raise the temperature of B and
lower that of A, in contradiction to the second law of thermodynamics.

The demon, thus, in producing difference, reduces entropy and eliminates
the disorder of chance.

Jean Hyppolite, toward the end of his life, read Mallarmé's *Un Coup
de dés* in conjunction with Norbert Wiener on cybernetics, and assimilated
the old man of that poem ("cadavre par le bras écarté du secret qu'il dé-
tient"), his fist clenched around the dice he will—perhaps—never throw, to
Maxwell's demon . . . in the process of going under. The poem would affirm
the irreducibility of the informational equivalent of entropy—noise—against
any effort to thwart that universal and transmit a message entire: "Un coup
de dés jamais n'abolira le hasard." Mallarmé's text, however, was, curiously
enough, a palinode: the culmination of a poetic career dedicated to the
proposition that poetry would allow one to eliminate chance, *le hasard,* word
by word. And the body of that poetry, I have demonstrated elsewhere, finds
its locus in the infinitesimal partition or window separating a mass of white
from a mass of red. The poems, that is, are superimposable as a virtually
abstract design, or as the action of Maxwell's chance-eradicating demon: a
perpetual motion machine endlessly, uncannily repeating the difference of its
partition.

Mallarmé's ultimate legacy, then, "Un Coup de dés," proposed the impossibility of eradicating chance or noise, the demise, in Hippolyte's terms,
of Maxwell's demon. The performance or legitimation of that legacy, its
transmission, however, would paradoxically entail its partial obliteration (by
noise). In 1920, Valéry, the privileged legatee, defended the legacy of "Un
Coup de dés" (against efforts to set it to music) in these terms: "that glory
[of Mallarmé] is not a *statistical* glory. It is not dependent on the size (*le
nombre*) of an indistinct audience. It is composed of solitary individuals who
do not resemble each other. Its possessor acquired it head by head, even as
he vanquished chance (*le hasard*) word by word." Thus does he simultaneously receive, protect, and obliterate the heritage of Mallarmé. But "the
statistical dimensions, numbers—population, surface area, raw materials"
were precisely those forces now triumphant at the expense of Europe and/
as Intelligence, the infinitely *probable* or random reality which Maxwell's
demon—borrowed from Poincaré—was to eradicate in "La Crise de l'esprit"

and, by implication, in "Le Vin perdu." The detour from the tear-work of Valéry's poetry—through politics and physics—has brought us to Mallarmé and the poetic tradition Valéry would perpetuate.

A curious junction between Mallarmé and politics occurs even earlier in Valéry's writings, in the first of his "quasi-political essays," "Une Conquête méthodique." The young Valéry, vacationing in London in 1896, visits, upon recommendation from Mallarmé, the British eccentric and poet, William Henley. Henley requests a curiously assigned article of his guest for a journal he is currently editing, *The New Review*. The journal has been running a series of statistically informative articles on the danger which German industrial competition poses for English commerce. Henley requests of Valéry a philosophical conclusion "in the French manner." The Frenchman, recipient of copious good wishes "for the good Stéphane," at first laughs off the assignment, but ends up writing an essay to which we shall presently turn.

The reality Valéry was invited to speculate on was essentially one of interstitial expropriation. Here, for instance, is the author of "Made in Germany" in a characteristic passage:

> Take observation, Gentle Reader, to your own surroundings: the mental exercise is recommended as an antidote to that form of self-sufficiency which our candid friends regard as indigenous to the British climate. Your investigations will work out somewhat in this fashion. You will find that the material of some of your own clothes was woven in Germany. Still more probable is it that some of your wife's garments are German importations; while it is practically beyond a doubt that the magnificent mantles and jackets wherein her maids array themselves on their Sundays out are German-made and German-sold, for only so could they be done at the figure. Your governess's *fiancé* is a clerk in the City; but he also was made in Germany.

By day's end:

> If you are imaginative and dyspeptic, you drop off to sleep only to dream that St. Peter (with a duly stamped halo around his head and a bunch of keys from Eison) has refused your admission into Paradise, because you bear not the Mark of the Beast upon your forehead, and are not of German make. But you console yourself with the thought that it was only a Bierhaus Paradise anyway; and you are awakened in the morning by the sonorous brass of a German band.

Thus E. Williams in the pre-text of Valéry's meditation, quoted at some length on the assumption of the usefulness—at the inception of the political writing of an author who has contributed as much as any to the contemporary esthetics of expropriation—of evoking the primal (political) shock informing that discourse, the privileged status of "made-in-Germany" as a floating signifier.

Valéry's essay is characterized above all by the desire to relegate "national bitterness" to a secondary status and indulge in a "special admiration" for an accomplishment as perfect as German industrial "method." He claims that the German achievement lay in organizing the economy with the same strategic awareness that had been employed in building Prussia's army. Two principal—and italicized—slogans motivate the German effort in Valéry's view: "*Inequality must be organized (Il faut organiser l'inégalité)*" and "*the real enemy is chance (le véritable ennemi, c'est le hasard).*" Although the essay, that is, is ultimately about the refinements of German marketing, its principle motifs are of a piece with those present at the intersection of poetry, politics, and physics with which we began. The hero of the new impersonal order, moreover, is neither Poe nor Leonardo, but Moltke, who "personifies the system." In fact, though, his greatest accomplishment is the achievement of his own superfluity in the German success; "It seems that the most profound of his designs has been not to die indispensable." Transposed into esthetics, the sentence yields Valéry's later pronouncements: "every work (*oeuvre*) is the work of many other things than an *author*" and "the true artisan of a splendid piece of work is absolutely no one." The author seems intent on affirming the mediocrity of his exemplary figure. The gifts of Moltke—like those of Maxwell's demon—are those of the second-rate: patience and attention. And yet it is precisely the intensity to which those banal aptitudes are brought which fascinates Valéry. By the essay's end, the author, in fact, extrapolates from the case of Moltke to a kind of incipient "method" no longer opposed to but at the heart of the great achievements of civilization: "Suppose, if you like, that several of those great minds, having made use of private methods (*méthodes intimes*), came to an awareness (*conscience*) of them." The case of "Moltke," then, would bring us to an understanding of the esthetic unconscious: the "phenomena of choice, substitution, and association that remain so obscure." And nowhere more so, we would suggest, than in the case of Valéry. For the essay on the "German conquest" has, in fact, brought us back to the Maxwellian program of organizing inequalities and eradicating chance which has been the focus of these notes from the beginning.

Return to "La Crise de l'esprit." One figure of the poet in that text is an "intellectual Hamlet" pondering the skulls of a host of illustrious men in Europe's imaginary graveyard: "If he picks up a skull, it is an illustrious skull.—*Whose was it?* This one was *Leonardo* . . . Hamlet has no idea of what to do with all those skulls. But if he abandons them! . . . Will he cease being himself?" Now that image of the Valéryan surrogate pondering the skulls of the great serves to remind us that in his youth Valéry, during an apprenticeship served under the anthropologist and craniometer Georges Vacher de Lapouge, measured 600 skulls exhumed from a disaffected cemetery. Indeed one of the editors of Valéry's correspondence dubs him an "anthropological Hamlet" on that occasion. As we approach Valéry's relation to Montpellier's most prestigious intellectual of the 1890s, probably its sole candidate to world renown, it should first be observed that the culmination of their relation appears to have been in 1892, the year Valéry—in Genoa—would deem poetry deleterious to intelligence and consequently unworthy of being pursued. Valéry, that year, not only attended the—packed—courses of the city's premier theoretician of intelligence, but lectured on Villiers de l'Isle-Adam at a session presided by him. Vacher subsequently published the following evocation of the evening:

> At the same time that Wagner's *Lohengrin* was being played, the Association listened to a reading of *Les Contes cruels* by Villiers de l'Isle-Adam, his friend and the first to have understood him in France. A calculated counterpoint, since the profound, strange, and mystical work of Villiers is the Wagnerianism of literature. Monsieur Valéry, through his infinitely skillful execution, was able to render the *Contes* accessible to the public. The literary analysis was impeccable in its substance, sculptural in its form. When the appearance of Asraël, the angel of death, was read, a shudder of fear passed over the room. All the mystical horror of Siva's temple, with its murderous nets, then descended on the audience. The impression left by this second gathering was profound and lasting.

Valéry's relation with Vacher, then, was of sufficient intensity to have attained a measure of mutuality.

And yet the name of Vacher is absent from Valéry's *oeuvre*, unmentioned in the *Cahiers,* appearing a single time in the published correspondence. That letter—to Gide, 13 January 1899—is alluded to on the final page of Derrida's essay on the poet's "divided sources" (Freud, Nietzsche), and is indeed worthy of reinvoking in the context of that topos. The bulk of the letter consists of two *post-scripta* relating Valéry's difficult relation to Nietzsche's "contradictions." In the first entry, the poet sorts out two incompatible strands in the philosopher's work: "Thus, on the whole, there are things that are admirable or naive or useless; one has to choose what's most suitable and return to either Stendhal or Descartes, for there's no middle ground possible." Energy or Mind, Stendhal or Descartes, impossible to reconcile. The second *post-scriptum,* however, offers a possible articulation of the two:

> You say he was in favor of unconsciousness (*tu dis qu'il prônait l'inconscience*). I don't believe it. There are even sentences that say just the opposite. It is simply that his dear *Uebermensch* is to have complete awareness (*conscience*) *with all* the "advantages" of UNCONSCIOUSNESS (*INCONSCIENCE*). That much is clear. Without that he wouldn't be an *Uebermensch;* he'd be, in one sense or the other, a simple enlargement of a given type, unconscious or conscious. Vacher or Poe, unbound (*démesurés*).
>
> That is how I personally would have proceeded to construct a character (Cf. *Teste*).

The suggestion here is that the Stendhal/Descartes gap that Nietzsche was unable to close was bridged—if only virtually—by Valéry in *Monsieur Teste.* But that articulation is imagined no longer in terms of Stendhal and Descartes, but of Vacher and Poe, respectively "*inconscience*" and "*conscience.*" As though the craniometer Vacher were at some level the unconscious of Valéry's hero of intelligence, Monsieur Teste.

Consider the context of that virtuality. "Monsieur Teste," more than a character, was the consolidation of an option to abandon poetry as deleterious to intelligence. That poetry, moreover, is conceivable as the tear-work which re-emerges—from repression—in *La Jeune Parque,* and that we evoked at the beginning of these pages. In Valéry's fantasmagoria, then, it is as though Intelligence were to Poetry as Consciousness is to the Unconscious. But the tear-work, we have seen, had a fundamental political coefficient. It embraced the threat to European superiority posed by the diffusion of its Intelligence outside itself. As Valéry puts it in the "Avant-Propos" to *Regards sur le monde actuel,* "Europe will not have had a politics worthy of its intellect." Poetry and Politics are deleterious to Mind, and the threat they together pose and that Monsieur Teste would repress is figurable as tear-work. But the menace to mind is above all a threat to European superiority, or rather to the preeminence of what Valéry, at the conclusion of "La Crise de l'esprit" calls "*Homo europaeus.*"

Which returns us to Vacher, the virtual "unconscious" of "Monsieur Teste." For *Homo europaeus* was the Linnaean term that Vacher had revived to designate what popular usage still obliged him to call the Aryan race. Indeed the major set of lectures that Vacher delivered at Montpellier, later published as *L'Aryen: son rôle social,* begins (in book-form): "This book is the monograph of *Homo europaeus,* that is, the racial variety to which the diverse names of dolichocephalic blond, Cymric, Galatic, Germanic, and Aryan have been given." It is therefore all the more significant that Valéry, immediately after concluding his essay with an encomium to the "astonishing inequality" enjoyed by *Homo europaeus,* should tack on the following denial: "It is remarkable that European man is defined by neither race, nor language, nor customs, but by desires and amplitude of will . . . Etc." For the choice of the technical racial term exempted from any reference to race is a further index of Vacher's role as "rejected source."

Monsieur Teste's "unconscious"? Perhaps the closest we come to a text figurable as such is the extraordinary and unfinished short piece entitled alternately *Agathe* and *Manuscript Found in a Brain.* For Valéry would later write to Gide that it constituted "the interior of Monsieur Teste's night." It relates the degenerating dream of a woman asleep for several years: "Now, for two, three . . . ten years, there have been no sensations for her: thus, study the impoverishment (or whatever) of the given with which she fell asleep. . . . The successive zones of alteration of images, etc., the variation of thought become gradually empty would be curious to do." The several pages that Valéry wrote but never published are probably as close as anything in the nineteenth century to the novelistic prose of Maurice Blanchot. Concerning them, several observations:

1. The figure who will sleep and dream in Monsieur Teste's night is plainly a version of the Jeune Parque. In her disorientation, she loses all sense of identity, asks: "Who asks? The same responds. The same writes, erases an identical line. They are but writings on the waters." Her future lies in a fascination with some internal vitiation of thought, an anticipation, I would suggest, of the Parque's tear: "an abstract pearl would roll, future, in the fold of ordinary thought: an astonishing law, confused with the one seeking it, would dwell therein: a single instant would deliver over that pearl. Outside of every path, unknown to every violence, it lies there (*elle est gisant*) exterior to every figure, every resemblance. . . . I have a desire of it (*J'ai d'elle le désir*). . . . I discover, infinitely, its lack, and already, out of that lack, I have made myself a useful sign." The night of Monsieur Teste is literally that of poetry, twenty years dormant.

2. The awakening of the Parque, we have seen from "Crise de l'esprit,"

was at some level the awakening of the threatened European in Valéry, *Homo europaeus*. The point of departure for the body of his political writings proper, *Regards sur le monde actuel,* moreover, was the newly acquired sense of being a European ... endangered in his essence by those two estranged manifestations of European might, the Japanese incursion against China (1895) and the American war with Spain (1898): "That indirect blow in the Far-East, and the direct blow in the Antilles thus made me perceive the existence of something that could be reached and disturbed by such events. I found myself 'sensitized' to contingencies that affected a kind of virtual idea of Europe that I was unaware until then of bearing within me." *La Jeune Parque* as *Homo europaeus*?

3. The title "Manuscript Found in a Brain" links up Poe, author of "MS. Found in a Bottle," with Vacher, technician of skull measurement, brain capacity, and cephalic indices. But Poe and Vacher, we have seen in the letter to Gide, were the two sides tendentially united in Teste. The Valéry text relates a dreamed obliteration of thought, born of sensory deprivation, in a seemingly endless night. The Poe tale, of course, imagines a ship drawn wildly through the white ice into a polar maelstrom. Valéryan thought, by (intertextual) implication, is whitened out. And Vacher's *Homo europaeus?* The most enigmatic trait of "European man," and the subject treated at greatest length in the chapter of Vacher's treatise on "L'Origine des Aryens," is depigmentation. The "superior race," in fact, is characterized first of all by a "kind of degeneration" of the normal "chromoblastic" capacity of its skin: "[The coloration] of *H. Europaeus* is a unique, abnormal, and, so to speak, pathological occurrence ... a phenomenon of etiolation." And it is a phenomenon attributable above all to a climate deprived of sun. Indeed much of Vacher's chapter situates its humanity somewhere between the random patterns of meteorology and the "Brownian movement" of protoplasmic "granulations of melanin" which color the skin. In between the two, a photographic technology for calibrating degrees of pigmentation is invoked. In some cases, the subject's extremities are registered at the expense of the rest of the body: "the remainder is expressed only by a nebulosity on the paper. This is the girl without a body (*la fille sans corps*)." In others, "the head and the hands come too quickly, and if one allows the exposure necessary for the body, the rest is lost. ... This is the trunk-girl (*la fille-tronc*)." Consider, then, that in Valéry (with Poe), we have a girl all but disarticulated by a whitening out of thought in the long night of her slumber. In Vacher, we find a girl scattered or dismembered as part of the analysis of a unique and pathological depigmentation of skin, the result of a prolonged absence of sun. Valéry's heroine will awaken from M. Teste's night during the War

as Poetry homologous to a Europe threatened—by diffusion—in its superiority. As for Vacher's *Homo europaeus,* he emerged in the Montpellier lectures as the protagonist of a racial tragedy whose outline was later sketched by the author in "Lois de la vie et de la mort des nations":

> But even as in a battery there is the zinc pole and the other, and the zinc is worn out early, so in a society with two terms, the active term is quick to grow weak. First, crossings that human nature makes inevitable alter the race of the conquerors. Drop by drop, the blood of the superior race departs into that of the inferior class (*Goutte à goutte, le sang de la race supérieure s'en va dans la classe inférieure*) and the servile blood infiltrates into the families of the conquerors.

This drama of racial decline, of the victory—already in France—of the servile, dark (brachycephalic) round-heads over the Aryan, blond (dolichocephalic) long-heads is the core of Vacher's version of social Darwinism. What is striking in the present context is the extent to which it reproduces the poetico-politico-physical node with which we began these notes: the decline of European man as a diffusion of wine into water; (but) the wine imaginable originally as blood ("songeant au sang, versant le vin"); the merging of "race" with "class" analysis; the scientific analogy invoked to convey decline as an erosion of difference. . . . The only missing element in the homology is Maxwell's demon, for which Vacher would substitute a particularly grisly program of eugenics.

The figure of Vacher as "rejected source," *source écartée,* in Valéry's fantasia of intelligence receives some sustenance from a consideration of the role of craniology—the science of skull measurement—in a still broader fantasmagoria of intelligence and/as inequality. Indeed the most recent inquiry into the history of craniology, S. J. Gould's *The Mismeasure of Man,* has succeeded in demonstrating that the ultimate legacy of that pseudo-science was the American IQ test. And since the name of Vacher figures on both sides of the divide, we shall do well to digress briefly to a consideration of that account. At the beginning of the sequence, we find Paul Broca leading the French scientific community in debate as to the proper correlations among cranial conformation, brain capacity, level of intelligence, and hierarchy of race. It was an odd debate, in which etiquette all but demanded that one be willing to submit one's brain to dissection and measurement after death, and in which the suspicion lingered that the ultimate worth of one's arguments was determined in the course of that posthumous exercise. The transition from "cranial" to "psychological" measurement of intelligence was the achievement of Alfred Binet early in the century, but it was in the United States that the twin legacies of craniology—reification and hereditarianism— were made to inflect the study of intelligence and the interpretation of the Binet scale. The stages of the Americanization of Binet's efforts to study, in their plurality, varieties of intelligence, though they will not detain us, are worth recalling: H. H. Goddard's importation of the Binet scale to America, his reification of its scores as innate intelligence and invention of the—om- nipresent—"moron"; L. M. Terman's dream of a rational society allocating professions in accordance with IQ scores; R. M. Yerkes's success in con- vincing the Army to test almost two million men in World War I, thus laying the "objective" basis for the hereditarian perspective that led to the Immi- gration Restriction Act of 1924, "with its low ceiling for lands suffering from the blight of poor genes." Now in one of the "classic" texts of tradition, A Study of American Intelligence (1923), C. C. Brigham was faced with an apparent threat to the thesis of essentially innate intelligence. For the results of Yerkes's mass-testing seemed to indicate that the immigrant groups that had been in the United States longer did better in proportion to the length of their stay. Environment, that is, and not heredity, would appear to be the key factor. It was at this juncture that the work of Vacher was adduced in order to save the hereditarian thesis. For what the test results demonstrated, it was argued, was not the priority of environment in the development of intelligence, but rather the historical circumstance that the innate intelligence of the various racial pools of immigrants the United States had been tapping had been gradually declining over the past twenty years. And it was Vacher's racial categories that were invoked to substantiate the thesis. The corrective Immigration Restriction Act would follow a year later, attempting to reverse the demographic impact of inferior immigrations. And shortly thereafter, Brigham would become Secretary of the College Entrance Examination Board, and develop the Scholastic Aptitude Tests on the model of the Army IQ Tests. All of which is to suggest that the impediments to a perception of the subliminal insistence of Vacher in the writings of Valéry may not be unrelated to the role played by the legacy of Vacher in the enabling conditions of academic discourse itself.

Return to the poetry: "Le Cimetière marin." Earlier we evoked the nodal figure of a tear (LARME) not quite lost in the retentive eye of the sea (LA MER). Whereby the poem enters into contact with the crisis of "Le Vin perdu" and "La Crise de l'esprit." That figure of randomness, however, is pitted against the stable and specular dualism of sun and cemetery. The cemetery: "Pères profonds, têtes inhabitées." The sun: "Tête complète et parfait diadème." The complex that emerges links up ideal intelligence, a fantasy of power, and the presence of the potentially perfect skull. A bracing communion with the poet's deceased father? Perhaps. Yet the complex would seem as well to refer us to Valéry's apprenticeship in craniometry, unearthing and measuring skulls—for their index of perfection—under Vacher. The general air of exaltation would bespeak the set of values destined to enter into an acute phase of crisis in that section of the poem we have read in terms of tear-work.

"Le Cimetière marin" as a poem of *Homo europaeus* threatened in his essence. . . . That interpretation may be sustained by a reading of a short text that is in many ways a prose rehearsal of the major poem of 1920. The piece is entitled "Le Yalou," dates from 1895, in all probability originated as the fragment of *Monsieur Teste* alluded to in the correspondence as "Teste en Chine," and finally found its place in *Regards sur le monde actuel.* "Yalou" is the French name of the river running between Korea and Manchuria, in whose delta the Chinese suffered a devastating defeat at the hands of the Japanese on 17 September 1894. Our text, in fact, is in large part a dialogue, overlooking the delta, between a European visitor and a Chinese sage prior to—and in anticipation of—that conflict. But it will be recalled from the "Avant-propos" to *Regards* that the Japanese attack on China lay at the inception of Valéry's sense of himself as European: "I found myself 'sensitized' to contingencies that affected a kind of virtual idea of Europe that I was unaware until then of bearing within me." For it was a Europeanized Japan that now attacked European interests in China. We approach here the motif of "La Crise de l'esprit": the diffusion of Europe's intellectual substance as a kind of entropy. Or as Valéry himself put it, in his *Cahier* of 1896: "Men of genius serve to put everything into the hands of imbeciles. The civilized nations cultivate the Japans." Valéry, that is, awakened as a European much as the Jeune Parque would later come to consciousness: threatened—and constituted—by the return of an estranged fragment of his own substance even as she would ponder the menacing strangeness of her tear.

"Le Cimetière marin," it has been suggested, may be read in terms of the relations among three poles: sun, cemetery, and sea. Between "sun" and "cemetery," "tête complète" and "têtes inhabitées," there is a specular relation of interdependence. The two registers have opposite affective charges (of immobility: *Midi sans mouvement,* and flight: *Allez! Tout fuit!*), but are perceived by Valéry as oddly complicitous. Thus does the Poet address the sun at high noon:

> Mais dans leur nuit toute lourde de marbres,
> Un peuple vague aux racines des arbres
> A pris déjà ton parti lentement.

(But in their night heavy with marble, / A vague people, at the trees' roots, / Has already, slowly, taken your side.)

The interdependence of sun and skull, then, fueling a fantasy of intellectual power, is opposed to the sea. Or rather less to the sea *per se* than to the play of tear-work—that crisis of (European) mind—which we have seen (through *La Jeune Parque,* "Le Vin perdu," and "La Crise de l'esprit") take the tranquil sea as its deceptive scene.

Consider now that in "Le Yalou," we find a precise homology with the system I have sketched in "Le Cimetière marin." A European intellectual is in dialogue with a Chinese sage in front of the body of water from which they both sense the Japanese will soon attack. The European views himself as a characteristic articulation of light, intellectual potency, and the immobility of immediacy: "for the group of luminosity and thought which constitutes me in this moment remains identical. Then, change is nil. Time no longer moves forward. My life comes to a rest." Transposed to the cemetery in Sète, we find:

> Midi là haut, Midi sans mouvement
> En soi se pense et convient à soi-même . . .
> Tête complète et parfait diadème.

(Noon above, Noon without motion / Thinks [in] itself and suits itself . . . / Complete head and perfect diadem.)

The other—Chinese—voice in the dialogue offers a radical critique of the violence of Western intelligence in the name of that solidarity with ancestry and earth which is the wisdom of China. Thus: "Intelligence, for you, is not a thing like others. You worship it like a preponderant beast. Every day it devours what exists." Better that capacity to feel one's almost passive solidarity with one's predecessors and the earth to which they have returned: "Every man here feels himself son and father . . . and sees himself appropriated into the people, dead, beneath him. Every man here knows that he is nothing without the fulness of that earth and outside of the marvelous construction of ancestors. . . . Here, everything is historical."

In our tripartite construct, then, the Chinese sage incarnates the cemetery even as the European may be superimposed on the sun. And just as our analysis of the poem posed a complicity between the two, so, in Valéry's political statement, was China the representative of Western interests. What then of the sea? It would appear in the two cases to be a source of infinite calm. "Le Yalou": "the sweet evenness (égalité) of the motion, of the calm takes hold of me." "Le Cimetière": "O recompense après une pensée / Qu'un long regard sur le calme des dieux! (Oh recompense after a thought: a long stare on the calm of the gods!)" Yet already our reading of the poem had detected the threatening tear at the surface of the sea's retentive eye. Consider in that light the following sentence of "Le Yalou": "And I lowered my eyelids, seeing no more of the brilliant sea than what one sees of a small glass of golden liquor (liqueur), borne to the eyes." Almost gratuitously, we find an image midway between the teardrop of La Jeune Parque and the image of diffusion in "Le Vin perdu": a tiny receptacle of liquid against the eye, in or of the sea. The tear-work, then, is once again emergent in a political context. But the politics of the circumstance are the same as those of "La Crise de l'esprit": the destruction of Europe through the diffusion of its intelligence outside itself. For the Japanese strike against China is an "indirect blow" against Europe. The Chinese sage comments: "Nippon . . . is making war on us. Her great white boats steam in our bad dreams. They will trouble our gulfs." The threat of war is indeed coming from the white boats on the water, and it is uncanny that Valéry in 1920 should have chosen the dove (of peace) as his metaphor of the white sails off the coast of the graveyard: "Ce toit tranquille où marchent les colombes." For he even invites us to doubt that peace in the verse: "Et quelle paix semble se concevoir!" In an earlier analysis, I have interpreted that semblance of peace as opening the way to a reading in terms of the violence of tear-work. But the logic of the present superimposition, while confirming that reading, also reveals the extent to which the historical reality of that "tear" was war.

From superimposition to superimposition, we have arrived at a Valéry whose poetry—at its most intense—is in perpetual—metaphorical—contact with a political concern: the crisis of inegalitarianism-cum-intelligence. To engage that poetry, moreover, is perhaps to encounter the texture of "Valéry's politics" more tellingly than in any inventory of his political options, be they disastrous (against Dreyfus in 1898, for Salazar in the 1930s) or commendable (the eulogy of Bergson in occupied Paris). Indeed a final series of methodological observations plays some havoc with the metalinguistic distance from which such options might be judged.

From superimposition to superimposition. . . . The technique of superimposing texts, first formulated explicitly by Charles Mauron, is intended to provide analytic access to that register of uncanny repetition midst extreme difference that is a touchstone of the effects of what Freud called "the unconscious." Thus the reading of "Le Yalou" with "Le Cimetière marin" has detected the complex repetition of the sun-skull-tear series in two otherwise unrelated texts. My initial delineation of Valéry's tear-work, moreover, in the essay already alluded to, was an effort to save Mauron's own remarkable superimpositions of Valéry's poems from regressing beneath their own most liberating potential. It ended with a reading of Mauron on an early poem, "Baignée," that takes up the series we have just encountered once again. The poem begins:

> Un fruit de chair se baigne en quelque jeune vasque,
> (Azur dans les jardins tremblants) mais hors de l'eau,
> Isolant la torsade aux puissances de casque,
> Luit ce chef d'or que tranche à la nuque un tombeau.

(A fruit of flesh bathes in some young basin, / [Azure in the trembling gardens] but outside the water, / Isolating the coil with its helmet-like powers, / Shines this golden head sliced at the nape by a tomb.)

In the luminous head ("chef d'or") above the grave ("tombeau"), we find the decor of "Le Cimetière marin." The poem ends, moreover, with the bather's arm brushing away an insect in orbit around her head:

> Si l'autre [bras], courbé sous le beau firmament
> Parmi la chevelure immense qu'il humecte,
> Capture dans l'or simple un vol ivre d'insecte.

(If the other [arm], curved beneath the beautiful firmament / Midst the immense head of hair it moistens, / Captures in the simple gold a drunken flight of an insect.)

The gesture is essentially that of the Parque at the beginning of her poem ("Cette main, sur mes traits qu'elle rêve effleurer"). The insect, that is, corresponds to the tear. Now in Mauron's interpretation that insect figures a "fascinated lucidity" spying on—and ultimately repressing—a "fascinating image." "Henceforth the witness will be opposed to the sleeping woman as the sun is to the skull. . . . Such a duality is characteristic of the poems of this period." The tripartite system (sun-skull-tear) has been reduced to a dualism, and the insect-tear has been absorbed centripetally by the solar head. That obliteration of the poem's disruptive tear-work by Mauron, I have argued, is a falling short—in the name of psychoanalysis—of the poet's own affinity with Freud at his most virulent. In absorbing the insect-tear back into the luminous head, Mauron has effaced the rudiments of a theory of the unconscious (dis)articulated by the poetry itself.

In the present poetico-political context, however, it seems worth observing a significant link between that act of absorption and the practice of superimposition itself. Mauron regarded that technique as the beginning of literary analysis, the necessary surrogate of the psychoanalyst's "free associations." It was to be a more radical procedure than "comparison," in which the individuality of texts was maintained: "Superimposition, on the contrary, blurs out each text, and one must be willing to attend only to the enigmatic coincidences." Whence the effect of uncanniness. Now Mauron's acknowledged "source" for the technique of superimposition was Francis Galton and his efforts at "composite portraiture." Galton managed to project simultaneously the photographs of several members of an actual or alleged family and derive therefrom a generic image. But the knowledge gained thereby had a rather precise political coefficient. Thus Galton, discoursing on one series of his composite portraits: "I have also various criminal types, composed from the photographs of men convicted of heinous crimes. They are instructive as showing the type of face that is apt to accompany criminal tendencies *before* (if I may be allowed the expression) the features have become brutalized by crime. The brands of Cain are varied; therefore the special expressions of different criminals do not reinforce one another in the composite, but disappear. What remains are types of faces on which some one of the many brands of Cain is frequently to be set." The original object of "superimposition," then, is skull type, sought in an effort to determine the innate and inherited inferiority—or superiority—of various racial types. Which is to suggest that the most characteristic technique of "literary Freudianism" was borrowed from the arsenal of "social Darwinism." It is a fact to which Mauron, in effacing Valéry's tear-work and the historical crisis in European self-confidence it mediates, pays unwitting and oblique homage.

The extent, in fact, to which composite portraiture was to find in skull type its ideal subject is revealed by the fact that it was introduced in France by Vacher de Lapouge. Indeed the first text of "anthroposociologie" proper to appear in his annotated bibliography begins with a summary of Galton's inquiries into heredity and ends with the description of an apparatus developed by Vacher "for the photographic production of images composed with the help of negatives." "Composite portraiture," the basis of "superimposition of texts," was to figure as a minor technique in the new science of "eugenics," which received its appellation from Galton and would form the core of Vacher's practical politics. Here, in conclusion, we allude but briefly to the horizon of this inquiry. Consider, on the one hand, Galton, at the end of his treatise on *Probability, the Foundation of Eugenics:* "When the desired fullness of information shall have been acquired, then, and not till then, will be the fit moment to proclaim a 'Jehad' or Holy War against customs and prejudices that impair the physical and moral faculties of our race." On the other hand, Vacher: "I am convinced that in the next century, people will be slaughtering each other by the thousands for one or two degrees more or less in cephalic index. . . . The last sentimental souls will be able to witness whole populations given to copious orgies of extermination." Somewhere between those two cries to race war, we find Mauron, heir to Galton's technique, (mis)encountering Valéry, Vacher's student, in the privileged medium of a human skull. That the near-sublimity of their exchange should figure so profoundly *within* the dialogue of our two craniometers, a virtual silence at the heart of their shrillness, is a circumstance sufficiently engaging in its distribution of political and esthetic values to sustain some hope of its usefulness, beyond the idiosyncratic case of Valéry, in future articulations of literature and/as history in general.

JAMES R. LAWLER

"An Ever Future Hollow in the Soul"

Amère, sombre et sonore citerne
Sonnant dans l'âme un creux toujours futur
—"Le Cimetière marin"

In a succinct formula Valéry defined what he held to be the difference between himself and Mallarmé: "For him, the work; for me, the self." He seized upon a polarity, nurtured it from his Genoese night of revolt that determined a basic orientation. Where Mallarmé sought to turn the poem into an absolute that subsumed memories and dreams in the language of beauty, Valéry made self-awareness his matter and method whose unachievable consummation might yet be considered an ultimate goal, to be possessed "once and for all." Forbears and descendants, past and future, had no place; what alone counted was the eventless time of inner constraint. "In a nutshell, I do not take up again, nor do I undertake."

The notes he made during the drama of his twenty-first year show thus, first and foremost, the solitude he claimed with fierce obstinacy. Consciousness as island, the domain of the shipwrecked Robinson, would banish alien gods: "I am between self and self." Pride refused allegiances, initiated rigor, rejected the thoughts of all and sundry. Yet this pursuit of self-sufficiency was marked by a critically anxious relationship to the past. Just as he explained Baudelaire with respect to Hugo and Poe, and Mallarmé with respect to Baudelaire, so he saw himself as the antithetical product of his predecessors. "Reading is a military operation," he wrote; again: "A man of value (in matters of the mind) is, in my opinion, one who has killed beneath him

From *Yale French Studies*, no. 66 (1984). © 1984 by Yale University.

a thousand books." So it was that, when he addressed his debt to Mallarmé, he spoke in similarly strong metaphor of "the one head to be lopped off so as to decapitate all Rome." Rimbaud was an element in his formation, the more so since the poet of "Le Bateau ivre" was a counterpoise to Mallarmé in the way that turbulence might respond to calm. But he maintained a fertile combat with Mallarmé for over fifty years. There could not be a clear break but an unresolved tension which, keeping him at a peak of alertness, underwent three subsequent crises—1898 (the year of Mallarmé's death, the "grief of the intellect," the "sadness . . . of not knowing something or of being unable to find," which was followed by his own silence as a poet), 1912 (the brusque confrontation with Mallarmé by way of Thibaudet's letters, and his own return to poetic creation), the early forties (the "Mallarmé question" took on grave resonance as shown in the notebooks and the last essay published in *Le Point* in early 1944)—that corresponded to pivotal moments in his life. He did not speak of "influence" for the word was too vague, and the figure of a transferred liquid misleading. Instead, he named a "decisive spiritual conquest," an "instantaneous intimate scandal" by which he had been "converted into a fanatic." The connection was analyzed in the notebooks and a series of essays, but the evidence of this revisionary bond is subtly inscribed in the whole range of his poetry itself. The structure—mind, poem—that resumes the world with a finality analogous to Mallarmé's "Work"; the mythical Narcissus who, like Hérodiade, discovers the terrors of an intrusive self-awareness; language, syntax, form; voice, tone, phrasing: all were explored with a jealous sidelong glance at the one poet he must, for his own reason's sake, resist.

The struggle, in a personality as egotistic as Valéry's, gave his thought unique denseness. We may apply to him the words he wrote of Verlaine: "His art, rather than heralding another, implies that a previous one is being fled." Nevertheless the poetry of his fortieth year was not allowed to emerge of its own accord like some fruit of natural growth: external events intervened with the outbreak of the First World War that brought history to the forefront of his concerns. Public turmoil became a condition of the genesis of *La Jeune Parque* and, indeed, its constant accompaniment. From a study of the manuscripts we see that the substance and vital charge of his poem were found in 1914 and 1915, and that their development coincided with the early dark period of the war. "Who would believe that certain verse was written by a man waiting on news bulletins, his thoughts at Verdun and uninterruptedly so?" "I well know I wrote it *sub signo Martis*. . . . I cannot conceive of its having been written otherwise than as a result of the war. . . . I had finally told myself I was carrying out a duty, paying homage to something about to disappear." In this way the sphere of reversibility posited in 1892—not the act itself but "my inviolable *Pure Possibility*" like the dice forever uncast—fractured under the pressure of the moment. Along the line by which the Young Fate would summon fresh resources and find the sensible dawn of her being, Valéry experienced poetry as temporal imperative.

It becomes important, then, to envisage *La Jeune Parque* and the group of poems composed in its margins as the expression of a disquietude that sought to encompass the authority of Mallarmé and much else. Valéry acknowledged a line of poets whom, in a sense, he wished to serve as guarantors: he named a cultural heritage, undertook to shore its imperilled state. Mallarmé was a preeminent part of this domain, but also Euripides, Virgil, Petrarch; and Racine, Chénier, Baudelaire; and Hugo, Rimbaud, Claudel. From such a point of view there could be no question of looking to a future tradition and some throng of disciples. "I likened myself to those monks of the early Middle Ages who heard the civilized world crumbling about their cloisters and who no longer believed in anything but the end of the world; and yet they took great pains to write, in solid and obscure hexameters, grandiose poems with no readers in view. I confess that French seemed to me a dying language and that I made a point of considering it *sub specie aeternitatis*." A series of fragments, mobile sheets, interchangeable digressions without beginning or end were his multiple variations on the single motif of the mind entwining the body and playing out, to the extreme point of the attitudes implied, the quivering patterns of a severely constituted self-knowledge. *La Jeune Parque* could literally be developed at will and endlessly: "an infinitely extensible hydra that may also be cut up into pieces." In the same manner, the poems of *Charmes* were at first arranged according to the alphabetical order of their titles, each no more than a moment of the ungraspable whole.

> Pris que je suis dans le corps de ce jour
> Comme le vers est pris dans le poème.

Yet if an elegance of diction and tone determines the crystal of thought, time's passage cannot be forgotten. The self of "Le Cimetière marin" begins its monologue with words of sensuous fullness, but it is led to savor the bitter waters of its inner sea. Such is the obverse of the instant, however pure: past and future are no solace to the mind for which consciousness is merely—the word is at the source of Valéry's notebooks—an abyss of "self-variance."

One poetic text of the very many that date from the war period illustrates the author's despair, in the face of which he pursued his creation.

"Aux vieux livres," included in early lists of titles for publication in *Charmes,* did not finally appear until after Valéry's death. It is his elegy dedicated to literature which, in alternate alexandrines and hexasyllables, establishes the measure of a thwarted aspiration. A noble age is expiring: wisdom and imaginative depth are evoked in a sequence of legendary names—Delphi, Plato, the Swan; at the same time, we come to be aware that this language has lost its vitality. The movement delineates a fatal decadence as "murmuring marbles" and the "splendor of former suns" succumb to a barbarous age.

> Le parfum de Platon lentement s'évapore
> Du souvenir humain.

The gravity of tone, the resonance of imagery are those of an achieved composition. Despite memorable lines, however, the text will not reach the promise of artistic unity it at times shows: it is as if the theme of civilization doomed had led lyricism to fail and to leave only its ruins.

Yet Valéry was not content to indulge in the disabused acceptance of fragmentation, and it is by this radical transition that his work found a new maturity. *La Jeune Parque* was not abandoned to its plurality of voices but brought to a final form. "J'y suivais un serpent qui venait de me mordre." The wounded sensibility discovers its past, past anterior, present, it calls forth the tear that reveals the hidden islands of thought—"Mères vierges toujours"—and an expectancy of fulfilment. Such temporal articulations enabled Valéry to transform his multiple moments of salvaged time—detached, reversible—into a continuum of the self that poignantly learns its fate as commingling mortality and vibrant élan. The movement culminates in the discovery of sea, and sun, and reborn innocence:

> Alors, malgré moi-même, il le faut, ô Soleil,
> Que j'adore mon coeur où tu te viens connaître,
> Doux et puissant retour du délice de naître,
> Feu vers qui se soulève une vierge de sang
> Sous les espèces d'or d'un sein reconnaissant.

> (Then, against my will, I must, oh Sun,
> Worship my heart where you come to know yourself,
> Sweet strong return of birth's delight,
> Fire to which a virgin of blood raises herself
> Beneath the golden species of a grateful breast.)

A law is found in the tracings of body and mind, a linear progression leads to light through an anxious maze: after being lost in her depths, the Parque affirms her identity in the enactment of a solemn rite.

One may in this respect examine the dramatic evolution of a single passage. The theme of spring comes towards the end of the first half (lines 218–42) and plays a crucial role in the Young Fate's process of self-discovery. It can be traced back to a much earlier manuscript, the paper and handwriting of which seem to indicate the late nineties or shortly thereafter. Under the title "Avril," some of the characteristic energy of the definitive text is already evident.

> Les arbres regonflés et recouverts d'écailles
> Aux plus jeunes des vents livrent d'âpres batailles
> Et brûlant de verdir jusques à l'horizon
> Meuvent sur le soleil leur entière toison,
> Montent dans l'air amer avec toutes les ailes
> De feuilles par milliers qu'ils se donnent (sentent) nouvelles,
> Et par tous les rameaux suprêmes de leurs fronts
> Ils poussent à l'azur à travers mille troncs
> Un fleuve tendre, immense et secret (vague) sous les herbes.

The development has at first reading a splendid force; and, indeed, the first line will remain unchanged throughout several versions and in the final text; lines 4, 5, 6 and 9 will receive only slight modifications; while the general syntactical pattern will be retained. The group of alexandrines is caught up in a single forward scheme as nature is personified and as subterranean waters rise to unite with the sky. Grounded in an urgent dynamism, the enabling metaphor is that of martial struggle ("livrent d'âpres batailles," "poussent à travers mille troncs") for which Valéry turned not to the Mallarméan tradition but to the Hugolian one of rhetorical and imaginative crescendo. And yet, when many years later the lines were considered for inclusion in La Jeune Parque, they were radically transformed. The working drafts that have come down to us show the poet taking his already reworked version and rehandling it as if it were a simple raw material. With ever more meticulous attention the trees come to be envisaged as bodies projecting their strength on high, delving into the humus of memory, dreaming the form that is the substance of their song to be.

> Un chant spirituel
> S'élève des châteaux de feuille et de vapeur.

This will lead to the theme of the later "Au Platane" of Charmes with its plane tree as the marvellous symbol of poetic creation; but it does not significantly further the assimilation of "Avril" into the corpus of the text. What Valéry needed was, first, the verbal play of "rameau" (branch) and "rame" (oar) which will underpin the sweeping curve of physical effort; secondly, the sexual element which will take priority over the martial and, consonant with a vast act of love, focus the tenderness discreetly suggested in the first draft ("Un fleuve tendre"). He later wrote: "In order to soften the poem somewhat, I was forced to insert unplanned fragments which I wrote after the fact. All the sexual elements were added; for example the central passage on spring which now seems to be of essential importance." The sequence becomes richer in rhythmic and musical scope, and tributary—in the manner of no other passage in *La Jeune Parque*—to Rimbaud still more than to Hugo in the expression of a panic violence ("L'étonnant printemps rit, viole," "Aux déchirants départs des archipels superbes"). But a further aspect is of no less interest: the lines are now seen, not merely as renewal and reawakening, but also as a step consciously taken towards death: the Young Fate turns to the joys of the flesh and, at the same time, realizes the mortal sense of her yearnings and the bitter aftertaste of tenderness ("O Mort, respire enfin cette esclave de roi," "Un fleuve tendre, ô Mort"). Hence her enthusiasm is inseparable from a pathos that reveals a wholly new dimension. The fragment can now have an organic place in the complex and equivocal evolution that forms the action of the poem.

In the case of *Charmes* the change from original to final versions was no less surprising. Valéry opted in 1922 for an arbitrary order ("L'Abeille," "Au Platane," "Aurore," "Le Cantique des colonnes," "La Ceinture"), a scheme that held good for the first eighteen poems, the remaining four ("Le Sylphe," "Ebauche d'un serpent," "Le Rameur," "Palme") spelling out a reversal of the pattern. But the two editions of 1926 offer a notable modification that was further adjusted in 1929 by the removal of "Air de Sémiramis" to the *Album de vers anciens*. The poet had rethought his entire collection; he had set the number of pieces in both the *Album* and *Charmes* at twenty-one so as to impose a balance; and, instead of the observance of the alphabet or—as for the *Album*—of the approximate dates of conception, he had written an implicit dynamics into the sequence. Pursuing the notion of the "livre composé" characteristic of the nineteenth century and elaborated by Baudelaire, he arrived at a scheme that may best be described in terms of his definition of the sonnet: "a rotation," he said, "of the same body around a point or axis." For the poems are no longer treated separately but as constituent parts of a whole whose extremes are "Aurore" and "Palme"—the morning ode of the intellect and sensibility, the parable of the creative act as inner reward. Time enters the collection, which has both origin and goal: the poems are arranged in six groups around the focal drama of "La Pythie," whose action engenders a new language in the manner of a dolorous parturition: "Honneur des Hommes, Saint LANGAGE." We follow step by step the creative self as it explores the forest of the senses, its "forêt sensuelle" ("Aurore," "Au Platane," "Cantique des colonnes"); plumbs the nature of desire ("L'Abeille," "Poésie," "Les Pas"); recognizes the tenuous interconnection between ideas and image, death and life ("La Ceinture," "La Dormeuse," "Fragments du Narcisse"); seduces the sensibility with lucid art, and is seduced ("Le Sylphe," "L'Insinuant," "La Fausse Morte," "Ebauche d'un serpent"); considers the interplay of poetry and abstract thought ("Les Grenades," "Le Vin perdu," "Intérieur," "Le Cimetière marin"); looks back at last on its achieved creation before turning to the artistic quest ever re-begun ("Ode secrète," "Le Rameur," "Palme"). Thus mind and senses, will and patience, revolt and submission, make the framework of a poem three times as long as *La Jeune Parque,* its structure more richly resolved than could be any chance accumulation. In "Aurore" a future is perceived that the reader will come to know; and the wisdom of "Palme," emerging from past endeavor, stands as the happy sign of self-integration.

We recognize that this ordered sequence goes beyond a particular an-ecdote or narrative curve or legendary progression in its depersonalization of the text. The self is seen—not in the partial fashion of the first *Charmes*—as universal; its acts are not those of one but of all. It is less than adequate to say that we here take to ourselves the poetic persona in the way of every great lyric expression, since Valéry builds into his writing a cycle of move-ments that discover mind and body in answer to the author's individually defined "knowledge of the living organism." Attention, patience, will, erotic desire are those of the intellectual sensibility which, eschewing the all-too-human, shows language disengaged from the quotidian cursus of thought. In this sense, led as we are by the system of poems, we realize that the collection is not only exemplary but didactic. The word would no doubt have hardly satisfied Valéry but nothing corresponds more closely to his effort to transform the art of poetry into the reader's own complete spiritual act. The book of poems proposes the scheme of a full and free and ideal exchange of sensuousness, feeling, intellection, so that, as he wrote, "it is not sufficient to explicate the text, we must also explain the thesis." In the revised *Parque* as in the definitive sequence of *Charmes,* this thesis is the implied one of sumptuous discovery of the resources of the self as it engages in the creative act. At the end of the collection, "Palme," with its Judeo-Christian symbol-

ism and exultant register, gives voice to a moral borne by its sensible strain
and thereby retroactively endows the twenty poems that precede it with an
implicit orientation.

> Patience, patience,
> Patience dans l'azur!
> Chaque atome de silence
> Est la chance d'un fruit mûr!

Again:

> Tu n'as pas perdu ces heures
> Si légère tu demeures
> Après ces beaux abandons.

All has become as simple and necessary as the knowledge that loss is gain,
that time is redeemed, that poetic meditation is the verdant season of a secret
ripening.

Valéry's pronouncements on the theory and practice of poetry were
frequent and various after the publication of *Charmes*. Strong with his own
experience, he enunciated the principle of artistic creation as a law of an-
nexation like Baudelaire faced by Hugo, himself faced by Mallarmé ("The
lion is made of the sheep he digests"); underlined the condition of poetry as
verbal act; insisted on the inventive potential of strict forms ("I am free,
therefore I fetter myself "); defined the conditions of the alliance of fine sound
and fine sense. His inaugural lecture at the Académie Française was a brilliant
statement of classicism as conceived and justified by a writer who could not
approach the rules in the fashion of a poet of Racine's time but for whom
skepticism aroused the need for order. "Doubt leads to form." The Surrealists found in him a figure of derision whose dicta they need merely reverse
to express what they themselves believed; but he could condemn Surrealism
for seeking "salvation by way of leftovers." Literary fashions, he knew, are
of a day, and he might still address a future reader who would be his loyal
adversary—"quelqu'un qui viendra après." "The poem must give the idea
of a perfect thought"; "Thought must be hidden in the verse like nutritional
virtue in a fruit"; "A metaphor is *what happens* when we *look at things in
a certain way,* just as we sneeze when we stare at the sun"; "Poets . . . you
may look down upon novelists, philosophers, and all who by credulousness
are enslaved by words—those who *must* believe that their discourse is *real*
by virtue of its contents and that it signifies some reality. But you know that
the reality of a discourse is words alone, and forms." His statements aim to
cut the fat from a critical practice still obeisant to the nineteenth century,

which was accustomed to explain the work by the man, or by the supposed feeling, or by the literary influence. Valéry spoke as an educator who could not but impart a lesson; he sought to *come clean* so as to ensure a future for art. At a time when poetry ran the risk of being engulfed, what was more urgent than to point to its myths?

From 1937 until a few months before his death in 1945, he was the Republic's official Professor of Poetics. In his courses at the Collège de France he developed ideas that had been sketched out in the notebooks but which lacked definitive shape. His teaching held poetry to be inseparable from awareness of the intellectual sensibility and the organically based laws of symmetry, complementarity and contrast; and herein lay the seed of a liberated rationale and practice. The paradox of this situation was only too apparent. The disabused skeptic had become a spokesman, the poet a draftsman of the poetics to be. His link with Mallarmé was in the final instance an earnest of the future: he could articulate a view alien to Surrealist and post-Surrealist tastes that could serve an art the exact character of which was as yet unclear. No doubt he felt painfully the end of his Europe and the imminent threat to values he had lived by; his anticipation was more and more enmeshed in anxiety. As he wrote in *Le Solitaire:* "I am weary of being a creature." How could he turn his mind to what he took to be the most inconceivable of thoughts, that "there will be men after us"? And yet he continued to write and, on the last pages of his notebook, stated his belief in the work he had completed: "After all, I have done what I could"; again: "*I am sure of that worth.*" The presentiment of Europe's doom, his own "Maladetta primavera" of love, the futility of hope: this is the groundnote constantly recurring; yet the spirit of his writing runs ahead of despair. Equivocal in its intensity, the flame is his figure of an art that lights the future yet itself is consumed. Still more eloquent is the symbol of the bottomless ocean like the poem ever to be achieved, although inherently resonant with the cadence of death.

> Amère, sombre et sonore citerne
> Sonnant dans l'âme un creux toujours futur

His attempt to separate the pure from the impure was not viable for the generation that came after his own. Yet tradition cannot suppress one of its strongest links as found in a thought that cultivates the ceaseless potential of the intellect, and poetry—"creux toujours futur"—its poignant exemplum.

ANSELM HAVERKAMP

Poetic Construction and Hermeneutic Tradition in "Le Cimetière marin"

O VIE,
Plus je pense à toi, VIE,
Moins tu te rends à la pensée
—"Paraboles"

Valéry's Socrates (1921), fallen into the post-Platonic aporia of a *Dialogue des morts* with Phaedrus, tells a story of the "objet ambigu" that as a child he found washed ashore, held in his hands, and threw back into the sea: the myth of the lost potential of a philosophical tradition caught in the "empirical opposition between philosophical intention and poetic form" in the belatedness of hermeneutic reflection. Valéry himself (1920), having returned to the subject of poetic form at the highpoint of his life, writes about the "cimetière marin" of his birthplace, Sète—"à peu près le seul de mes poèmes où j'aie mis quelque chose de ma propre vie": his cemetery by the sea is the autobiographically determined location of that hermeneutic reflection that only reaches the Platonic Socrates in the finality of Hades because Valéry could recapture it only in a retrospective glance over the process of philosophical tradition. The autobiographical reflection on the critical moments and turning-points of his life ("Ce n'est pas un rêve"), which Valéry demands of Socrates in the story of the "objet ambigu," can serve as a hermeneutic model for the historical efficacy of tradition (as *wirkungsgeschichtlicher Zusammenhang*) only because it presupposes a reflection on the opposition

From *Text und Applikation—Theologie, Jurisprudenz und Literaturwissenschaft im hermeneutischen Gespräch: Poetik und Hermeneutik 9,* edited by Manfred Fuhrmann, Hans Robert Jauss, and Wolfhart Pannenberg. © 1981 by Wilhelm Fink.

between philosophical intention and poetic form factually experienced in the course of his life. In *La Jeune Parque* (1917), after twenty years of silence, Valéry takes up the philosophical motif of the "constitution of self-consciousness," "of a 'conscious consciousness' conditioned by waking and coming-to-oneself out of sleep, this living death." About the same time, he wrote to Lefèvre what was to become the first stanzas of "Le Cimetière marin."

II

"Ce cimetière existe," Valéry conceded to occasional questioning, while noting more precisely in a letter to Gide: "*Le Cimetière marin* serait donc le type de ma *poésie* vraie et surtout les parties plus abstraites de ce poème." This autobiographical occasion is as clearly insufficient for the reading of the poem as its author is without authority: "Pas d'autorité de l'auteur," Valéry wrote, rejecting the credibility of certain interpretations, in this case [Gustave] Cohen's academic "explication" of the text (1933): "il n'y a pas de vrai sens d'un texte." The refusal of the author Valéry to accept responsibility for the readings of his readers is not the "hermeneutic nihilism" that [Hans-Georg] Gadamer had in mind. The incriminating sentence in the *Commentaires de Charmes* to Alain's annotated edition (1929)—"Mes vers ont le sens qu'on leur prête"—has an openly polemical meaning. He directs his attack against "l'invention de l'exercice scolaire absurde qui consiste à faire mettre des vers en prose," a practice that even Gadamer doesn't favor, especially when he urges that hermeneutics must do justice to "the experience of art." Yet what becomes of Gadamer's postulate—"Aesthetics must become part of hermeneutics"—when the relationship between aesthetic experience and hermeneutic reflection no longer coincides with the relationship between poetics and hermeneutics entailed by this project? Valéry: "Si l'auteur se connaît un peu trop, si le lecteur se fait actif, que devient le plaisir, que devient la Littérature?" That aesthetic experience must rely on hermeneutic reflection, that it finally got caught vis-à-vis hermeneutic reflection in an irreversible relationship of dependence: this was Hegel's most general diagnosis, a problematic not remote from Valéry's own.

But neither could Valéry's point be that hermeneutic reflection must be totally adequate to aesthetic experience: "poetic construction" barricades itself against the universal hermeneutic mediation of aesthetic experience. If it presupposes reflection in order to come into being, the reverse is not true: aesthetic experience is not bound to reflection in order to make itself "understood"; hermeneutics remains external to its efficacy. For Valéry, this has well-known implications not only for linguistic theory but also for the theory of history (independent of Hegel). While he spoke in detail about the linguistic implications, the historical implications (which remain largely unthematic in his theoretical statements) become exemplary in such texts as "Le Cimetière marin" and *Eupalinos*. Less that is new can be said about his linguistic theory than about its historical implications, especially when the two, history and theory, are questioned together.

"Observons que des conditions de forme précises ne sont autre chose que l'expression de l'intelligence et de la conscience que nous avons des *moyens* dont nous pouvons disposer, et de leur portée, comme de leurs limites et de leurs defauts." So runs the pertinent sentence "au sujet du Cimetière marin" with which Valéry elucidates "la plus poétique des idées, l'idée de composition." Above all, poetic form is seen as composition because it arises constructively from the poet's mastery of his material, a condition which for its part explains the priority of construction over the inspiration of the author. In the emphasis on the constructive character of poetics, both stages of reflection (as conscious consciousness) are superimposed: in the process of poetic composition the conscious manipulation of subject matter presupposes a consciousness of its operational range, and the reflexivity of the procedure becomes the reflection of the hermeneutic condition of composition. The reflection of poetic form (as form) thus surpasses the "harmless traditionalism" associated with Hegel that Gadamer's hermeneutics still favors. It alters the hermeneutic character of poetry and leaves the framework of hermeneutic reflection behind in that (as an "aesthetic" moment) it goes from being a mere *a posteriori* application to a constructive moment of poetics.

[Theodor W.] Adorno speaks of a "second reflection" that arises in opposition to the first, hermeneutic one, raising it to a higher power at the expense of its hermeneutic returns: "Second reflection takes hold of the mode of procedure, the language of the work of art in the widest sense, but it aims towards blindness [. . .]: with the ascendence of reflection and through its increased force, the subject matter itself is obscured." Unlike traditional poetry of reflection (pejoratively, "*Gedankenlyrik*"), which requires from the reader's reflection a payment in the same currency as that deposited in the poem, the reflection constructively transacted in the poem is preserved only in the reflex of poetic composition: "reduced to an element of mere intuition [*Anschauung*]." This reflex also sparks reflection: it awakens it more than it needs it. Yet through the needle's eye of the poem no path leads back to the reflection of the author whose opinions must be solicited only by those who can't deal with the freedom of reading or, obligated to professional classroom teaching, do not want to trust their own intuition precisely when it is required to set another in motion. Valéry, in the midst of such conflicting demands, felt very strange and explained his ambivalence to Cohen's interpretation in terms of this estrangement, when he witnessed how his poem, inextricably bound with his own reflection, was treated *ex cathedra* as a scholarly object.

If it is correct that the specifically "aesthetic" reflection of poetry (as poetry) is the reflection of its own hermeneutic framing, then poetic construction presupposes more than mere linguistic awareness in dealing with language. If one reduces Valéry's linguistic insights to the intimation of modern linguistics, one gets only the linguistic "positive" of the hermeneutic "negative" that has served as a commonplace of the modern lyric since Mallarmé. Such positivity allows only for a hermeneutically "naive," that is, thematic distinction between Mallarmé and Valéry, either in terms of thematic rigor or thematic flexibility. Retrospectively (1931), Valéry writes that his debt to Mallarmé is "la possession consciente de la fonction du langage et le sentiment d'une liberté supérieure de l'expression au regard de laquelle toute pensée n'est qu'un incident, un événement particulier." Bound with the conscious possession of the function of language is the feeling of a higher freedom of expression: one becomes aware of language, the "most basic of all phenomena," as the horizon of the possibility of all thought, as the poetically available space of expression, "la condition verbale de la littérature."

Yet a problem arises here. Measured by the ideal of musical composition, the thematic weakness of literature hampers poetic construction. While the model of mathematical construction can be applied in music without diminution, the analogous poetic construction is tied to a thematic substrate upon which language is firmly established. This is true even in the "reificational effect" (*Verdinglichung*) resulting from the "materiality" of signification. Consequently, mere conscious departure from the accidentally received conventions of expression, as well as from the linguistic self-thematization of language (as language), won't do; Valéry's "skepticism of language" and Mallarmé's "magic of language" can agree here only negatively. Rather, thematic concentration (rigorous or flexible) can only be the result of composition, not of some "subject matter" to which composition conforms: "Je rêve donc que je trouve progressivement mon ouvrage à partir de pures conditions de forme, de plus en plus réfléchies,—précisées jusqu'au point qu'elles proposent ou imposent presque ... un *sujet*—ou du moins, une famille de sujets." This, however, does not mean that there are, occasionally, no thematic opportunities for composition: "Fabrication d'un poème—se place dans les mots—autour d'un mot-sujet ou d'une impression laisser venir les mots appelés à divers titres." Paraphrases like Valéry's aloof commentaries encounter, as far as possible, the thematic element of the poem, yet lack its specific poetic composition. They assume from the outset that the poem wants to "say" something where it wants to "make" something: "Si donc l'on m'interroge; si l'on s'inquiète (comme il arrive, et parfois assez vivement) de ce que j'ai 'voulu dire' dans tel poème, je réponds que je n'ai pas *voulu dire,* mais *voulu faire,* et que ce fut l'intention de *faire* qui *a voulu* ce que j'ai *dit.*"

As the constructive moment of poetics, the *poietic* (in the strict sense) necessarily presupposes the opposition of immanent poetics to the linguistic situation of the age. Contrary to a denotational semantics of teleological explanation, it posits the pragmatically unrestricted ambiguity of linguistic possibilities: "univers de relations réciproques, analogue à l'univers des sons, dans lequel naît et se meut la pensée musicale. Dans cet univers poétique, la résonance l'emporte sur la causalité, et la 'forme,' loin de s'évanouir dans son effet, est comme *redemandée* par lui." That which was indiscriminately conceived of as the one imitation of nature in the traditional concept of mimesis falls apart in the moment of non-mimetic construction and mimetic "resonance." The musical metaphorics of composition and resonance bring the "dialectic" of mimesis and rationality into an orientational schema that clarifies the complementary participation of poetic construction and poetic language in poetic form: whereas the metaphor of composition implies the nonmimetic relation of poetic composition to nature, the metaphor of resonance implies the mimetic relation of poetic language to nature whereby the constructively constituted form, as an artificially resonant body, brings the poetic qualities of language to reverberation. The "resonance phenomenon" of language is thereby to be thought of as a kind of "biofeedback" that first adapts mimetically to the natural environment and confirms the linguistic constitution of consciousness as the "self-constituting momentum of man."

Valéry is indebted to Mallarmé for this conscious perception of the resonance phenomenon of language. Poetic construction, however, also presupposes a conscious consciousness beyond the "mechanism," as he sometimes calls it, to which the resonance phenomenon of language yields in hermeneutic reflection. Valéry's anti-Platonic, anti-Cartesian turn against the traditional oppositions of nature and art, Being and consciousness, is the consequence of a consciousness that sees the contradiction of rationality and mimetic resonance firmly established in the belatedness of hermeneutic reflection. Hence the anti-historical affect of poetic construction against all traditional stabilizers. If poetic construction is to help bring about the mi-

metic resonance of language, it must raze disturbing interferences, free the
reader from the ground-in hermeneutic attitude in which the thematic reception of poetry is fixed on the representation of poetic images. For the
thematic weakness of poetry is the weakness of its interpreters for "images."
One takes the representation of poetic images generated in reading as a
semantic substrate thematically like the objects of perception in everyday
communication. But the image is first of all a mode through which representation (*Vorstellung*) comes into being in reading, not an object perceived
in it; perception is only feigned by the image and the representation of its
objects is later interpreted only as if it were perception. In the impression of
immediate perception, the image mediates the momentary presence of objects
whose actual absence it presupposes.

Strictly speaking, poetic images function representationally only because
what is represented in them is not (no longer) the object of the perception
within whose horizon it is represented. The hermeneutic prejudice therefore
has it that the images conveyed in poetry have a metaphorical meaning that
refers to an imaginary object in the same way the meaning of everyday expressions refers to the object of sensory perception. This is supported by an
optical background metaphorics of aesthetic effect according to which the
cognitive achievement of poetry is analogous to the perception of external
objects in the quasi-sensory communication of inner images. But what is
most decisive here is not the positing of a copying relation of poetry to
reality so much as the belief in a semantic horizon common to both in which
the aesthetic experience is to be hermeneutically reflected and communica-
tively resolved.

The "sensory effect" of mimetic resonance, however, has nothing to do
with the hermeneutic relation in which poetic images are interpreted. Mimetic resonance comes into being not through poetic images but rather
through poetic form, which before all visual effects is developed from the
phonetic qualities of linguistic materials, not from the semantic qualities that
make them interpretable; it is mediated through construction, not through
the interpretation of previously constituted images. To bring resonance to
reverberation requires a vehicular capacity of poetic form—requires such
"sensory effects" as the fiction of sign-free references to objects grounded
in images linguistically motivated through what Valéry names "le sens du
son": "une correspondance mystérieusement exacte entre les *causes* sensi-
bles, qui constituent la forme et les *effets* intelligibles, qui sont le *fond*."

Valéry's own statements on *Poésie pure* (1928), however, have furthered
the substantialist misunderstanding that poetry conveys a uniquely precious
substrate: "substance noble et vivante" authenticated without adulteration

in poetic form. In this case, the visual orientation of poetry would only be replaced by an acoustic one. The so-called clarity of poetic images would only be replaced by a so-called darkness of poetic tones that no longer would serve the emotive coloring or rhetorical heightening of cognitive acts but rather would constitute self-standing poetic "substances" in their own right. In the structural reification of poetic coloration, mimetic resonance becomes only the trusted negative of what was formerly understood as mimetic evidence, i.e., the manifest qualities of perceptual imagery. The result is heightened hermeneutic reflections, not their dismantling, as one knows from the way the so-called "symbolists" were received by literary criticism.

Valéry's theoretical initiative reaches further than these contradictions, but the question remains how his poetic praxis copes with them. Theoretically, it would be no trouble to refer the substantialist explanation of "poésie pure" back to a functional determination of its semantic ambiguity. Mimetic resonance, as the original quality of poetic language, would thus only be the mythically robed version of the anthropological hypothesis according to which it is a function of man's linguistic relation to the world. Viewed as a semantic correlate of the affinity between inner and outer nature brought to resonance in poetic form, ambiguity would not be the goal so much as the surface reflection of the "aesthetic back-formation of the real in the horizon of possibilities" achieved in poetic composition: "it mediates a consciousness of aesthetic freedom itself." However, the fact that more is at stake here than the freedom of the constructively active poet, a constructively opened free space of reception in which the diligence of the reader rivals the construction of the author, is not yet guaranteed by mere ambiguity but rather depends on the mode of reading provoked by it in the text.

III

At first glance "Le Cimetière marin" reads like a piece of traditional poetry of reflection: a poetry that has maintained itself selectively to tradition, on the one hand cited, on the other rejected, but in each case appropriating reflection in the same measure, whether in demanding or dismissing it. In its best works, such poetry had often exploited an artfully arranged obscurity, "beau désordre," remote from philosophical clarity and counter to any thematic order of consistency. Obscurity had already resulted from the representational process of presenting an object to consciousness (*Vergegenwärtigung*) in moments determining, for their part, the historical efficacy of tradition. Reflection itself obscured the most obvious sense of ordinary linguistic understanding, the most easily paraphrasable content of poetic diction. Such reflection at work in poetry resisted the rhetorical model of metaphor and paraphrase and instead dealt with the hermeneutic model of an *allegoresis* within which poetic and hermeneutic reflection could together fuse a horizon of common tradition beyond the abysses of historical discontinuity. Thus the obscurity of tradition required allegorical clarification and exemplary generalization. To interpreters having undergone the requisite hermeneutic asceticism, such a dark inscrutability of tradition offered, as an added attraction, the quiet pleasure of an always new glass bead game.

Nevertheless, with every application to new contexts such allegorical reading meets the resistance of an irreducible remainder of tradition. This remainder appears not in the contents of a work so much as in the lingering tones of past texts that, like a kind of "preverbal melody" and before every representational activity, guide every appropriation and transformation of tradition in the poem. In this way, the alleged "substance" of tradition is again reduced to a rhetorical function of the lyrically articulated consciousness.

How much in this respect Valéry can be distinguished from Petrarch is difficult to say. More precisely, the question here concerns that which separates "Le Cimetière marin" from the allegorical reading of traditional poetry of reflection. Valéry defines his intention: "Il n'y a pas un temps pour le 'fond' et un temps de la 'forme': et la composition en ce genre ne s'oppose pas seulement au désordre ou à la disproportion, mais à la *décomposition*." That on first reading "Le Cimetière marin" appears meant to be read and interpreted in a deeper, traditionally allegorical sense cannot be refuted by any formal contradiction of the text encountered in the first reading. A richer, more complex repertoire of word plays and allusions maintained over twenty-four stanzas could hardly be contemplated, nor the challenges of traditional poetry of reflection brought to a more outstanding realization.

Moreover, the poem's pre-Socratic epigram opens a horizon of hermeneutic tradition whose Pindaric signature holds in enigmatic distance what the modern paraphrase makes trivially familiar: "O mon âme, n'aspire pas à la vie éternelle mais épuise le possible!" In the language of the earliest beginnings of the lyric, this sentence brings out something it has in common with the poem, an intended effect that in the Greek quotation is more obscure than enlightening. Literally the cemetery of Sète, "Le Cimetière marin" appears in the light of a warning to live in the finite rather than to strive for eternity. It is the perfect allegorical locale that tradition foresees for such reflections: "that 'sea cemetery' reminiscent of the Ambrosian landscape which becomes successively a roof covered with white pigeons, a temple of Time, a flock of sheep with a shepherd dog, a multicolored hydra; all this is based on the same Christian poetics of kaleidoscopic transformation of symbols," as Spitzer says. Valéry's title thus receives from Pindar's motto a hermeneutic commentary on the logic of interpretation to which the reading of the poem must yield. In the relation between allegorical landscape and hermeneutic application, landscape becomes the flexible vehicle of a reflection whose hermeneutic interest aims at the allegorical deep-structure of a thematic surface:

> Ce toit tranquille, où marchent des colombes,
> Entre les pins palpite, entre les tombes;
> Midi le juste y compose de feux
> La mer, la mer, toujours recommencée!
> O récompense après une pensée
> Qu'un long regard sur le calme des dieux!
>
> (st. 1)

The process of interpretation follows in the text the interactive structure of thematic "vehicle" and reflexive "tenor": in the first stanza two lines of commentary follow four lines of text. The metaphorical qualities of the thematic fields of cemetery and sea—both a "focus," the boundary of sea and eternity—mark the hermeneutic frames that guide the allegorical perspective of the reading. In the course of consistent allegorical organization, the metaphorical possibilities of the poem are transformed into a continuous pattern of imagery, into the tendentious equivocality of a verbal metaphorics that is nothing but the relative flexibility of thematic fields fixed by certain images. This occurs with the help of the tenor of reflection activated in the poem: "Le rôle du vrai poète philosophe," comments Cohen, "n'est pas de créer des systèmes . . . , mais d'éprouver et de nous faire éprouver, à propos des notions métaphysiques les plus abstraites, des sensations profondes et vivantes, traduites en images neuves et fortes." His version of an allegorical reading turns "Le Cimetière marin" into a drama of the history of ideas in which "Non-Etre ou Néant" ("symbolisée par Midi") and "conscience" ("celle du poète sans doute, celle de l'homme aussi") are bound up with the author ("acteur à la fois et spectateur de ce drame"), namely, in the following four acts: "Immobilité," "Mobilité," "Mort ou Immortalité?," "Triomphe du momentané" (and, of course, "de la création poétique").

This kind of overworked obscurity of the poem belongs to the semantic structure of the text (or so it is supposed). To interpretation it appears as a "quality" of the poem's allegorical workmanship or, better, as a quality of the images transplanted in the text to thematic fields whose reflexive tenor leads to underlying "ideas." Clearly, the obscurity with which the allegorical reading of "Cimetière marin" is involved concerns that constitutive equivocality of hermeneutic tradition in which the historical efficacy of consciousness not unwillingly ensnares itself. One can thus also understand Valéry's references to the accidental ending of the poem and the similar arbitrariness in the series of individual stanzas, including the conclusion "il n'y a pas de vrai sens d'un texte," which leaves the equivocality of the text up to the reader to figure out. As superficial reflex of the reflection transacted in poetic composition, this equivocality testifies to a hermeneutic tradition that is no longer the "contents" of the text but now rather only a "pretext" for its allegorical reading. In this manner, equivocality becomes the touchstone of the hermeneutic attitude of reading: either in the intention of allegorical interrogation of tradition or in the intention of its critical resolution, hermeneutically generalizing or critically distancing. Historically oriented, poetic construction becomes a criticism that maintains itself destructively rather than selectively to tradition. It persists in the process of desedimenting tradition, inciting those conflicts, played out between old and new readings, that characterize the structure of the modern lyric. In the opposition of immanent poetics to the paradigmatic fixations of contemporary linguistic usage, the critique of this historically transmitted hermeneutic tradition opens the space of its operations, its "deconstruction" of received readings. From Gnostic "pseudomorphosis" to hermeneutic "fusion of horizons," the means of this critique have been the allegorical procedure of interpretation; its anticritical function—to propagate truth with method—has been evident since the Gnostic generalization of the Platonic horizon of late antiquity.

But "Le Cimetière marin" cannot be read anti-allegorically in this manner merely because it leads on first reading to the equivocal pretext of tradition. Despite all attempts, in the variable course of tradition, to exhaust the interactive potential between thematic vehicle and reflexive tenor, an unavailing residue remains, one which becomes the critical moment of reading. In that it confirms in the equivocality of the poem the excess of tradition (of which the poem is an allegorical exemplar), this remainder frustrates the allegorical fulfillment of reading. It lets the equivocality of the text turn into the equivocality of a pretext; it guides allegorical interpretation away from the text itself and prevents reading from coming to rest.

The anti-allegorical moment of this mobilization of reading can be easily tested in dialogical schemas of question and answer that reduce the interactive structure of vehicle and tenor to its hermeneutic denominator. The hermeneutic reflection of lines 5–6 presupposes as answer to the experience of lines 1–4 a question that does not follow from the allegorical interpretation of these lines but rather must contradict them, since allegory is always an answer. The supplementarity of the relationship between title and motto now becomes clearer: in that the lyrical quotation helps allegorically to localize the allegorical locale, it contradicts the allegorical aim and the hermeneutic interest in it. If one understands the "logic" of question and answer as the rhetorical postulate of the interactions allegorically realized in the relationship between vehicle and tenor, one can begin to articulate the latent resistance in which the way for the anti-allegorical turning of the poem is prepared. This resistance of course does not become obvious before the "livre" and "vivre" rhyme of the last stanza. The line "Le vent se lève! . . . Il faut tenter de vivre!" moreover repeats the same schema and resolves it. In this stanza (24) the relationship between vehicle and tenor is no longer decidable.

From this angle, the poem lets itself be read differently in the second reading: what was before only a literal surface for allegorical meaning becomes a literal meaning for an allegorical surface. "Ce toit tranquille, où marchent des colombes" is no longer an excerpt of an ambrosial landscape: "Quiet that roof, where the doves are walking." Taking up the first stanza again in the last, the text reads: "Ce toit tranquille où picoraient des focs!" The most obscure word presents itself as the most literal, not the one that is allegorically most profound but rather the one that is contingently bound to the marine location. "Ce cimetière existe," Valéry explains: "Il domine la mer sur laquelle on voit les colombes, c'est-à-dire les barques des pêcheurs, errer, *picorer.* . . . Ce mot a scandalisé. Les marins disent d'un navire qui plonge de l'avant dans la lame, qu'il *pique du nez.* L'image est analogue. Elle s'impose à qui a vu la chose."

Beneath this Greek inscription no allegorical landscape with doves (les colombes) and the reflections to which they give rise, but the cemetery by the sea at Sète? Valéry seems at times to have been in doubt about the possibly misleading effect of the Pindar quotation, for in the early editions of the poem it is sometimes deleted. In any case, left in the Greek original it strengthens what the French translation compresses into a false single meaning: the linguistic link to the Mediterranean scene. Exhaustion of the possible means here exhaustion of the water displaced beneath the holds of ships. Following a commonplace influential since Vico, Valéry posits the "original metaphorical nature" of language, which in his statements on "poésie pure" he considers to be its poetic substance. It remains contradictory how the archaic pragmatics of language should serve the depragmatization of the modern linguistic situation. For the reading of "Le Cimetière marin," however, such obscurities of theory are not that important. What links Pindar's language with the language of the fishermen in Sète is a common practical relationship to the primordial mastery of nature. In relation to this, all conventional formalizations of modern linguistic usage are secondary, all hermeneutic reflections irrelevant, and hermeneutic tradition itself becomes nothing but a long drawn-out process of alienation.

In the relation between thematic vehicle and reflexive tenor, hermeneutic reflection yields to the mechanism of allegorical interpretation—first reading teaches this. Valéry's "conscious consciousness," on the other hand, sets into motion a second reflection that reduces the allegorical image to the rules by which it is produced. The second reflection completed in the "conscious possession of linguistic functions" thus thematizes the hermeneutic conditions controlling the allegorical reading. Its theme is the interactive structure of vehicle and tenor built into poetic construction; its reflex the equivocality engendered by poetic composition. The first four lines of the poem therefore do not deliver any "immediate intuition," presupposed by every hermeneutic reflection, but rather a representational image that, as an allegorical result, is adapted to hermeneutically schooled procedures of reading much like the "hinge figures" (*Kippfiguren*) of Gestalt psychology on which one can train one's eye. "Ce toit tranquille": the horizon of the sea with fishing boats whose peculiar movement lets the familiar picture tilt into the image with doves: "Elle s'impose à qui a vu la chose." Extended across the perspective between pines and graves, the allegorical image becomes the image of its own allegorical arrangement in which the flexibility of allegorical interpretation becomes the thematic vehicle for the potentiality of aesthetic experience. The insight into the hermeneutic forestructure of perception is consequently its reflexive tenor "récompense après une pensée," the result of a reflexive effort in which reflecting consciousness comes to reflexively heightened intuition: "Qu'un long regard sur le calme des dieux!"

IV

"Just as the eyes reduce all things to visibility, so the mind returns them to possibility," so goes the relation between the thematic vehicle of landscape and the reflexive tenor of construction in second reading: "On the height of the cemetery, looking down on the blinding sea, situated between the immense vacuum of death and the unbearable vacuum of burning space, Valéry, deploring the impurity of life to thought and of thought to itself, conceives a symbol denoting pure possibility, and transcending all his other images of the monotonous circle or of the snake biting its own tail. It is the view of the southern sun motionless at noon: 'Midi là-haut, Midi sans mouvement /

En soi se pense et convient à soi-même'" (G. Hartman, *The Unmediated Vision*).

The "phenomenon" of the previously mentioned hinge effect works, as Valéry says in another passage, like a Kantian "symbol of reflection" that makes intuitable the mode according to which mimetic resonance reverberates in the equivocality of poetic composition. Analogous to the semantic equivocality of language, visibility becomes a symbol of the kind of perception belonging to second reading and conceptualized in second reflection. The impression of immediate intuition is thus only the result of the first reading worked through in the allegorical mode, not of immediate evidence so much as of the momentary "afterimage" (*Nachbild*) of allegorical reading that establishes for reflection the symbolic coincidence of sensory appearance and supersensory meaning. The afterimage left by first reading confirms that this reflection consists of a "regression to an unreflected dimension," to that which is an "unreflected underground" in the first reading and which in the traditional repetition of the allegorical mode "constituted an original past" that, as Merleau adds, "was never present." The disappointment produced by the hinge effect in the first reading comes to no definitive result in any renewal of the same process. Rather, in becoming the horizon of a second reading, reflection itself now becomes the moment of aesthetic experience.

"Je garde quelque temps dans le regard la présence restante de ce mouvement prodigieux," Valéry describes the moment after a sunset. "Je ressens fortement l'impression de nécessité, rigueur, d'horaire inflexible, de puissance inerte précise." Such lived experience clearly differentiates itself from poetry. Second reading does not aim for any "identity in perception" in which the repetition of an original perception simulates another embodied by a quasi-hallucinatory symbol. The afterimage of tradition, which first reading makes manifest, is no longer a "natural symbol" but rather only a "sign of remembrance" in which second reflection finds a temporary refuge. The autobiographical localization of "Cimetière marin" thus does not lead back to the "source" of the experience that has gone into the poem but rather only to the reflection that has come to consciousness at this place. To be sure, it marks the site on which the poem takes place as the equivalent of this experience but does so in such a way as to strengthen the inaccessibility of the experience buried within it. In that the hermeneutic reflection in the poem thus fails, its failure becomes accessible in second reflection and, within this, to aesthetic experience as well.

Of course, this does not occur immediately and without detours. "With a shock, the literalization of the prior symbol [as one allegorically mediated] liberates that moment made spiritually autonomous in second reflection, as the latter becomes productive in its rupture with representability." Such autonomy, however, remains a mere postulation, does not yield the second reading in which it could become productive. Second reading is held back by second reflection in that in the latter it remains in a rhetorical syncrisis of hermeneutic effort in which reflection can only bring it into the field of aesthetic experience as an "intellectual moment" whose renewal produces nothing. In second reading, second reflection completes the rupture with the representability of what, after first reading, it has grown to expect as the afterimage of tradition. Second reflection becomes aesthetic not in the re-production of what is "represented" imitatively in the structure of the text but rather in the act of reading itself.

This is because second reading does not reproduce the first reading. Rather, the former repeats the latter in that it engenders reflection in it and sets it in relation to itself. "Not an inessential condition for the innovation engendered by reading consists in the fact that the operational mode through which the semantic form has been originally realized is not reproduced in second reading." The fact that "momentary evidence" appears in the imi-tation of tradition thus indicates, above all, that what has been transmitted here "is precisely only the momentary": like the afterimage of the sun de-scribed by Valéry that not only heightens the impression of its overpowering presence, which masters "Le Cimetière marin," but also signifies that it has, without pause, run its course and set.

This absence of the transmitted element in the afterimage of tradition provokes second reading to a reflexively heightened intuition. To the extent to which second reflection is thereby dependent on the completion of second reading and is determined by it, reading for its part remains irresolvably bound with reflection. As much as second reading "still reduces reflection to an element of mere intuition," it can no longer leave it behind "in order to bring a world established by reflection unreflectively to intuition," which again would be the allegorical aim of "reclaiming the past in the presence of a total situation." By means of second reflection, reading is not related to something lying outside it but rather is placed, second to first, in a relation-ship that is no longer the "object" but rather the "form" of reading in the act of reading. Reading does not empty into reflection but the other way round: reflection empties into reading.

The presupposition for this, that now second reflection can become the moment of aesthetic experience, lies in the afterimage of first reading, which marks the beginning of the second. In that the hinge effect, at the moment it shows itself, contradicts the first reading, it produces in the afterimage an orientational schema that serves the purpose of reflexive "visual guidance" in the second reading. Functioning in this manner in the first stanzas of "Cimetière marin" is the architectonic "background metaphorics" of roof and temple (sts. 1–4) whose constructive function is further employed in *Eupalinos*. It guides reflection without leading it any further to the success of a definitive meaning. The hinge effect keeps the metaphorical flexibility of the text in the second reading free from forming a consistent allegory and does this through irresolvable oscillation between underlying metaphorical patterns. The metaphorical qualities of this effect are thus not in any way taken back so much as set free from the limitations to which the paradigmatic associations were subordinated in the course of the first reading. The hinge effect liquidates meaning by dissolving it in the possibilities of suggestion brought out by mimetic resonance.

The visual guidance provided by the belated construction of images ("afterimages")—advancing from the secondary rhetorical to the primary aesthetic function—also supports the motivation of the "sens du son" so that now second reflection (as aesthetic) turns from the primary hermeneutic to the secondary rhetorical function. In response to this movement, Valéry dedicates his own sophistical point in the stanza to Zenon. The metaphorical interconnection of the afterimages—which is nothing other than the negative of the allegorical pattern transformed again into rhetorical ornament—lures one to the impressionistic interpretation of symbols that can be discovered on the micrological level of verse and metaphor. Second reading, however, cannot come to rest with this kind of relaxing conclusion. At the end of the first reading, its lyrical "subject" had already abandoned the text and thrown the reader back upon himself. This becomes clearly evident in the repetition of the last stanza, where the efficacy of the afterimages has faded. There this efficacy is attributed to the traditional metaphor of the book that, as its ironic (not allegorical) vehicle, becomes the self-reflexive tenor in the hermeneutic difference between life and reading.

> Le vent se lève! . . . Il faut tenter de vivre!
> L'air immense ouvre et referme mon livre,
> La vague en poudre ose jaillir des rocs!
> Envolez-vous, pages tout éblouies!
> Rompez, vagues! Rompez d'eaux réjouies
> Ce toit tranquille où picoraient des focs!
>
> (st. 24)

Wind rises, perceptual stimulant of movement; nature intrudes into the book of "second nature," of tradition: what could become, in the light of the Mediterranean locale, the aesthetic frustration of hermeneutic reflection reduces itself again to the familiar view of gently moving fishing boats on the horizon. The poem simulates a lyrical "I" whose ghostliness scares away the old hermeneutic attitudes that, having become second nature, have attached themselves to the afterimages of tradition. The book of nature sets itself up in the second reading as a book of second nature in which aesthetic experience, like "phenomena" in the book of nature, is realized through a delay in the course of tradition, through a pause of the sun in its trajectory.

What remains as a moral washed up and left over under the clear sky of the Mediterranean is Pindar's motto, from which the poem can be derived in advance and without remainder. If the motto was a preliminary instruction for the reading of the poem, the poem now appears as commentary to this introduction. However, this indicates that something in the reading has been added to the poem that was not contained in the text. In the experience of repeated reading, the preliminary instructions for reading gain retrospectively the quality of an introduction, better, a transition to life. According to its allegorical mode, reading was always directed towards eternal life; in the mode of repetition the anagogical perspective is reflected in its vanity and retrieved in the life of the here and now, where it can never be entirely done with hermeneutic reflection: "Plus je pense à toi, VIE, / Moins tu te rends à la pensée."

Second nature—"a world from whose all-embracing power only the innermost recesses of the soul are exempt; a world which is present everywhere in a multiplicity of forms too complex for understanding, and whose strict laws, both in becoming and in being, are necessarily evident to the thinking subject; but a world which, despite all this regularity, offers itself neither as meaning to the goal-directed subject nor as the material of sensuous immediacy to the practical subject"—would have "no lyrical substantiality." Thus the appraisal of Lukács's *Theory of the Novel,* which appeared at the same time as "Le Cimetière marin." Confirming this state of affairs from the inverted perspective of the modern poem, Valéry wrote: "Il ne faut donc jamais conclure de l'oeuvre à un homme—mais de l'oeuvre à un masque—et du masque à la machine." Behind the mask of the lyrical "I" Valéry practices a hermeneutic mimicry in the book of second nature, secures for reading a mimetic resonance serving not the first but the second nature of tradition. In this way, the poem thematizes not only the indigenousness (*Naturwüchsigkeit*) of tradition and the allegorical mechanism of reading through which it advances, but also the role of the lyrical consciousness inscribed within these structures like the Cartesian "ghost in the machine."

"Le Cimetière marin" represents the continuity of tradition conceived of in its historical efficacy not in any objective functional model of a dialectic like the "unmoved Nothing" and the "moved Being," "death and immortality," "poetry and life" (my paraphrase of Cohen). Rather, the afterimages of the first reading of this poem help to complete this continuity by making use of the hermeneutic attitudes of ever-changing, historically efficacious consciousness—e.g., the antique certainty of "momentary evidence" (light metaphorics), the Christian expectation of an "individual eschatology" (death metaphorics), the modern commonplace of a philosophy of life (kinetic metaphorics)—that make them available to second reading in order that they may be finally surpassed in the experience of reading as well as of life. The "regard marin" (st. 4) mediates this momentary evidence for the observer; the latecomer reflects individual eschatology in the remembrance of "les âmes singulières" (st. 15); the contemporary philosophizes about life on the basis of Zénon's paradoxes (st. 21).

The last of these instances raises the problem, one of special importance for the "coloring" of time in philosophies of life, of the rehabilitation of "intuitive movement." However one wishes to elucidate the thematic substrate of the poem, Zénon, like Pindar, leads beyond the boundaries of poetic construction into a contemporary discussion in which "la méditation d'un certain *moi*" shifts from the historical role of the lyrical "I" to the hermeneutic interests of Valéry, thereby fusing the most remote horizon of tradition with that of the author. Valéry gives some credence to a paraphrase: "J'ai débauché les quelques images de Zénon à exprimer la rébellion contre la durée et l'acuité d'une méditation qui fait sentir trop cruellement l'écart entre l'être et le *connaître* que developpe la conscience de la conscience. L'âme naïvement veut épuiser l'infini de l'Eléate." Now, Zénon's argument is anything but naive; it refutes intuitive movement by showing it to be only an apparent effect that owes its vividness to a belated reflection. Here one encounters the temporal structure of allegorical reading that reconstructs in hermeneutic belatedness a continuum between the remembered past and the expected future. "That the moving arrow remains at rest," as Aristotle cites Zeno, reduces the result of allegorical reading to the paradoxical denominator of the image created by the hinge effect in which hermeneutic reflection offers to individual destiny an illusionary exile in the shadows of the tortoise. In life it is just as certain that Achilles in a few steps can catch up with the tortoise as also in life reading is already overtaken and surpassed—a circumstance that was not true of allegorical reading, which in life could be neither caught nor surpassed.

By quoting Zénon, Valéry describes in the repetition of the paradox the paradoxical repetition of second reading that in the act of reading always overshoots the text. The repeated appeal to Zénon thus simulates the continuity of tradition as the very apparent movement that Zénon had rejected: "Zénon!"; "Cruel Zénon!" allegorically, "Zénon d'Elée!" academically (st. 21). Just as Zénon saw continuous motion refuted in repetition, so living movement is postponed in reading. Repeating commonplaces of contemporary discourse, the poem caricatures the futility of the repeated reflections in antique anamnesis and Christian anagogy. Thus it is a pensive pause before the decisive step into life, a step in which the author, in the end, is ahead of the reader.

V

The author exits the scene, bequeathing the premises to the reader. In doing so, the inversion of the allegorical reading—which had placed the poem's locale in the perspective of the remembrance of a past scene preserved for future expectations—is perfected. The precondition for this is the reversibility of *allegoresis:* the structural analogy in which the hermeneutic process of tradition in "Le Cimetière marin," as the process of a consciousness historically determined by its effectual operations, is unlocked through the autobiographical experience of the author coming to "conscious consciousness." Valéry used the same homology of individual and collective eschatology—which as allegorical remainder determines poetic construction—as the schema for the fictive biography of Socrates in *Eupalinos*. In that work "what is sought is the inversion of the tradition of fundamental aesthetic concepts that can no longer be taken as fact but rather only made intelligible through their projection into the history of an identical person (identical beyond death), of a Socrates who sees beyond the sum of the whole tradition (as originally conceived by him) compressed into his own life."

Also indebted to inverted *allegoresis* is the Socratic prefiguration of the Valéryan forms of the fulfillment of historically efficacious consciousness. The reciprocal process of clarification between life and reading assumes that, though neither fulfilled in remembrance nor successfully integrated in reading, what comes to consciousness in life is remembered in reading. Otherwise, the reader of "Cimetière marin" would not be able to take advantage (with the same kind of flexibility as dramatic roles) of the hermeneutic attitudes mediated through poetic construction, nor accept the traditional mask of lyrical subjectivity for the duration of the reading. A more important extension of this offer is the anagogy contracted into a locale that offers, instead of a paradigmatically remembered scene, a constant view manifest to the eye: "absence de temps" mystifies place as reading absorbs time. This occurs in Valéry not without those ideological distortions through which the vanishing efficacy of his lyric is also to be explained. Landscape becomes once again the vehicle by means of which Valéry belatedly adduces "the suffused meaning" of a myth that, as if it now lay open to the light of day, has finally left behind the shells of its pseudoforms that had obscured all previous attempts to read and work through the text of tradition.

The attempt of all philosophies of life to keep their distance vis-à-vis the "transmission of tradition" for the purpose of achieving supremacy over it cannot get along without the mythic analogue that pretends to give pure evidence instead of a historically effectuated situation. Like the impossible flight of Zénon's arrow, the impossible space of such a distance arises out of Valéry's dilemma, not from his poem, out of the predicament of the author that reminds the reader, not without embarrassment, of himself. By means of a reading that resolves itself only in the sense that it gives back the horizon for a life that lives to see another day, the reader becomes independent of the experience of the poem. For the poet, on the other hand, it follows from this that the individual experience of the living subject becomes entirely unrecognizable in the horizon of what lies before him—read. The work would thus represent the dead shells of experiences that provided its occasion, the library in which the poet found an entrance to the cemetery where the reader gets his experiences at the expense of the author: like the living in place of the dead, writes Sartre in Valéry's place, "qui publiait depuis vingt-cinq ans des livres posthumes." The author, posthumous in his own lifetime, provides himself with a likewise minimal as well as esoteric preserve in his thematic fixation on a field of perception, which brings before the eyes of hermeneutical sympathizers not yet denatured by the general public, what Valéry himself names "my Mediterranean experience."

One can read about the "regard marin" in greater detail in the *Inspirations méditerranéennes:*

> Let us ask ourselves briefly how a philosophical thought comes into being? What happens to me when I ask myself this question is that hardly before I attempt an answer I am immediately transported to the shore of some wonderfully illuminated sea. There one finds gathered together the perceptible ingredients, the elements (or aliments) of spiritual states in which the most universal thought, the most comprehensive question can germinate: light and scope, leisure and rhythm, transparency and depth. . . . What he sees is impressed upon his mind, what he can possess or wish according to his essence. Unexpectedly, the view of the sea creates in him a farther reaching wish than that which the attainment of

any particular thing could satisfy. It is as if he were seduced, initiated into universal thoughts. . . . It is well known that behind all of our abstractions stand such personal and unique experiences; all expressions of highest abstract thought originate from quite simple, ordinary usage of language, which we must rid ourselves of if we are to philosophize. . . . We know from the history of language that such abstractions also occur in our personal experiences; and it is the same process through which this sky, this sea, this sun—everything that I have just named the pure elements of day—have given to contemplative minds the ideas of eternity, profundity, knowledge, and the universe, which always have been the object of metaphysical or physical speculation . . .

All these essential factors of European civilization are thus products of this conditioning, i.e., the fact that local occurrences have had a recognizable efficacy of universal interest and value. In particular, however, the creation of the ideals of the most complete and consummate development of man stem from these shores as the blueprint or realization of the construction of human personality. Man, the measure of all things; man as political element, as city dweller; man as a being capable of justice; man, who before God and *sub specie aeternitatis* becomes everyman, all this is almost entirely a Mediterranean creation.

Chronology

1871   October 30, Paul-Ambroise Valéry is born in Sète, on the western Mediterranean coast of France. Father, Barthélemy Valéry, is Corsican; mother, Fanny Grassi, Italian.

1878   Valéry attends the Collège de Sète.

1884   Valéry family resettles in Montpellier, where Paul enters the lycée and begins to write poetry.

1887   Death of Barthélemy Valéry.

1888   Having received his undergraduate degree, Valéry begins law school at the University of Montpellier.

1889   Valéry discovers Mallarmé's poetry. He must interrupt his studies in November for a year of military service.

1890   Valéry meets Pierre Louÿs, through whom he will meet André Gide. Small reviews begin to publish his poetry.

1891   "Narcisse parle" and "La Fileuse" are published and receive much praise. Valéry travels to Paris and meets Mallarmé.

1892   Receives law degree. In early October, he experiences an intellectual crisis which compels him to renounce poetry as an occupation.

1894   Settles in Paris. Attends Mallarmé's Tuesday night gatherings. Begins keeping a literary journal, which will eventually become the 257 *Cahiers*.

1895   Applies for a position at the War Office but is not actually appointed until 1897. His prose work *Introduction à la méthode de Léonard de Vinci* is published by the *Nouvelle Revue*.

1896   *La Soirée avec Monsieur Teste* is published.

1898   Mallarmé's death profoundly affects Valéry.

1900   Valéry marries Jeannie Gobillard, a friend of Mallarmé's daughter. Becomes private secretary to Edouard Lebey, director of the French press association, Agence Havas. *Poètes d'aujourd'hui,* an important anthology of poetry, publishes some of Valéry's early poems.

1902   Valéry moves to 40 rue de Villejust, his lifelong residence. The street is now rue Paul-Valéry.

1909   Gide's newly established *Nouvelle Revue Française* publishes Valéry's "Etudes," an essay on dreams.

1912   Gide and his associate Gallimard convince Valéry to let them publish a volume of his poetry and prose. In revising his early work, Valéry recommences writing. Inspired by Gluck's recitatives, he begins the long poem which is to become *La Jeune Parque.*

1915   "Une Conquête méthodique" is republished eighteen years after its first publication as "La Conquête allemande." During the First World War, this work will be considered prophetic.

1917   *La Jeune Parque* published. During the next three to four years, other works are published in various reviews, among them *Littérature,* the surrealist review. The poems of this period will eventually become the collection *Charmes.*

1920   *La Nouvelle Revue Française* publishes "Le Cimetière marin." Valéry's early poems, in revised form, are published in the *Album de vers anciens.*

1921   The dialogues *Eupalinos ou l'architecte* and *L'Ame et la danse* published.

1922   *Charmes* published. With the death of Edouard Lebey, Valéry becomes unemployed. Decides to make his living exclusively by writing, publishing, and lecturing throughout Europe.

1924   *Variété,* collected essays, published, first of five such volumes. With Valéry Larbaud and Léon-Paul Fargue, Valéry becomes a coeditor of *Commerce,* a literary review. Portions of his journals published.

1925   Valéry elected to the Académie française.

1926   *Rhumbs,* another volume of extracts from the *Cahiers,* is published.

1927   Valéry surprises his audience with his reception speech at the Académie française: he criticizes rather than lauds his famous predecessor, Anatole France.

1931   Valéry gives the welcoming address for Maréchal Pétain at the Académie française. His "mélodrame" *Amphion* is produced by the opera, with music by Honegger.

1932   *L'idée fixe* published.

1933   The newly established Centre Universitaire Méditerranéen at Nice names Valéry as its administrator.

1934   Another "mélodrame," *Sémiramis,* is produced by the opera, again with music by Honegger.

1937   The Collège de France names Valéry to newly created chair of poetics. He gives the first lecture of a poetry course that he will offer every winter until just before his death.

1940   Valéry moves to Dinard during the occupation of Paris. Returns to Paris in September and remains there for most of the remainder of World War II.

1941   Valéry's eulogy for Henri Bérgson, delivered to the Académie, is received as a brave statement of resistance.

1944   Last important lecture at the Sorbonne in December, "Discours sur Voltaire."

1945   Valéry dies on July 20. At his funeral he receives national honors. He is buried in the cimetière marin in Sète.

Contributors

HAROLD BLOOM, Sterling Professor of the Humanities at Yale University, is the author of *The Anxiety of Influence, Poetry and Repression,* and many other volumes of literary criticism. His forthcoming study, *Freud: Transference and Authority,* attempts a full-scale reading of all of Freud's major writings. A MacArthur Prize Fellow, he is the general editor of five series of literary criticism published by Chelsea House. During 1987–88, he served as Charles Eliot Norton Professor of Poetry at Harvard University.

GEOFFREY H. HARTMAN is Karl Young Professor of English and Comparative Literature at Yale University. His many volumes of literary criticism include *André Malraux, Beyond Formalism, Wordsworth's Poetry, Criticism in the Wilderness,* and *Saving the Text.*

WALLACE STEVENS, one of the most significant poets of the twentieth century, was known for such works as *The Auroras of Autumn, Harmonium,* and "The Man with the Blue Guitar."

OCTAVE NADAL's many works include *A mesure haute, Paul Verlaine, Le Sentiment de l'amour dans l'oeuvre de Pierre Corneille,* and an edition of the correspondence of Paul Valéry.

LLOYD JAMES AUSTIN is the author of *Paul Bourget: Sa vie et son oeuvre jusqu'à 1889* and has edited volumes of Baudelaire's and Mallarmé's writings.

W. N. INCE is Professor of French at Soton University. He is the author of *Hérédia* and *The Poetic Theory of Paul Valéry.*

CHARLES G. WHITING is Professor of French at Northwestern University. He has written two studies of Paul Valéry: *Paul Valéry* and *Valéry, jeune poète.*

GÉRARD GENETTE is, with Barthes and Todorov, best known as one of the French critics affiliated with the Ecole Pratique des Hautes Etudes in Paris and the journal *Poétique*. He is the author of many books on the study of narrative, among them: *Mimologiques, Palimpsestes, Narrative Discourse* (a translation of *Discours du récit: Essai de méthode*), and *Figures of Discourse* (called simply *Figures* in French).

RENÉ WELLEK is Sterling Professor Emeritus of Comparative Literature at Yale University. Among his works are *A History of Modern Criticism* and, with Austin Warren, *Theory of Literature*.

JEFFREY MEHLMAN is Professor of Romance Languages at Boston University. He is the author of *Cataract: A Study in Diderot, A Structural Study of Autobiography*, and *Legacies of Anti-Semitism in France*. He has also edited the collection *French Freud: Structural Studies in Psychoanalysis*.

JAMES R. LAWLER is Professor of Romance Languages and Literature at the University of Chicago. His books include *Form and Meaning in Valéry's "Le Cimetière marin," The Language of French Symbolism, The Poet as Analyst, Essays on Paul Valéry*, and *René Char: The Myth and the Poem*.

ANSELM HAVERKAMP is Professor of German and Comparative Literature at the University of Constance and has been Visiting Professor of Comparative Literature at Yale, Minnesota, Oregon, and other American universities. His next book, *Second Readings or Reading beyond the Page*, will soon be published by the University of Minnesota Press.

Bibliography

Arnold, A. James. *Paul Valéry and His Critics, a Bibliography: French Language Criticism 1890–1927.* Charlottesville: University Press of Virginia, 1970.

Asselineau, Roger. "The Impact of American Literature on French Writers." *Comparative Literature Studies* 14 (1977): 119–34.

Austin, Lloyd James. "La genèse du 'Cimetière marin.'" *Cahiers de l'Association Internationale des Etudes Françaises* (July 1953): 253–69.

———. "Paul Valéry compose 'Le Cimetière marin.'" *Mercure de France* nos. 1076 and 1080 (January and May 1953): 577–608, 47–52.

———. *Paul Valéry: "Le Cimetière marin."* Grenoble: Roissard, 1954.

Beeker, Jon. "Paul Valéry's Use of Forest Imagery." *Language Quarterly* 19, nos. 3–4 (Spring–Summer 1981): 37–40.

———. "Symbolism of Ternary Structures in Paul Valéry's *Charmes.*" *Kentucky Romance Quarterly* 14 (1977): 441–48.

———. "Water Imagery in Paul Valéry's Poetry." *Degré Second: Studies in French Literature* 7 (1983): 41–55.

Bemol, Maurice. *La Parque et le serpent.* Paris: Les Belles Lettres, 1955.

———. *Paul Valéry.* Paris: Les Belles Lettres, 1950.

Bilen, M. "Introduction à la méthode de Paul Valéry." *Europe* no. 507 (1971): 22–37.

Boa, Peter. "Valéry's 'ego poeta': Towards a Biography of the Authorial Self." *Neophilologus* 62 (1978): 51–62.

Chiari, Joseph. *Contemporary French Poetry.* Manchester, Eng.: Manchester University Press, 1952.

Cohen, Gustave. *Essai d'explication du "Cimetière marin": Avant-propos de Paul Valéry au sujet du "Cimetière marin."* Paris: Gallimard, 1933.

Cox, Richard. *Figures of Transformation: Rilke and the Example of Valéry.* London: Institute of Germanic Studies, University of London, 1979.

Crow, Christine. *Paul Valéry and the Poetry of Voice.* Cambridge: Cambridge University Press, 1982.

———. *Paul Valéry: Consciousness and Nature.* Cambridge: Cambridge University Press, 1972.

Cruickshank, John. "Valéry and the Great War." In *Baudelaire, Mallarmé, Valéry: New Essays in Honor of Lloyd Austin,* edited by Malcolm Bowie, Alison Fairlie, and Alison Finch, 346–64. Cambridge: Cambridge University Press, 1982.

Delbouille, P. "Paul Valéry et le mythe des sonorités." *Zeitschrift für französische Sprache und Literatur* 70 (1960): 129–38.

Derrida, Jacques. *Margins of Philosophy.* Translated by Alan Bass. Chicago: University of Chicago Press, 1982.

Dragonetti, Roger. "Rythme et silence chez Paul Valéry." In *Aux frontières du langage poétique,* 157–68. Ghent: Rijksuniversitat te Ghent, 1961.

Duchesne-Guillemin, Jacques. *Essai sur La Jeune Parque de Paul Valéry.* Brussels: L'Ecran du monde, 1947.

——. *Etude de Charmes de Paul Valéry.* Liège: Desoer, 1947.

——. *Etudes pour un Paul Valéry.* Neuchâtel: La Baconnière, 1964.

——. "Paul Valéry et la musique." *Revue Musicale* no. 210 (January 1952): 113–21.

——. "Valéry et Léonard." *Essays in French Literature* 8 (1971): 57–71.

Dutton, K. R. "Valéry's *La Jeune Parque:* Towards a Critical Close Reading." *Australian Journal of French Studies* 11 (1974): 83–108.

Eliot, T. S. "Leçon de Valéry." In *Paul Valéry vivant,* 74–81. Marseille: Cahiers du Sud, 1946.

Fahnrich, Herrman. "Music in the Letters of Paul Valéry." *Music and Letters* 55 (1971): 48–66.

Feuser, Willifred F. " 'The Birth of Venus': Rilke and Valéry." *Neohelicon* 5, no. 2 (1977): 83–102.

Franklin, Ursula. "The ABC's of Literary Criticism: Valéry's *Alphabet.*" *Romance Notes* 22 (1981): 3–9.

——. "Mallarméan Affinities in an Early Valéry Prose Poem." *The French Review* 51 (1977): 221–32.

——. "Valéry's Broken Angel." *Romanic Review* 74 (1983): 355–73.

Gaede, Edouard. *Nietzsche et Valéry.* Paris: Gallimard, 1962.

Geen, Renée G. "Views on Education in Valéry's *Cahiers.*" *French Studies* 33 (1974): 420–31.

Genette, Gérard. "La Littérature comme telle." In *Figures I,* 253–65. Paris: Seuil, 1966.

Grubbs, Henry A. "Two Treatments of a Subject: Proust's 'La regarder dormir' and Valéry's 'La Dormeuse.' " *PMLA* 71 (1956): 900–909.

Hessenauer, Anita. "Narcissism in the Poetry and Thought of Paul Valéry." *Research Studies* 50 (1982): 21–31.

Ince, Walter N. "Composition in Valéry's Writings on Monsieur Teste." *L'Esprit Créateur* 4 (1964): 19–27.

——. *The Poetic Theory of Paul Valéry: Inspiration and Technique.* Leicester, Eng.: Leicester University Press, 1961.

——. "Resonance in Valéry." *Essays in French Literature* 5 (November 1968): 38–57.

Karpinski, Joanne B. "An Endless Meditation: A Reading of Wallace Stevens' Prefaces to the Dialogues of Paul Valéry." *The Wallace Stevens Journal* 7, nos. 1–2 (Spring 1983): 30–35.

Lawler, James. *Form and Meaning in Valéry's "Le Cimetière marin."* Melbourne: Melbourne University Press, 1959.

————. *The Poet as Analyst: Essays on Paul Valéry*. Berkeley: University of California Press, 1974.

————. "Valéry's 'Un feu distinct.'" *French Studies* 28 (1974): 169–76.

Lyotard, Jean-François. "Theory as Art: A Pragmatic Point of View." In *Image and Code*, edited by Wendy Steiner, 71–77. Ann Arbor: University of Michigan Press, 1981.

McCutchan, Garrett. "Sun, Consciousness, Sound and Identity in 'Le Cimetière marin.'" *Kentucky Romance Quarterly* 25 (1978): 195–204.

McDowell, Judith H. "Intellect and Imagination: The Poetry of Paul Valéry and Wallace Stevens." *CLA Journal* 26 (1982): 58–75.

Marshall, David. "Reading, Tasting." *Glyph* no. 6 (1979): 123–40.

Martin, Graham D. "Valéry's 'Ode secrète': The Enigma Solved." *French Studies* 31 (1977): 425–36.

MLN 87 (1972). Special Valéry issue.

Moore, W. G. "France: Valéry at Dawn." *London Magazine* n.s. 17, no. 1 (April–May 1977): 92–96.

Nash, Suzanne. *Paul Valéry's Album de vers anciens: A Past Transfigured*. Princeton: Princeton University Press, 1983.

Noulet, Emilie. *Paul Valéry (Etudes)*. Paris: 1938. Reprint. Brussels: La Renaissance du Livre, 1951.

Peyre, Henri. "Edgar Allan Poe and Twentieth-Century French Poetry: Paul Valéry." *Laurels* 51 (1980): 73–87.

Pickering, Robert. "Energy and Integrated Poetic Experience in the Abstract Poetic Prose of Valéry's *Cahiers*." *Australian Journal of French Studies* 16 (1979): 244–56.

Posnock, Ross. "Beckett, Valéry and Watt." *Journal of Beckett Studies* 6 (Autumn 1980): 58–63.

Poulet, Georges. *Studies in Human Time*. Translated by Elliott Coleman. Baltimore: Johns Hopkins University Press, 1956.

Raymond, Marcel. *Paul Valéry et la tentation de l'esprit*. Paris: La Baconnière, 1964.

Riffaterre, Michael. "Syllepsis." *Critical Inquiry* 6 (1980): 625–38.

Rinsler, Norma. "The Defense of the Self: Stillness and Movement in Valéry's Poetry." *Essays in French Literature* 6 (November 1969): 36–56.

Scott, David. "Valéry and the Sonnet: A Critical Re-examination of His Theory and Practice." *Australian Journal of French Studies* 14 (1977): 264–77.

Shaw, Priscilla Washburn. *Rilke, Valéry and Yeats: The Domain of the Self*. New Brunswick, N. J.: Rutgers University Press, 1964.

Subrahamanian, K. "Paul Valéry on Prose and Poetry." *The Literary Criterion* 14, no. 3 (1979): 58–63.

Suckling, Norman. *Paul Valéry and the Civilized Mind*. Oxford: Oxford University Press, 1954.

Tison-Braun, Micheline. "Scientist and Poet: Two Views of Chance." *Dada/Surrealism* 7 (1977): 66–75.

Trimpi, Helen P. "Contexts for 'Being,' 'Divinity,' and 'Self' in Valéry and Edgar Bowers." *The Southern Review* 13 (1977): 48–87.

Vines, Lois. "Dupin–Teste: Poe's Direct Influence on Valéry." *French Forum* 2 (1977): 147–59.

Virtanen, Reino. "The Egocentric Predicament: Paul Valéry and Some Contemporaries." *Dalhousie French Studies* 1 (October 1981): 91–117.

———. "On the Dichotomy Between Genius and Talent." *Comparative Literature Studies* 18 (1981): 69–90.

Weinberg, Kurt. *The Figure of Faust in Valéry and Goethe: An Exegesis of "Mon Faust."* Princeton: Princeton University Press, 1979.

Wilson, Edmund. "Paul Valéry." In *Axel's Castle,* 64–92. New York: Scribners, 1931.

Yale French Studies 44 (1970). Special Valéry issue.

Acknowledgments

"La Dormeuse" (originally entitled "Valéry") by Geoffrey H. Hartman from *The Unmediated Vision: An Interpretation of Wordsworth, Hopkins, Rilke and Valéry* by Geoffrey H. Hartman, © 1954 by Yale University Press, © 1966 by Geoffrey H. Hartman. Reprinted by permission.

"Two Prefaces" by Wallace Stevens from *Paul Valéry: Dialogues* (Bollingen Series 45, no. 4), translated by William McCausland Steward, © 1956, 1984 by Princeton University Press. Reprinted by permission.

"Introduction to *Poems in the Rough*" (originally entitled "Introduction") by Octave Nadal from *Paul Valéry: Poems in the Rough* (Bollingen Series 45, no. 2), translated by Hilary Corke, © 1969 by Princeton University Press. Reprinted by permission.

"Modulation and Movement in Valéry's Verse" by Lloyd James Austin from *Yale French Studies*, no. 44 (1970), © 1970 by *Yale French Studies*. Reprinted by permission.

"*La Promenade avec Monsieur Teste*" by W. N. Ince from *Yale French Studies*, no. 44 (1970), © 1970 by *Yale French Studies*. Reprinted by permission.

"*La Jeune Parque*" by Charles G. Whiting from *Paul Valéry* by Charles G. Whiting, © 1978 by Charles G. Whiting. Reprinted by permission of the Athlone Press.

"Valéry and the Poetics of Language" by Gérard Genette and translated from the French by Josue Harari from *Textual Strategies: Perspectives in Post-Structuralist Criticism*, edited by Josué V. Harari, © 1979 by Cornell University. Reprinted by permission of Methuen & Co. Ltd. and Cornell University Press. This essay originally appeared in French under the title "Valéry et la poetique du langage" in *MLN* 87 (May 1972), © 1972 by the Johns Hopkins University Press, Baltimore / London. Reprinted by permission.

"Paul Valéry's Poetic Theory" by René Wellek from *Four Critics: Croce, Valéry, Lukács, and Ingarden* by René Wellek, © 1981 by the University of Washington Press. Reprinted by permission of the University of Washington Press.

"Craniometry and Criticism: Notes on a Valéryan Criss-Cross" (originally entitled "Craniometry and Criticism: A Valéryan Criss-Cross") by Jeffrey Mehlman from *boundary* 2 11, no. 1 (Fall 1982), © 1982 by *boundary* 2. Reprinted by permission.

" 'An Ever Future Hollow in the Soul' " by James R. Lawler from *Yale French Studies,* no. 66 (1984), © 1984 by Yale University. Reprinted by permission.

"Poetic Construction and Hermeneutic Tradition in *Le Cimetière marin*" (originally entitled "Valéry in Second Reading: Poetic Construction and Hermeneutic Tradition in *Le Cimetière marin*") by Anselm Haverkamp and translated by Vernon Chadwick from *Text und Applikation—Theologie, Jurisprudenz und Literaturwissenschaft im hermeneutischen Gespräch: Poetik und Hermeneutik 9,* edited by Manfred Fuhrmann, Hans Robert Jauss, and Wolfhart Pannenberg, © 1981 by Wilhelm Fink GmbH & Co. Reprinted by permission. Footnotes (including attributions to Hans Blumenberg and Theodor W. Adorno on pages 161, 167, 173, and 178) have been omitted by the editors.

Index

ABC, 58
"Abeille, L'," 97, 156–57. *See also Charmes*
Adorno, Theodor W., 163
Agathe: background of, 55–56, 140; *La Jeune Parque* compared to, 55–56; style of, 57, 141
"Air de Sémiramis," 28, 98, 156. *See also Charmes*
Alain (Emile-Auguste Chartier): Valéry's works as viewed by, 44, 47, 129, 162
Album de vers anciens, 156. *See also specific poems*
Ame et la danse, L': Athikté's role in, 22, 33–36, 74; Eryximachus' role in, 33, 35; *Eupalinos ou l'architecte* compared to, 33–34; immortality vs. mortality as theme in, 3–5; readers' role in, 34–35; Socrates' role in, 3–4, 5, 33–35, 74; style of, 22, 34–35, 74
Amphion, 22
Analecta, 2–3
Andromaque (Racine), 91
"Ange, L'," 54, 58–59
"Angel at the Sepulchre, The," 54
"Anne," 27, 72. *See also Album de vers anciens*
Aristotle, 177
Aryen, L': son rôle social (Vacher de Lapouge), 140–42
"Au Platane," 155–57. *See also Charmes*
"Aurore," 156; modulation in, 64–65; sensuality and sexuality in, 65, 93, 157. *See also Charmes*

"Aux vieux livres," 154. *See also Charmes*
"Avril," 156–56. *See also Jeune Parque, La*

"Baignée," 147–48
Barthes, Roland, 104
"Bateau ivre, Le" (Rimbaud), 100
Baudelaire, Charles: prose poems of, 50, 57; and Valéry, 95, 153, 156
Bergson, Henri, 146
Bertrand, Aloysius, 50
Beyle, Henri. *See* Stendhal
Binet, Alfred, 143
Blanchot, Maurice, 6, 140
Brigham, C. C., 143
Broca, Paul, 142
Broken Stories. See Histoires Brisées
Brosses, Charles de, 106

Cahiers: general themes in, 64, 91, 144, 153; poetry in, 48–49
Cain, Lucienne, 97
Calypso, 58
Cantate de Narcisse, 13
"Cantique des colonnes, Le," 156–57. *See also Charmes*
Carnot, Sadi, 134
"Ceinture, La," 156; general themes in, 67–68, 157; modulation in, 68–69, 73; style of, 67–68. *See also Charmes*
Cézanne, Paul, 50
Char, René, 51
Charmes: general themes in, 131, 156–57; *La Jeune Parque* compared to, 97, 131, 157; manuscripts of, 156;

Charmes (continued)
structure of, 153, 156–57; title of, 10, 125. *See also specific poems*
Chartier, Emile-Auguste. *See* Alain
Chénier, André-Marie de, 153
"Cimetière marin, Le," 47, 63; allegory in, 168–78; autobiographical elements in, 161–62, 168, 173; consciousness and mind as themes in, 13, 55, 61, 153, 177; "Crise de l'esprit" compared to, 143, 145; epigraph to, 168, 171, 176; *Eupalinos ou l'architecte* compared to, 175, 178; form as theme in, 13, 16; general themes in, 14, 28, 70, 72, 157, 163; hermeneutic interpretation of, 169, 170–79; *La Jeune Parque* compared to, 69–70, 99, 132, 145; landscape's role in, 178–79; metaphor in, 29, 169, 174–75; modulation in, 65–66, 69–70, 73–74; readers' role in, 168, 170–79; sea's role in, 14, 19, 145–46; sight and vision as themes in, 15–16, 18–19, 29; style of, 109, 178; sun's role in, 145, 172, 174, 176; tears as theme in, 131–32, 143, 145; as traditional poem of reflection, 167–68, 170, 173–77, 179; "Vin perdu" compared to, 143–45; "Yalou" compared to, 145, 147. *See also Charmes*
Claudel, Paul, 51, 114, 153
Cohen, Gustave: "Le Cimetière marin" as viewed by, 29, 129, 162, 164, 169, 176
Coleridge, Samuel Taylor, 130
Connaissance de la déesse (Fabre), 122–23
"Conquête méthodique, Une," 136–37
Contes cruels, Les (Villiers de l'Isle-Adam), 138
Corneille, Pierre, 92
"Coup de dés, Un" (Mallarmé), 52, 135
Course in General Linguistics (Saussure), 104
Court de Gébelin, Antoine, 106
Cratylism, 104–5, 111–12. *See also* Mallarmé, Stéphane: as poet and writer; *Mots anglais, Les* (Mal-
larmé); Valéry's works: Cratylism in
Cratylus (Plato), 103–5, 112
"Crise de l'esprit, La": background of, 137–38; "Le Cimetière marin" compared to, 143, 145; *La Jeune Parque* compared to, 140–41; politics as discussed in, 2, 132, 135–36, 139–40, 144, 146
"Crise de vers" (Mallarmé), 107
Criticism, literary. *See* Hermeneutics; *specific articles, books, and critics*
Croce, Benedetto, 117

Dance and the Soul. See Ame et la danse, L'
Danse grecque antique, La (Séchan), 31–32
Degas, Edgar, 124
Derrida, Jacques, 6, 138
Descartes, René, 3; and Valéry, 2, 15, 130
Divagations (Mallarmé), 32, 52–54
"Dormeuse, La": consciousness and mind as themes in, 28, 30; form as theme in, 12–13, 15–16, 22–23; general themes in, 12, 19, 22, 157; prolepsis in, 22, 30; rhythm of, 8–11; sight and vision as themes in, 12–13, 15, 28, 30; sound in, 9–12; style of, 10, 12, 20, 72; text of, 7–8. *See also Charmes*
Dreyfus, Alfred, 146
Ducasse, Isidore-Lucien. *See* Lautréamont, Comte de
Duchesne-Guillemin, Jacques: "La Ceinture" as viewed by, 68–69; *La Jeune Parque* as viewed by, 91–92, 94

"Ebauche d'un serpent," 47, 156–57; modulation in, 66, 74. *See also Charmes*
Eclogues (Virgil), 48
Eliot, T. S., 120
Emerson, Ralph Waldo, 2
"Episode," 96. *See also Album de vers anciens*
"Eté," 71; consciousness and mind as themes in, 13, 26; continuity and homogeneity as themes in, 24, 26; general themes in, 13–14, 29–30;

sound in, 17, 29. *See also Album de vers anciens*

Eupalinos ou l'architecte: L'Ame et la danse compared to, 32–34; architecture as discussed in, 41–42; background of, 37–38; "Le Cimetière marin" compared to, 175, 178; construction and substitution as themes in, 24–25; the divine as discussed in, 42–43; Eupalinos' role in, 22, 35–36, 41–43; general themes in, 38–40, 163; language in, 36, 44; Phaedrus' role in, 33, 36, 43; Socrates' role in, 36–37, 40–45, 178

Eureka (Poe), 23, 119

Euripides, 153

Evening with Monsieur Teste, An. See Soirée avec Monsieur Teste, La

Explication du Cimetière marin (Cohen), 29

Faraday, Michael, 24

"Fausse Morte, La," 157. *See also Charmes*

Félix, Elisa. *See* Rachel, Mademoiselle

"Fileuse, La," 28

Flaubert, Gustave, 125

Fónagy, Ivan, 104

Fourment, Gustave, 54

"Fragments du Narcisse," 157; "Angel" compared to, 58–59; modulation in, 67–69; style of, 67–68. *See also Charmes*

Freud, Sigmund, 5, 146–47

Gadamer, Hans-Georg, 162–63

Gallimard, Gaston, 89

Galton, Sir Francis, 148–49

Gide, André: and Valéry, 54, 56, 61, 89, 92, 109, 131, 138, 140–41, 162

Gluck, Christoph Willibald von, 11, 90–91

Goddard, Henry Herbert, 143

Goethe, Johann Wolfgang von, 119

"Graveyard by the Sea." *See* "Cimetière marin, Le"

"Grenades, Les," 157. *See also Charmes*

Hegel, Georg Wilhelm Friedrich, 162–63

Henley, W. E., 136

Hermeneutics, 166. *See also* "Cimetière marin, Le": hermeneutic interpretation of

Hérodiade (Mallarmé), 99

Histoires brisées, 58

Homer, 123

Hugo, Victor: literary influence on Valéry of, 28, 153, 155–56; as writer, 121–22, 124

Hume, David, 23

Huysmans, Joris-Karl, 48

Hyppolite, Jean, 135

Hytier, Jean, 64

Illuminations (Rimbaud), 48, 50, 52

Immigration Restriction Act of 1924, 143

In Memory of Myself, 54

"Insinuant, L'," 157. *See also Charmes*

Inspirations méditerranéennes, 179–80

"Intérieur," 157. *See also Charmes*

Introduction à la méthode de Léonard de Vinci, 53, 119; consciousness and mind as discussed in, 23, 67; continuity and homogeneity as discussed in, 24–25; general themes in, 28–29, 41

It Must Be Abstract (Stevens), 1. *See also Notes toward a Supreme Fiction*

Jacob, Max, 51

Jakobson, Roman, 104, 114

James, William, 104

"Je disais quelquefois à Stéphane Mallarmé," 110–11

Jespersen, Otto, 104

Jeune Parque, La: "Agathe" compared to, 55–56; background of, 55, 89–90, 131–32, 152, 155–56; body imagery in, 14–15, 72, 80, 90, 93, 95, 97–100, 155; *Charmes* compared to, 97, 131, 157; "Le Cimetière marin" compared to, 69–70, 99, 132, 145; consciousness and mind as themes in, 13–15, 55, 61, 63, 71, 90, 94, 100, 157, 162; "Crise de l'esprit" compared to, 140–41; general themes in, 13, 27, 72, 98, 154; immortality vs. mortality as theme in, 70–71, 90, 93, 95–96, 98–99, 101, 156; land-

Jeune Parque, La (continued)
scape in, 92, 98, 100, 101; as major work, 47, 89; manuscripts of, 93, 155; modulation in, 20, 63–64, 69–72; mythological allusions in, 92, 94, 96–99; Parque's role in, 70, 80, 92–101, 140–41, 144, 154–55; prolepsis in, 20, 21; rhythm of, 92, 94–95, 99; sea's role in, 145, 154; sensuality and sexuality in, 93, 94–97, 100–101, 156; serpent's role in, 72, 93–94, 100; *La Soirée avec Monsieur Teste* compared to, 93, 140; sound in, 17–18; springtime passage in, 96–97, 155; structure of, 91–92, 153–54; style of, 71, 93, 97, 99, 100; suicide as theme in, 98, 100; tears as theme in, 17–18, 92, 97–98, 131, 139–40, 146–47, 154; temptation as theme in, 14–15; title of, 92, 98. *See also Charmes*

Kandinsky, Wassily, 50
Kant, Immanuel, 23–24
Keats, John, 20
Klee, Paul, 50

Lamartine, Alphonse-Marie-Louis de Prat de, 47
Lautréamont, Comte de, 51
Lebey, Edouard, 89
Le Breton, Georges, 117
Lefèvre, Frédéric, 162
Léger, Alexis Saint-Léger. *See* Perse, Saint-John
Leonardo Poe Mallarmé, 1
"Letter about Mallarmé," 3
Lettre de Madame Emilie Teste, 76. *See also Promenade avec Monsieur Teste, La; Soirée avec Monsieur Teste, La;* "Teste en Chine"
Levinson, André, 35
"Linguistics and Poetics" (Jakobson), 114
"Lois de la vie et de la mort des nations" (Vacher de Lapouge), 142
Louÿs, Pierre, 52, 54
Lucien Leuwen (Stendhal), 122
Lucretius, 123

"Made in Germany" (Williams), 136

Mallarmé, Stéphane: language as viewed by, 50, 106, 108–10, 114; as poet and writer, 5, 48, 106–8, 114, 125; and Valéry, 2, 9, 11, 44, 48, 50–54, 64, 94, 99, 106, 108–10, 124–25, 135, 151–53, 159, 164–65
Manet, Edouard, 50
"MS. Found in a Bottle" (Poe), 141
Manuscript Found in a Brain. See Agathe
Mauron, Charles, 146–49
Maxwell, James Clerk: theories of, 134–35, 137, 142
Mélange, 13, 58, 117–18
"Mémoires d'un poème," 121
Merleau-Ponty, Maurice, 173
Milton, John, 15
Misérables, Les (Hugo), 122
Mismeasure of Man, The (Gould), 142
Mistral, Frédéric, 124
Mixture. See Mélange
Moltke, Helmuth Karl Bernhard von, 137
Monet, Claude, 50
Mon Faust, 86
Montaigne, Michel de, 3, 47
Mots anglais, Les (Mallarmé), 105–7
Musset, Alfred de, 122

Nadal, Octave, 93
Naissance de Venus, 27
New Review, The, 136
Nietzsche, Friedrich, 33, 138–39
Notebooks. See Cahiers
Notes toward a Supreme Fiction (Stevens), 1, 5
Noulet, Emilie, 91

"Ode sécrete," 157. *See also Charmes*
"Of Mere Being" (Stevens), 1
Old Alleys, The, 48
"Orphée," 51, 57–58. *See also Paradoxe sur l'architecte*

"Palme," 156; general themes in, 5, 157–58; style of, 1, 157–58. *See also Charmes*
Paradoxe sur l'architecte, 51, 62. *See also specific poems*
"Pas, Les," 72–73, 157. *See also Charmes*
Pascal, Blaise, 47, 61–62, 122

Péguy, Charles-Pierre, 51
Peirce, Charles Sanders, 104
Perse, Saint-John, 51
Petrarch, 153, 168
Phèdre (Racine), 126–27
Pièces sur l'art, 117
Pindar: literary influence on Valéry of, 14, 168, 171–72, 176–77
Plato, 103–4
Poe, Edgar Allan, 5, 23, 119, 141
Poème sur le désastre de Lisbonne (Voltaire), 74
Poësie, 117
"Poésie," 157. *See also Charmes*
"Poésie et pensée abstraite," 113
Poincaré, Jules-Henri, 25, 134–35
Point, Le (journal), 152
Ponge, Francis, 51
Pope, Alexander, 114
"Prince et la Jeune Parque, Le," 91. *See also Jeune Parque, La*
Probability, the Foundation of Eugenics (Galton), 148–49
Promenade avec Monsieur Teste, La: background of, 75–77; manuscripts of, 76–79, 81–84, 86–87; Monsieur Teste's role in, 78–79; narrator's role in, 78–79, 81–83; onlooker vs. scene as theme in, 78–86. *See also Soirée avec Monsieur Teste, La*; "Teste en Chine"
Proust, Marcel, 109, 114, 127
Psyché (Corneille), 92
Pure Dramas, 48, 53–54
"Pythie, La," 70, 95, 157. *See also Charmes*

Rachel, Mademoiselle, 91
Racine, Jean, 8, 91, 153
"Rameur, Le," 156–57. *See also Charmes*
Raymond, Marcel, 61
"Recueillement" (Baudelaire), 69
"Réflexions sur l'art," 117
Regards sur le monde actuel, 139, 141, 144
"Renaissance," 96. *See also Jeune Parque, La*
Rilke, Rainer Maria, 20, 44–45
Rimbaud, Arthur, 47; literary influence on Valéry of, 48, 51–54, 152–53, 156; as poet, 50–51

Ronsard, Pierre de, 10

Salazar, Antonio de Oliveira, 146
Sapir, Edward, 104
Sartre, Jean-Paul, 6, 114, 179
Saurat, Denis, 36
Saussure, Ferdinand de, 112
Schopenhauer, Arthur, 33
Séchan, Louis: *Ame et la danse* as viewed by, 31–35
"Serpent, Le." *See* "Ebauche d'un serpent"
"Sleeper, The." *See* "Dormeuse, La"
Socrates, 106
Soirée avec Monsieur Teste, La: background of, 53, 140; *La Jeune Parque* compared to, 93, 140; Monsieur Teste's role in, 76, 79, 93, 119, 134, 139, 141. *See also Promenade avec Monsieur Teste, La*; "Teste en Chine"; "Yalou, Le"
Solitaire, Le, 67, 159
Souday, Paul, 33, 37–38
Spleen de Paris, Le (Baudelaire), 50, 57
Staël, Madame de, 12
Stendhal, 122
Stevens, Wallace, 1–3, 5
Study of American Intelligence, A (Brigham), 143
Supervielle, Jules, 48
Swann's Way (Proust), 109
"Sylphe, Le," 156–57. *See also Charmes*
Symposium (Plato), 33

Tel Quel, 109, 117–18
Terman, Lewis Madison, 143
"Teste en Chine," 144. *See also Lettre de Madame Emilie Teste*; *Promenade avec Monsieur Teste, La*; *Soirée avec Monsieur Teste, La*
Theory of Heat (Maxwell), 134–35
Theory of the Novel (Lukács), 176
Thibaudet, Albert, 152

Vacher de Lapouge, Georges: literary influence on Valéry of, 138–44; theories of, 140, 143, 148–49
Valéry, Paul: air and sea as viewed by, 24–25; architecture as viewed by, 62–63; background of, 48, 51, 53, 138, 144; and Baudelaire, 95, 153, 156; Blanchot compared to, 6,

Valéry, Paul (*continued*)
140; the body as viewed by, 15,
22–23; Chénier's influence on,
153; Claudel's influence on, 153;
consciousness and mind as viewed
by, 2, 5–6, 19–20, 23–25, 28, 52,
54–55, 62, 89–90; continuity and
homogeneity as viewed by, 24–25,
28; Corneille's influence on, 92;
and Descartes, 2, 15, 130; Euripides' influence on, 153; form as
viewed by, 25, 64, 90, 124–26;
and Gide, 54, 56, 61, 89, 92, 109,
131, 138, 140–41, 162; and
Gluck, 11, 90–91; Hegel compared
to, 162–63; and Hugo, 28, 121–
22, 124, 153, 155–56; language as
viewed by, 109–10, 112–14, 162–
64; letters of, 31–32, 37–38, 52,
109, 138–41, 144, 162; and Mallarmé, 2, 9, 11, 44, 48, 50–54,
64, 94, 99, 106, 108–10, 124–25,
135, 151–52, 153, 159, 164–65;
music as viewed by, 62–63;
Nietzsche's influence on, 33, 138–
39; novels as viewed by, 126–29;
and Pascal, 61–62, 122; personality of, 3, 49; and Petrarch, 153,
168; *Phèdre* as viewed by, 126–
27; philosophy of, 2–3, 15, 28,
128–30; Pindar's influence on, 14,
168, 171–72, 176–77; Poe's influence on, 141; as poet and writer,
26–27, 45, 48–51, 53, 56, 58, 62,
91; poetry as viewed by, 10, 49–
50, 117–29, 138, 158–59, 166–
67; Poincaré's influence on, 25,
134–35; politics as viewed by,
132–34, 146, 152–53, 159;
Rachel's influence on, 91; and Racine, 8, 91, 153; Rimbaud's influence on, 48, 51–54, 152–53, 156;
Stendhal's influence on, 122; and
Stevens, 1–2, 5; as teacher, 117,
159; Vacher de Lapouge's influence
on, 138–44; Virgil's influence on,
153; Wagner's influence on, 91;
Zeno of Elea's influence on, 175,
177–79; Zola as viewed by, 128–
29

Valéry's works: Cratylism in, 109–10,
112, 114; critical writings, 49; ero-
tica, 48–49; general themes in, 15,
17, 18, 86, 146; modulation in,
64, 69; prose poems, 53–55, 58,
59; sound in, 17, 18; style of, 16–
17, 20–21, 29, 72, 93; translations of, 44–45. *See also specific
works*

Valeur de la science, La (Poincaré), 134

Variété, 117

Verlaine, Paul, 106, 152

Vico, Giambattista, 171

Vielé-Griffin, Francis, 107–8

Vigny, Alfred-Victor de, 121

Villiers de l'Isle-Adam, Auguste de, 138

"Vin perdu, Le": "Le Cimetière marin"
compared to, 143, 145; general
themes in, 135–36, 145, 157; tears
as theme in, 132–34, 146. *See also
Charmes*

Virgil, 153

Wagner, Richard, 91

Wahl, Jean, 44

Whitman, Walt, 2

Whitney, W. D., 104

Wiener, Norbert, 135

Williams, E., 137

"Yalou, Le": background of, 144; "Le
Cimetière marin" compared to,
145, 147; general themes in, 145–
46. *See also Regards sur le monde
actuel*; *Soirée avec Monsieur Teste,
La*

Yerkes, Robert Mearns, 143

Ygdrassil (journal), 117

Zeno of Elea, 175, 177–79

Zola, Émile, 128–29